CANADIAN DREAMS

CANADIAN DREAMS

The Making and Marketing of Independent Films

■

MICHAEL POSNER

Foreword by Norman Jewison

Douglas & McIntyre
Vancouver/Toronto

Douglas & McIntyre Ltd.
1615 Venables Street
Vancouver, British Columbia V5L 2H1

Canadian Cataloguing in Publication Data

Posner, Michael, 1947-
  Canadian dreams

ISBN 1-55054-114-5

  1. Motion pictures, Canadian. 2. Motion pictures,
Canadian—Marketing. 3. Motion picture industry—Canada.
I. Title.
PN1993.5.C2P68 1993   791.43'0971   C93- 091627-1

Editing by Brian Scrivener
Cover design by Rick Staehling
Text design by Tom Brown
Typeset at Vancouver Desktop Publishing Centre
Printed and bound in Canada by Best-Gagné Book Manufacturers Inc.
Printed on acid-free paper ∞

Contents

Acknowledgement

Canadian Dreams was initiated by The Canadian Independent Film Caucus. Created in 1983, the CIFC is an association of 200 independent Canadian filmmakers, with chapters in Toronto, Montreal and Vancouver and members across the country. It acts primarily as a lobby group and is devoted to developing and promoting the production and marketing of Canadian film and video.

The Canadian Independent Film Caucus would like to thank the following for their financial contribution to the research and writing of *Canadian Dreams*:

Department of Secretary of State of Canada, Canadian Studies and Special Projects Directorate

      Ontario Film Development Corporation
      Ontario Ministry of Culture and Communications
      Film House Group
      Kodak of Canada
      Outerbridge and Miller, Barristers and Solicitors

Foreword

Norman Jewison

MAKING A FILM is like going to war. It requires courage, confidence, dedication and sacrifice. Film borrows from all the older art forms; literature, dance, music and painting. As a consequence, it has become the central art of our century.

Feature films drive television, video and compact discs. They create a country's myths, celebrate its heroes and examine its defeats. They express, through the filmmaker, the very soul of a culture. That is why, in the last 50 years, film production has grown to play the most important role in the global communications industry.

Over the past half-century Canada has developed a technical infrastructure which makes possible quality feature filmmaking. First, through the National Film Board, our filmmakers earned an enviable reputation for excellent English and French documentaries. But it is only in the past few years that a whole new approach to the art and business of making feature films in Canada has been developed.

Yet despite the recognized proof of talented film artists in Canada, one critical question remains: How will the films created by our filmmakers find their way to the cinema and television screens of the world? Feature films in Canada are almost all independent productions. Unlike the United States, where several international studios dominate production, in Canada the filmmaker is forced to deal with government agencies and small domestic distributors. We need Canadian film distributors who have the financial backing and marketing expertise to exploit the emerging creative talent.

Canadian independent filmmakers too often are forced to find support from foreign distributors through exposure at film festivals, American theatrical agencies and industry screenings. Our government agencies supply the basic seed money for development, but until we can attract significant investment from our banks and financial institutions, we will always be left to struggle in this highly competitive area dominated by the United States.

American studios, distributors and television networks have been successful in obtaining huge investments of capital from American, European and Asian banks. This, in part, is why American films dominate the cinema and television screens of the world.

Where is the Canadian investment in *Canadian* feature films? For some reason our Canadian banks and financial institutions have not played an important role in financing original Canadian film and television production. Perhaps Canadians are too conservative to have the confidence and courage to step up to the table. Investment in the arts is a high-risk undertaking. Films are expensive to make, and there is no guarantee of profit. Banks do not lend money to an industry which does not return a profit. Yet, in the United States economy, the communications industry is now the second largest gross earner of dollars. Why don't we have a bigger slice of this ever-expanding industry? To participate in this business, many talented Canadian artists are forced to work and live in the United States.

Some courageous Canadian film executives, such as Robert Lantos of Alliance Communications and Harold Greenberg of Astral Communications, are building their companies to be more aggressive in the areas of distribution and production. Other organizations of note are Biosphere, The Beacon Group, Maxfilms, Norstar and Cineplex. But until we gain more control over our own distribution and exhibition it will continue to be difficult for our Canadian films to be seen by a wide audience.

The most important asset for a young Canadian filmmaker is confidence. You must possess a deep belief in yourself and your project, and the ability to keep striving toward the making of that film. My advice is: surround yourself with people who support you, believe in you and share your dream. If you are going to make a film happen, you've got to believe. Faith in yourself and your visualization has to be deep and complete. It's a little bit like believing in miracles. Maybe that's what films really are—magical, mysterious flights of fancy that somehow happen because someone has unshakable faith.

Your feature motion picture, to be successful, must capture the imagination of a worldwide cinema audience. It must communicate across cultures, and provide a good story filled with joy, anxiety, suspense, action and, you hope, some insight into the human condition. As a good book embraces readers throughout the world, or a great work of painting or sculpture thrills the viewer, your film must also inspire a global audience.

It may seem a daunting prospect, but don't be discouraged. Take heart and inspiration from the fact that all great filmmakers share the same struggle and have endured the same problems. Martin Scorsese tells of how he went, hat in hand, pleading for money to make his next film—*after* he had made *Raging Bull*. Bergman, Fellini, Cassavetes, all had to find independent financial backing for their films. Even when we have made successful commercial films, we must continue to prove ourselves; to push and sell our next project just as hard as the first.

Filmmaking is not for the faint of heart. You need the courage of Daniel and the tenacity of Terry Fox. Canada is full of talent. With confidence and the right amount of ambition, we *will* stun the world with our brilliance.

For Lauren, Susan and Samuel, my dreams

Introduction

IT IS AN AXIOM of existence that no group of people will ever recount the history of any shared event in precisely the same way. The more people who participated in that event, the more viewpoints, interpretations and histories inevitably result—like the three versions of 'reality' recollected in Kurosawa's *Rashomon*. Any accurate chronicle of what occurred must therefore be constructed by weighting the testimony of the witnesses, deciding who is reliable and who is not; whose memory is trustworthy and whose is fallible; and who, for a variety of reasons, has chosen to filter the past through the distorting prism of time. That has been my task in sifting through the facts and opinions assembled for this book.

In the beginning, *Canadian Dreams* was intended as something of a primer, illuminating the lessons learned by Canadian directors, producers and writers in making and marketing films during the late 1980s. The movies included were selected because each had a strong and instructive story to tell—stories focussed not so much on moviemaking as on dealmaking, particularly the intricacies of financing and distribution. Some obvious and important talents are not here—David Cronenberg, Anne Wheeler, Atom Egoyan, Léa Pool, Micheline Lanctôt, Jean-Claude Lauzon, Bill MacGillivray, Bruce MacDonald, Phillip Borsos, among many others. In some cases, the filmmakers were gratifyingly too busy with new projects to make themselves available for interviews; in others, the filmmakers evinced no particular enthusiasm for telling their story, no matter how compelling or educational it might have been. The final selection attempts to offer a range of films that is particularly instructive or inspirational, and that reflects different regions, budgets and genres.

The ultimate value of lessons, of course, lies in their application—taking the knowledge gained and applying it to one's benefit. That approach presupposes an ideal universe, fixed and predictable, where the rules of the film game are clear, consistent and always fair. The reality, however, is somewhat different. Rules are not always clear or fair and, like rules everywhere, they can be remarkably elastic, depending on circumstance. If they weren't, filmmaking in this country would be even more daunting an enterprise than it already is. It may resemble a level playing field but, like everything else in the world of celluloid, it's just an illusion. Or, as film distributor Jeff Sackman says bluntly, the only rule in Canadian cinema is that "there are no rules by which to go."

Among the films examined in this book, for example, are Patricia Rozema's charming *I've Heard the Mermaids Singing*, which was financed and produced despite antipathy for its script within the funding agencies, yet became one of the decade's most successful Canadian films; Michel Brault's affecting *Les Noces de Papier*, which was initially considered suitable only for the home television movie market, but later won wide and popular theatrical release and was sold to more than 40 countries around the world; and Denys Arcand's enduring masterpiece, *The Decline of the American Empire*, arguably the most important Canadian film of the 1980s, which consists—against virtually every rule of the cinema—of 90 minutes of conversation.

Indeed, in almost every instance, the films explored herein owe their success, critical or (more rarely) commercial, to defiance of conventional wisdom. When no distributor would touch *A Rustling of Leaves*, a heart-of-darkness documentary about the Philippine revolution, director Nettie Wild mounted her own release campaign. When Guy Maddin's cinematographer on *Tales from the Gimli Hospital* refused to get out of bed for a scheduled shoot one afternoon, Maddin—already a novice producer, director, screenwriter, sound recordist and lighting technician—quickly learned how to use a movie camera. When everyone told director Simcha Jacobovici that distributors never put additional funds beyond the original minimum guarantee into productions, he managed to persuade Cineplex–Odeon to inject another $69,000, needed to finish work on his powerful feature documentary on the Middle East, *Deadly Currents*. By and large, the vocabulary of the men and women who made these films happen does not include the word "no."

Of course, there are those who argue that the very notion of a successful Canadian feature film is fanciful, if not preposterous. In box-office terms, they say, these dreams are far from being fulfilled. The argument is valid, as far as it goes, but it does not go terribly far. In fact, the primary market for most non-Hollywood films today—Canadian, American or European, it hardly matters—is no longer the front-end theatres, but the back-end television sets and VCRs. That's where investments are now typically recouped, if they are recouped at all.

Moreover, it seems fundamentally unfair to compare the box office gross of the average Canadian film with that of the average Hollywood movie; the latter is backed by launch and marketing campaigns that generally cost more than the entire production budget of Canadian films. And while there may be no correlation between a film's quality and what is spent to launch it, there is a strong correlation between promotional budgets and the number of people who buy tickets in the fortnight after a film's release—the period that usually determines the film's theatrical success.

Although competition for available dollars is fierce, the creation of Telefilm Canada and the various provincial film agencies has been an undeniable boon for the nation's filmmakers, yet it is the commercial after-life of a film that engenders the most heated discussions. To survive beyond the first few weeks in the theatres, films must rely either on saturation marketing campaigns, of the kind only Hollywood films can typically afford, or on word-of-mouth advertising. Clearly, the cumulative benefits of word-of-mouth cannot accrue to a film that disappears after two weeks in the theatres. A certain critical mass is needed—five or six weeks minimum—and to reach it, a certain threshold of promotion and advertising is required. That is a threshold few Canadian films—with launch campaigns worth an average $75,000—ever approach.

All of that being the case, perhaps the more valid benchmark to apply to these Canadian dreams is critical reception. And while there are (and will always be) naysayers and caveats, the vast majority of reviews that greeted the release of the ten films included in this book were extraordinarily positive. And those audiences that managed to see the films generally loved them. The core problem of Canadian cinema is not the talent to make the movies, but the expertise to market and promote them. Marketing and promotion is, anatomically, the Achilles heel of Canadian cinema.

Still, it will not take long for readers to discern an undercurrent of complaint in the remarks of writers and directors, producers and distributors interviewed for this book. It does not matter that they represent a privileged minority—among scores of aspirants—that was actually given the chance to realize their dreams. It does not matter that, for all the real and imagined sins of government-subsidized financing, independent filmmakers in Canada would mightily protest any sustained assault on Telefilm Canada and the Ontario Film Development Corporation—the two institutions without which the phrase 'Canadian film industry' could scarcely be spoken. Indeed, independent filmmakers in Canada probably have a better shot at making movies than do their counterparts anywhere else in the world. It does not matter that they have managed to scale an Everest of obstacles—financial, bureaucratic, creative—in order to assemble the elements needed to make their films. In fact, having devoted years of their lives to conquering the mountain, they are all the more frustrated by the reward that typically awaits them at the top—a too-brief moment in the sunlight and then a very fast descent into obscurity.

They are, as a consequence, an often disputatious lot—and, even when their opinions threaten to jeopardize their relationships with powerful forces in the industry, they have not been reluctant to speak out. The writers are unhappy with the producers for skewering their scripts. The producers are unhappy with the distributors, either for not knowing how to promote their film, or for knowing how—and then doing next to nothing about it. The distributors are unhappy with the exhibitors for being insensitive to the needs of Canadian features—taking the first opportunity to find a product that will fill more seats. And remarkably—remarkably because it is their principal source of income—almost no one has a kind word to say about the institutions that make the films possible—the government funding agencies, whose sins are alleged to include interference, incoherence, mismanagement, indecision and interminable delay. In fact, the cinecrats seem to have the worst of all possible worlds—on one side, reviled by their beneficiaries, who seem to resent the dependency that has been created; and on the other, under mounting pressure from their patrons in government to show 'Results'—measured as an investment that actually earns a few dollars, instead of yet another blue ribbon of excellence at yet another film festival.

How valid are these complaints? Readers must form their own judgements. In doing so, however, you should remember that among the individuals profiled in these pages, ego is not in short supply. Quiet or loud, subtle or direct, smooth or abrasive, all of them are perfectionists, driven and tenacious. They never quit—which is almost certainly the reason they managed to get their project on the greenlighted list in the first place. It is not altogether surprising, therefore, that they are also hyper-alert to the merest hint of neglect or mistreatment by agencies, distributors, exhibitors or anyone having contact with their creation.

According to Richard Davis, who co-produced *The Outside Chance of Maximilian Glick*, one of the "really interesting things about looking back on a movie is that issues that loomed very large at the time, personality conflicts and conflicts with the agencies, go one way or the other; they either get the rosy glow of things remembered and it's past us. Or they cast even longer and darker shadows, edged in bitterness and despair." That may finally be too severe and categorical a judgement, but it certainly describes many of the relationships explored in this book. Moreover, Davis is surely right in noting that "revisionist history wasn't really invented by the Marxists. It's something we all have, particularly this industry, which is 30 percent reality and 70 percent bullshit." All of that—the ego imperative, flawed memories, new agendas, and Davis' BS factor—is worth remembering as one delves into the pages that follow.

All that aside, the case histories of these films contain other common themes and characteristics. None of these elements provides any guarantee that a film will be made, let alone prosper. But unless you think seriously about them, you may find yourself handicapped even before you begin.

Scripts: There is simply no substitute for a 24-karat, quality script. This is where the film begins—and often ends. No amount of brilliant acting or direction, no amount of money lavished on prints and ads, will rescue a bad script. The more time taken to develop a script that everyone immediately recognizes as being a cut above the crowd, the better off you will be. The caveat: official evaluations are always prone to error, so that even a brilliant script may not be recognized as such.

Champions: Money is scarce and competition intense; however meritorious your project, it has a much better chance of achieving lift-off if there is a measure of real bureaucratic power behind it. If the distributor is only going through the motions, you will need to find or develop an ally within the funding agencies to maintain its drive to the screen. Building coalitions may not be your idea of what filmmaking is all about, but it is now an essential part of the process. The caveat: agency regimes change, frequently, and today's influential champion can be tomorrow's impotent UI recipient.

Stars: Outside of Quebec, *bona fide* homegrown movie stars (such as Michael J. Fox, Keanu Reeves, Donald Sutherland, Kate Nelligan) tend to go to Hollywood and soon become too expensive for low-budget Canadian films. Foreign actors are acceptable, but may force you to redesign the financing structure, because Telefilm's maximum 49 percent investment is usually contingent on using native talent in the principal roles. However, attaching a legitimate star to your project—as Michel Brault did with Geneviève Bujold in *Les Noces de Papier*, for a nominal fee of $50,000—will pay dividends at every step. The caveat: we have not yet discovered how to clone Geneviève Bujold.

Distributors: Ask the right questions and choose wisely. Recognizing that most films are neither blockbusters nor duds, can your distributor maximize your film's potential? And will it? Does it know the target market? Has it developed a coherent strategy for reaching that audience? Does the poster effectively sell the film? It's not necessarily the money budgeted for prints and ads that matters; it's how wisely the dollars are spent. The caveat: even if you don't like the answers to your questions, there may not be much you can do.

Festivals: The promotional razzmatazz is wonderful, but it's also deceiving. There is no direct correlation between how a film festival audience receives a film, and how it will perform at the box office. Too many Canadian movies focus too intensely on festivals. The goal is laudable—to generate press, buzz, word-of-mouth advertising—but something is often lost in the process, resources and enthusiasm that might be better saved for the commercial release. Moreover, a film that plays too often at festivals may also be administering self-inflicted wounds, eroding its own core audience. The caveat: some art and specialty films can never capture a huge commercial audience, and are therefore best suited to the festival circuit.

However, when Canadian films occupy only three percent of the total screen time available, it is clear that in large part the problems that confront Canadian filmmakers are structural. The very support programs which help make films possible can undermine their chances for success. Consider, for example, the whole issue of minimum guarantees—what distributors pay for the rights to market films. As of July 1993, three-quarters of the distributor's advance for a Canadian feature is covered by Telefilm's Distribution Fund, using taxpayer money; the distributor is therefore at risk for only 25 percent, which is normally recouped through sales of video rights and broadcast licenses. As a safety net, the structure is almost flawless—but there are no risk-reward incentives attached that might motivate a distributor to go the extra mile for the film.

Moreover, eligibility for the Fund has depended simply on the number of Canadian titles a distributor acquires, rather than on how the films perform at the box office. Hence, the potential commercial value of any film property is not the key determinant in any decision to acquire the rights. The key determinant is maintaining eligibility for the Fund. In effect, distributors are encouraged to buy Canadian films, but are under few obligations to market them aggressively. That protects distributors from financial injury, but leaves the film ill-equipped to compete in the theatrical marketplace.

With no expectation of significant box-office returns, distributors have no inclination to spend more than token amounts on marketing. And, with nothing more than minimum outlays on promotion, films rarely survive more than two weeks in Toronto, Montreal and Vancouver. Thus does the negligible (some might say lamentable) distribution of Canadian feature films become a self-fulfilling prophecy. Nor is that the end of the story. The buying decisions of video store managers are often based on how well the film performed in theatres. Hence, lack of commercial success in one venue helps create lack of commercial success in the next.

Spending more generously on behalf of Canadian films would obviously be less problematic if independent Canadian distributors had access to the many millions of revenue dollars generated by Hollywood movies; regrettably, they do not—the major chains being effectively owned or controlled by Hollywood, and the Canadian market being regarded for bookkeeping purposes as simply the fifty-first state. And such is the apparent power of celebrity lobbyist Jack Valenti and the Motion Picture Guild of America, that no federal government has yet mustered the political will needed to patriate the nation's theatres. Unless and until distributors are given an opportunity to earn a reasonable share of those revenues, it is probably unrealistic to expect them to fill their ledger books with the red ink that usually flows from Canadian movies.

In the interim, it is clear to the industry's senior policy-makers that the current system of feature film financing and distribution is no longer sustainable. "Some significant changes are going to have to be made," says Peter Katadotis, head of English-language production at Telefilm Canada. "I'm not sure what we are going to do. But can the system work this way? The answer is no." Among the most obvious problems, Katadotis concedes, is that most Canadian feature films are really movies-of-the-week in masquerade. "When you're paying eight bucks," he says, "you want to see something that you won't see at eight o'clock on television. You want to see something really different." To make such films theatrical, bigger production budgets will be required. "It's important to keep a healthy amount of low-budget films, so that younger people can start up," Katadotis says. "But basically my philosophy is that a film's anticipated revenues should be commensurate with its budgets."

Crossing the quagmire of distribution is a more formidable challenge. "We're caught in a bind," Katadotis admits, "and I don't know the way out of it, actually." The bind is that production financing now typically consists of 49 percent from Telefilm, 20 percent from a provincial film development agency and 10 percent for deferrals. Part of the shortfall can sometimes be met by resorting to what remains of Ottawa's capital cost allowance tax shelter. More commonly, it's the Distribution Fund that is used to fill the final 20-30 percent of every film—the money flowing to producers in the form of the distributor's advance against minimum guarantees. "Without the Fund, those feature films cannot be made," says Katadotis. "So when you change it, what you're doing is affecting the ability of the producer to put together a film. There's a missing piece here. We have to figure out how to get the incentives right. They're not right yet, there's no question about it."

For other industry voices, what Canada needs is not more subsidies, but less. Danny Weinzweig, former president of the now-defunct distributor Cinephile, maintains that filmmaking in Canada is already too dominated by agencies like Telefilm. Agency officials, he says, are "intelligent and well-meaning," but "they think the film industry is all about going to film festivals. Their backgrounds tend to be documentaries, National Film Board, arts organizations. And that does dictate the style of moviemaking that we are doing; it's not market driven." Weinzweig insists that Telefilm provides a valuable service, and applauds its backing of such talented filmmakers as Atom Egoyan, Patricia Rozema and Bruce MacDonald. He simply wishes it were not the only game in town—that some other means, such as tax credits for private capital investment, were available to finance production.

Katadotis and Weinzweig, of course, are only two voices in the continuing national debate about how best to foster the making of successful Canadian films. That debate encompasses everything from script-writing and development to marketing and exhibition, and it will not end soon. In the meantime, our filmmakers will continue to be impelled by their dreams.

Between the dream and the reality lie a thousand obstacles, setbacks, disappointments. For the producers and directors in this book, there were many times when the sheer accumulation of adversity tempted them to quit. They categorically refused to yield to this temptation. The sole consideration was getting the film made, and they were prepared to make whatever sacrifice was required to fulfill that objective. And that perhaps is the ultimate lesson—that the dream must never be surrendered.

Film is a team effort, and this book was faithful to that process. I owe a debt of gratitude, in the first instance, to all of the writers, directors, producers, editors, distributors and film agency officials interviewed—the leading actors in the unfolding drama of these films. They were generous with their time and with their candour. I acknowledge with thanks the members of the Canadian Independent Film Caucus committee who created and financed the project—Colin Browne, Wayne Clarkson, Katherine Gilday, Don Haig, Bob Lang, Tom Perlmutter, Yolande Rosiggnol, John Walker, Peter Wintonick. They facilitated access, read the text, and made many helpful suggestions; they, in turn, benefitted from the wisdom and scholarship of D.J. Turner of the National Archives of Canada. Let me thank particularly the committee's chairman and one of the founding members of the Film Caucus, independent filmaker Peter Raymont, who did all of that and also deftly steered the manuscript through the inevitable reefs of the publishing process. I am indebted to Jane Logan, who introduced me to the Caucus; to coordinators Avrel Fisher, Cristina Senjug, Eva Percewicz and Nina Sparks, who were helpful in countless, logistical ways; to David Groskind, for his patient tutorials in computer literacy; to my agent, Bella Pomer, for her unfailingly sound counsel; to Carole Leopold, who never ceased to encourage; to Scott McIntrye, for his patience, and to my editor, Brian Scrivener, for his sensitive handling of the material. This book was their Canadian Dream, and it would not have been realized without them. They are, of course, to be absolved of whatever sins I have inadvertently committed.

Michael Posner
July 1993

1
The Little Movie That Did

I've Heard the Mermaids Singing

DIRECTOR:	Ann-Marie
Patricia Rozema	MacDonald, Richard
PRODUCER:	Monette
Alexandra Raffé	**DISTRIBUTOR:**
EXECUTIVE PRODUCER:	Cinephile (Canada);
Don Haig	Miramax (USA);
WRITER:	Films Transit (world)
Patricia Rozema	**RELEASE DATE:**
DIRECTOR OF PHOTOGRAPHY:	September 11, 1987
Douglas Koch	**RUNNING TIME:**
SOUND:	82 minutes
Gordon Thompson,	**BUDGET:**
Michele Moses	$362,109
EDITOR:	
Patricia Rozema,	
Ronald Sanders	
ACTORS:	
Sheila McCarthy,	
Paule Baillargeon,	

"At Cannes, it was very clear quite quickly that people were liking it. And we thought, 'Okay, we won't be laughed out of here in ten minutes.' And then it just went on for ten minutes, the ovation, people hooting and hollering, and people on their feet, and they put the spotlight on us in the balcony, and below they were sort of saying, 'Stand up. Stand up.' And in fact, you know at that moment somehow that you will never be taken by surprise like that again. You will never have something so wonderful. Other wonderful or equally wonderful things may happen. But never again will I not expect it. It's like a loss of virginity, a strange sadness, for I can never be this uncomplicatedly delighted again. It never crossed our minds. That was the beauty of it."
— Alex Raffé, producer

"Mermaids did well across the board, wherever it had the opportunity to show. The problem with Mermaids was, it didn't show everywhere."
— Andre Bennett, distributor

SYNOPSIS Polly Vandersma, a socially awkward, 'organizationally impaired' temporary secretary—Everywoman—takes a job in an art gallery. She leads a rich fantasy life, including episodes in which she seems to fly. Eventually, she uncovers a minor fraud, and learns to love herself.

ORIGINS It is a lamentable truth that there are few genuine success stories in Canadian cinema. Movies that actually make significant money for their investors are rare; those that do, by every artistic standard, are usually execrable. Many more films win critical acclaim, but these seldom find an audience. The typical pattern is a two-week run in three or four major

Patricia Rozema, director and writer,
I've Heard the Mermaids Singing.

cities, after which they are consigned to cinematic oblivion—the repertory houses and the back shelves of the video stores.

I've Heard the Mermaids Singing was different. It won consistently favourable reviews from critics, including a standing ovation from the not-easily-impressed *glitterati* at its premiere in Cannes in 1987. It did well in both Quebec and the rest of Canada, as few English-Canadians films do. And it made money—not mega-dollar amounts, but real money nonetheless, going into the black six months after its release, from the proceeds of its theatrical run alone. In the 1980s, the number of quality Canadians films that did that could be counted on the fingers of one hand.

Even more remarkably, *Mermaids* was largely the work of two women who had never directed or produced a feature film. They were given a grand total of $362,109 in public money and, with minimal interference from the funding agencies, were allowed to make their movie. Before she turned to cinema, producer Alex Raffé had been a paralegal clerk and had worked for 10 years in contract administration for the Xerox organization. Writer/director Patricia Rozema did not even see her first movie until she was 16. Later, the perception would be fostered, says Rozema, that "I was this incredible ignoramus who suddenly makes movies," a sort of idiot savant of Canadian cinema. The perception was false. In fact, although she had been born and raised in a strict Calvinist home in Sarnia, Ontario—a town which then had only one movie theatre—she had acted lead roles in high school theatre productions, attended drama camp in summer, and performed and studied dramatic literature in college. Far more than most directors, she had, by her early 20s, gained a solid grounding in the dramatic arts—"how to act and work with actors, what's dramatic structure, what's story structure. I was steeped in it."

Rozema was working on the CBC's public affairs show The Journal when she started writing film scripts in 1983. Her earliest efforts were unanimously rejected by funding agencies. There were several, none-too-subtle suggestions that she consider a new line of endeavour, and not until 1985 was she able to win financial backing for *Passion—A Letter in 16 MM*, about a successful career woman. The 26-minute black-and-white film would later win a Silver Plaque at the Chicago International Film Festival and provide a springboard of credibility for her next project.

Mermaids began with the invention of its lead character, "Polly"—an unsuccessful career woman. Rozema had tired of the presentation, in film, of competent, intelligent, world-conquering women. She was more drawn to characters who were less articulate, less self-confident. She wanted these characters to address the same subjects as the educated and the articulate, but she wanted them to speak "in a real, simple, bumbly kind of wisdom, that was less aggressive or snotty." Or as she told the *New York Times* on the eve of the film's opening there in 1987, "I wanted to take seriously someone you wouldn't talk to at a dinner party."

Rozema started writing while working as a third assistant director on David Cronenberg's *The Fly*. When that film went into post-production, Rozema was given what she calls an honourable discharge and went back to writing her script. In the beginning, Rozema envisaged Polly as being very conservative—in dress, manner and speech—and completely alone. And she conceived the tone of the film as being "a lot sadder" than the final result. "But I knew very early on that it was going to be about a temporary secretary who works at an art gallery and that she would have this inner life, of adventure and things I thought would be fun to do, like fly."

Right from the start, *Mermaids* also had a strong anti-authority motif, a theme that stemmed in part from one very harsh review of *Passion* in the *Globe and Mail*. Stung by the review, and "pathologically sensitive to criticism," as she told the *New York Times*, Rozema resolved to essentially destroy the notion that objectivist standards in art have any meaning. A temporary secretary's opinion on art, *Mermaids* seems to say, is as valid as anyone else's. "The point of the film," she told one interviewer, "is to trust yourself—whatever *they* say."

DEVELOPMENT Rozema began with a thin skeleton of a script and just kept adding, trying to make sure that the additions all served the same purpose. Her goal was to make it "dense and rich, an interesting screenplay with interesting things in it. Every interesting thing I'd see or a line of dialogue overheard on the streetcar, I'd come home and put it in," she recalls. When she finished her first draft, Rozema circulated it among friends in the arts community, including actress Anne Marie Macdonald, who would later be cast in the film.

In soliciting comment, Rozema asked readers to make notes of their reactions as they read. For example, "someone reading the script might think 'this character is starting to seem very ignorant to me,' or have some other question. I may want them to have that question at that point, or I may want to delay that question until later. But to get the process is the hardest thing, because your perception of a film is totally diferent by the end of a film, when your questions have been answered."

SELECTED FOR DIRECTORS FORTNIGHT·CANNES 1987

SHEILA McCARTHY IN

I'VE HEARD
THE MERMAIDS
· SINGING ·

ISN'T LIFE THE
STRANGEST
THING YOU'VE
EVER SEEN?

WRITTEN & DIRECTED BY
PATRICIA ROZEMA

· LE CHANT DES SIRÈNES ·
WITH PAULE BAILLARGEON & ANN-MARIE MACDONALD
DIRECTOR OF PHOTOGRAPHY DOUGLAS KOCH MUSIC MARK KORVEN
ART DIRECTOR VALANNE RIDGEWAY EDITOR PATRICIA ROZEMA
EXECUTIVE PRODUCER DON HAIG PRODUCERS ALEXANDRA RAFFÉ & PATRICIA ROZEMA
INTERNATIONAL SALES FILMS TRANSIT CANADIAN DISTRIBUTION CINEPHILE LIMITED
MADE WITH THE PARTICIPATION OF TELEFILM CANADA·ONTARIO FILM DEVELOPMENT CORP.
CANADA COUNCIL·ONTARIO ARTS COUNCIL·NATIONAL FILM BOARD (PAFFPS)

Effective, evocative, Magritte-style image developed for promotion by Rozema and graphic artist Robbie Goulden was used successfully by the film's distributors worldwide.

4 CANADIAN DREAMS

Rozema's writing was financed by two grants, totalling about $48,000, from the Canada Council and the Ontario Arts Council. Originally, she intended to make a one-hour film, probably for television. But the finished script timed out at 65 minutes, too long for a TV hour. Her obvious choice was either to cut it or to add 15 minutes, making it just long enough for a short feature and qualifying, in theory at least, for the feature film funds that were just being established at the government financing agencies. "Really," concedes Rozema, "it became a feature because there was feature money."

In June 1986, with her script revised, she approached the Ontario Film Development Corporation for production financing. The newly-formed agency had been given an initial endowment of $20 million to invest in feature films over three years. As part of that grant, the OFDC had set up a special projects fund designed expressly for low-budget features (under $500,000) and other more experimental films, under the direction of Debbie Nightingale. "We thought," says Bill House, then the OFDC's executive coordinator of production and development, "that we would do a small number of films out of this program and that it would be less rigorous in all of its terms than the main feature fund."

Rozema and Raffé were living together when they created a company, Vos Productions, and filed their production financing application. Vos— meaning Fox in Dutch—had been Rozema's mother's maiden name. The application came accompanied by letters of support from the likes of David Cronenberg, *Fly* producer Stuart Cornfeld and, says Rozema, "anyone I could think of who had any credibility in the industry." The endorsements were not officially required, but she correctly reckoned they could not hurt. On the numbers side, the proposal was exhaustive—a characteristic that would come to mark all of Alex Raffé's submissions. "With Alex, any question you can think of is already answered," says Louise Clark, who succeeded House as the OFDC's head of production and development. Every budget cost had been sourced and double-checked. Raffé's initial request from the agency: $85,000.

The script itself arrived with a somewhat improbable title (*Oh, The Things I've Seen*) and was accompanied by what may have been the single most important factor in its launch. More than a treatment, this document was a kind of director's manifesto, a detailed breakdown of the film, its characters, tone, format, thesis, visual style, references. This was as much an intellectual exercise for Rozema as it was a selling document—"that was the hard thing," Rozema says, "to get a clear vision"—but there is no doubt that it impressed Debbie Nightingale and others at the OFDC. Nightingale was equally taken with Rozema and Raffé themselves. "They just had a real persistence about them," she recalls, "a real conviction. I knew they would get it done, with or without us. They weren't wacky or wild-eyed, just determined."

Despite Nightingale's support, others within the agency were skeptical. "Certain people felt that Patricia's first film, *Passion*, was very pretentious,"

Rozema and lead actress Sheila McCarthy head up the aisle at the Cannes Film Festival following a standing ovation for their film.

recalls Bill House. "And although Patricia was determined that *Mermaids* would not be pretentious," the OFDC's in-house critics (including legal affairs officer Jonathon Barker) focused precisely on that point, calling the script 'precious.' The official reader's report on the script was also quite negative, and advised the agency not to finance the film, saying it had no commercial potential. (The same reader later saw the movie at a screening for cast and friends and loved it.) Nightingale concedes that the Rozema script was difficult to read, but she was not persuaded that anyone could tell whether the script would or would not make a good movie. And she trusted the filmmakers, and their belief in their own material. Nightingale's endorsement was therefore crucial. Film projects without a champion in the agencies, facing committees with a dozen reasons to say 'No,' are doomed to fail. "If everybody's sort of like, 'it's okay,' I don't think it happens," says Raffé, "because there are too many cookies that are available for the same dollars."

The distinction may have been subtle, but what also helped *Mermaids* was that, on paper at least, it had a modicum of commercial potential. Almost from the beginning, remembers Louise Clark, the new agency was besieged by young filmmakers looking for money for off-beat, experimental films, that were more properly the territory of the arts councils. "We wanted something that could play to a mainstream audience, even if it was at the Carlton Cinema. We turned down a lot of good filmmakers on that basis."

At the key decision-making meeting, Nightingale made what amounted to an emotional pitch for support. Jonathon Barker resisted her, calling the script "a piece of shit that would never do anything." Four factors ultimately persuaded the OFDC to invest: *Passion*, Rozema's respected if not loved first film; Nightingale's enthusiasm for the project; the director's manifesto, Rozema's statement of the film's intent, which was written with bell-like clarity of purpose; and perhaps most important for the agency—new and risk-averse custodians of public money—the sheer miniscule size of the proposal.

As House says, the film's projected budget was "so tiny" as to make the OFDC's financial risk negligible. "At that level, and at that size, you knew that the film would be what it was going to be." Indeed, that was the whole point of the special projects fund—to make films so low in budget that the OFDC's financial exposure would be minimal. Certainly no one at the OFDC ever entertained the notion that *Mermaids* would become the critical and commercial success that it did. At best, House concedes, "we were thinking that we would have a nice small movie at the end of the day." Nightingale concurs. "We all believed it was a nice little art picture that would show at the Bloor Cinema, and maybe go to a couple of festivals." The OFDC therefore consented to invest $85,000, the board agreeing with Debbie Nightingale's recommendation that the film "was unusual enough to be intriguing, but with enough of a commercial element to make it a worthy special project investment." The agency's investment was subsequently raised to $100,000.

Initially, Rozema and Raffé were reluctant to approach Telefilm, which, then under the administration of Peter Pearson, had a reputation for being philosophically averse to low-budget, *auteur*-driven films. But Telefilm's funding, they knew, was indispensable; without it, *Mermaids* would never be made. They filed production financing applications in the spring of 1986.

Juliani's support, however, was offset by the opposition of Pearson, who simply felt the material did not fit the mould of Telefilm's celluloid ambitions. "I guess it just didn't hit his bone the way it hit my bone," explains Juliani. Nor was Pearson the only obstacle. Raffé recalls one meeting at which Rozema tried to explain the movie to the agency's head of script development. "He didn't get it. He couldn't make head or tail of it. It was really patronizing. Patricia was banging her head in the corridor afterward." Later, Raffé and Rozema heard from Juliani that Pearson himself had stomped out of committee meetings, flatly declaring that Telefilm should not be financing these kind of minimalist, student films.

The Telefilm jury remained out for several weeks, a delay that caused Rozema and Raffé an appropriate amount of anxiety. "When are we going to hear," Rozema recalls complaining to Juliani during one meeting. "We're scheduled to start shooting in September." Juliani laughed. "What is she laughing at," Rozema wondered. "And then I thought, 'Of course. She's laughing because unless she says yes, I can't shoot.' "

For a time, one problem at Telefilm was the film's lack of a distributor—a precondition for any agency investment. Rozema and Raffé had shopped the project widely, without satisfactory result. By the time it reached Andre Bennett, president of Cinephile, a largely unknown art film distribution company run from the basement of his family home, more than a dozen mainstream distributors and broadcasters had taken a polite pass, including Global and CITY-TV.

Bennett, a native of California, was a latecomer to the film distribution game. By training, he was an academic, a professor of political philosophy both at the University of Toronto and at McMaster. In 1983, he attended his first film festival in Peterborough, Ontario, and became excited by a Japanese film (*Keiko*), made by Quebec director Claude Gagnon. Bennett subsequently paid Gagnon a visit in Montreal and returned home thinking he would try to find an art house cinema to screen the film. *Keiko* "did marvellously well," and before he knew it other French directors were asking him to represent their work in English Canada; Andre Bennett had found a new profession.

Rozema remembers vividly that Bennett was "ecstatic" about the script. "He read it, and he got it, and he just loved it." Bennett's own recollection is slightly different. The script, he says, "was relatively uneven, but I didn't care. Both Patricia and Alex were incredibly enthusiastic about this project. It was more listening to them talk than reading the script" that persuaded him to get involved.

For Bennett—with a wife and kids, scratching out a living renting obscure art films to university campuses and film societies—the $5,000 minimum guarantee he pledged to commit was "an event." He had never before invested a single dime in any project, and in fact was "quite upset" when he learned that he had to put money into the Rozema film. He assumed the distribution fee could be paid out of future revenues. Later, Bennett would sell *Mermaids* to First Choice, the pay–TV channel, for $150,000 and to the CBC for $120,000.

Cinephile's $5,000 guarantee was the absolute minimum required to satisfy the agencies. In fact, Telefilm wanted more, and asked Raffé and Rozema to persuade Bennett to raise it to $25,000, payable over three years. He refused. Telefilm's request for a higher distribution fee reflected its concern that the film could not be completed on the proposed budget. Raffé regarded this suggestion as not very constructive. She and Rozema had already deferred $20,000 in salary, and were living on a $25,000 producer's fee, which they had split. "So saying you should have more money was not a helpful comment, unless you're also saying 'we'll give you more money,' which you can't because we've already taken the maximum, 49 percent." In the meantime, Raffé was taking crash courses on Lotus 1,2,3, "because if I had to type the budget one more time, I was going to throw up."

After a series of meetings, Telefilm was finally leaning in the yes direction. Then, only a few weeks before the start of principal photography, Raffé was summoned to the office of the agency's head of business affairs, Gwen Iveson—"I remember feeling like I was in the headmistress' office because I'd done something wrong"—and told, as a requirement of Telefilm's participation, to hire a seasoned executive producer to oversee the project.

"Well, we don't want one," Raffé said. "And we can't afford one."

"Well, you have to have one," said Iveson, "and here's a list of candidates. Choose."

None of the names on the agency's list were acceptable—Vos would have had to relinquish too much creative control—so at 7:30 the next morning, Raffé and Rozema called on Don Haig, a savvy film producer known as an avid supporter of emerging talent. "Don's belief," says Raffé, "has always been that first-time filmmakers will sell their mother, their cat, their aunt and their sisters to finish their first film. And that's the one to take the risk on." Haig, predictably, was keen to help—for an absurdly modest fee (in keeping with the scale of the production) of $7,000. He knew Rozema's early work and liked it, and had been "impressed by her ability to finish her films, piecemeal, and twist peoples' arms." Haig's only caveat was that he was already committed "on about eight other projects. So I told them I would open as many doors as I could, but don't expect me to be running out there trying to find money."

Essentially, Haig served as an administrative umbrella, a first line of defense against the demands of the agencies, principally Telefilm. At one point, the agency raised a host of questions about how Rozema was going to shoot a scene set in a commercial office building. "You'll need to hire police," the agency said. "You'll need to budget for insurance." Haig says he initially spent a lot of time with Telefilm's production people trying to convince them, "Look, nothing's going to happen. The film will be made. All we need is your miserly support." These were speeches two rank novices could write, but not deliver.

Haig was an acceptable choice at Telefilm, but not unanimously. In the agency's eyes, he was too nice, too *laissez-faire*, too willing to let amateurs run riot with public money. Telefilm would have preferred a tougher, more hands-on producer, counter-signing every expenditure cheque. Their other concern was that Haig, the benign godfather of young talent, was over-committed, and simply would not have time to properly shepherd the project. Eventually appeased, if not completely satisfied, Telefilm agreed to commit $163,000 to the production's budget. But the final agreements were not complete until the fall of 1986. In fact, Rozema had already finished shooting before the first agency cheque arrived. That delay forced Raffé to take a bank overdraft for $25,000, backed by an OFDC pledge to remit its production funds to the bank until the overdraft debt was retired.

The production financing, therefore, broke down as follows:

> Telefilm: $163,000
> OFDC: $100,000
> Arts Council grants: . . . .$ 79,000
> Deferrals: . . . .$ 20,000

The National Film Board contributed editing facilities.

At one point in these discussions, Rozema and Raffé also gave the film its final title. The line was taken from one of Rozema's favourite T.S. Eliot poems, "The Love Song of J. Alfred Prufrock."

CASTING Eager to help a young filmmaker on a tight budget, Maria Armstrong, an independent casting director, had cast Rozema's first film, *Passion*, for no cost. They had had a major disagreement about the lead actress; Armstrong had recommended Helen Shaver; Rozema wanted to go with Linda Griffiths; inevitably, Rozema won the argument. But Armstrong believes Rozema later regretted that decision, so when it came time to cast her next film, "Patricia was really cautious, overly cautious, and she and Alex were bound and determined to see every actress in the city who could possibly play the role of Polly." Dozens of actresses actually read for the part; many more were looked at in photographs or videos. Rozema even drafted a questionnaire, asking the candidates what movies they liked, the last three books they had read, what kind of characters they liked to play. "Patricia wanted to see everybody that every agent had suggested," says Armstrong, "plus people she had seen walking down Queen St. West that maybe fit the role. She was a young, ambitious director who felt this is how you find stars—serving coffee or working in little stores. That's not how you find them."

For *Mermaids*, Armstrong recalls, a budget of only $500 had been set aside for casting. For that fee, Armstrong told Rozema, "I'll recommend people I think will work, set up appointments and loan my studio for auditions, and you can do it on your own." Armstrong submitted a list of six or seven actresses, including Sheila McCarthy. In her opinion, those were the only actresses who needed to be auditioned. Why had she recommended McCarthy? "I had a vision of what I felt Polly should be and Sheila was that vision. I'm not sure Patricia had a vision, because she didn't know a lot of actresses. But I was not going to let her make the same mistake she had made with *Passion*." According to Armstrong, Rozema liked McCarthy's reading, but "she wasn't jumping up and down. Sheila was just one of a a couple of people she was considering." It took several readings before McCarthy was chosen.

THE SHOOT The shoot began September 24, 1986, lasted four weeks and a day, and went exceedingly well, complicated only by some technical problems in transforming the Rozema script into reality. "Because we didn't have anything to compare it with," says Raffé, "I don't think we understood at the time how uncommonly well the shoot went." Several scenes called for paintings that glowed, which required lengthy set-ups. The scene in which Polly conducts an orchestra ran into difficulty when the real conductor, hired to teach McCarthy the proper technique, was injured in a car accident; he conducted his tutorial from a hospital telephone. The now-famous flying sequences—"my little fantasy" says Rozema—were done "for a song," with large fans and the director yelling above the noise "this is amazing," trying to get her actress into the spirit of the scene. The film was shot in 16MM; shooting in 35MM was out of the question because of cost. So, for the same reasons, was the other option—super 16—which would have made the final blow-up less grainy.

While Rozema shot, Raffé rented a $200-a-month production office and some adjacent storage space and became production manager, coordinator, secretary, accountant, everything. She seldom left the office. When principal shooting was wrapped, Rozema, McCarthy and the first assistant director did four or five days running around Toronto for location shots. And while everyone looked at the rushes, no one was quite sure how to evaluate the material on film. "We saw it as raw material that the editing would shape," says Raffé. In one instance, Rozema shot multiple takes without sound of Polly leaving her kitchen to enter a golden forest. The extra takes were deliberate, because Rozema was trying two or three different styles. Raffé recalls watching Don Haig watch that set of rushes and thinking, "I wonder what the hell is going through your mind. We're taking your good name here, and you're probably thinking, 'what's this about?'" But Haig, convinced that young filmmakers must be encouraged to experiment, never wavered in his support.

POST-PRODUCTION Rozema edited the film at studios provided, without cost, by the National Film Board, through the winter of 1986–87. She found the process very slow at first, owing in part to her reluctance to cut the material. When she showed a rough assembly to Film Board friends, they were impressed—perhaps too much so. "I was frustrated because I didn't get as much criticism as I wanted," she says. Later, the NFB offered to pay for a professional editor to consult on the film, an offer Rozema accepted with alacrity. At that point, editor Ron Sanders came in, went through the film with her and helped her tighten it. Sanders' constant refrain was "cut to the money." His rationale was that the maximum impact of any shot is the first moment it is seen. In one important scene, Rozema had Polly walk into frame and stare at the luminescent painting in the gallery. Cut to the money, Sanders suggested. Just show her standing looking at the painting. The result, Rozema agreed, was "so much more poetic." Generally, she was afraid to have the film look like every other movie, but had unconsciously become much more conservative. "Sanders taught me to let go, to free up."

Occasionally, watching colleagues enjoy the film, it occurred to Rozema that *Mermaids* might find a larger audience than she expected. "I can remember thinking, 'What if this hits?'" But she tried to repress the question, telling herself: "Don't indulge in that. Make it good. Imagine that the audience is made up of your mentors, the perfect cinema-goer in the sky, and then forget the rest." Eventually, by mid-January 1987, she had a rough-cut ready to show the agencies.

Among his friends and colleagues, a good-natured debate continues to this day about the first reaction of the OFDC's Bill House. According to some, House returned from a rough-cut screening calling the film "lugubriously slow." Rozema, in fact, remembers him coming back to the projection booth while the film was running to ask when it would finish. "Bad sign," she says. "Bad sign." House himself acknowledges that he said the film needed to move "faster, faster, faster." But he insists that, on balance, he thought *Mermaids* was "working nicely," and encouraged Rozema to keep going. Others, including Donna Wong Juliani, were even more positive, although Rozema has no recollection that "anyone was ecstatic." Don Haig thought the rough cut had a certain kind of charm. "It was a cute, little, experimental, personal kind of film. If I had been watching as a distributor or an exhibitor, I'd have thought, 'It'll play on the CBC some time. It's not a blockbuster by any means.' "

But Rozema nursed serious misgivings about the process itself—the ad hoc, post-screening evaluations, in which one voice would often dominate the floor, or the discussion would segue into reactions to reactions to reactions, or speakers would digress on issues tangential to the film. The problem with test screenings, Rozema found, was that "people weren't there the way they would be at a movie at a Friday night. They were there with a job to do, watching with an especially critical eye, thinking of too many things. There were too many artificial criteria."

She had steeled herself for criticism, was prepared in fact to have the film rejected because the Polly character was too inconsequential to care about; or because "the gay thing was bugging people; or because things about art are flaky and pretentious—things outside the film that would have protected me." In her judgement, the American system of pre-release test screenings seemed sounder, where viewers were asked to record their reactions in writing. In the absence of that, Rozema trusted most the opinions of those with "real, good, strong gut reactions," and looked for a commonality of viewpoint among them.

It was after one rough-cut screening in February 1987 that Andre Bennett suggested the film be entered in the Directors' Fortnight at Cannes. At the time, Raffé had never even heard of that category; Rozema was not sure where it ranked in the festival hierarchy. Still in mid-edit, Rozema decided to pass up the first chance to be selected for Cannes, because "I just wasn't ready to show it." But after the generally favourable reviews of the rough cut, she decided to submit the film to a selection committee that met in Montreal in March.

The film was then in the final stages of sound editing, preparing for its mix. The day it was chosen for screening in the Directors' Fortnight, Don Haig was scheduled to have lunch with Bill House and Ian Birnie, an OFDC development officer. House wanted the meeting to clarify exactly how many projects Haig was involved with. At the stroke of noon, just as Haig was leaving his office, Telefilm's festival bureau called from Montreal to announce the good news. He was naturally elated. It was the third film in five years that he had been associated with to be selected in the Fortnight category (the others were Clay Borris' *Alligator Shoes* and Leon Marr's *Dancing in the Dark*).

The first person Haig told was Birnie—House had not yet arrived—"and Ian just about fell off his chair. I don't think he ever imagined it could be accepted." In fact, "it was probably the one film they thought had the least chance of being accepted." Birnie went off to call House, who arrived panting and equally incredulous. Indeed, according to Haig, if Birnie had been stunned, House was positively speechless. "And needless to say, he didn't bother to interrogate me further about my endeavours."

House concedes that he was "amazed" that it was chosen by the Cannes committee, "who must have seen a film not any farther advanced than what I saw." He immediately telephoned his OFDC boss, Wayne Clarkson. "It was beyond our wildest dreams," says House. "Here we were, less than a year old, and one of the first movies we've made out of the fund was going to Cannes. It was extraordinary. All of a sudden, there was this sanction, not only to the film but to the program and to the agency. It gave us instant credibility in the world."

Raffé and Rozema, out of contact through the lunch hour, did not hear the news until 3:30 that afternoon. When they did, they floated down the street to a pub and, as Raffé recalls, "sat there a bit stunned," and then, for lack of anyone else to tell, told the waitress, who promptly came back with liqueurs saying, "I can't figure out what you're so excited about, but you just seem so excited, these are on the house."

The Cannes confirmation gave Raffé, Rozema and Haig less than six weeks to finish the film. They spent the weekend immersed in technical questions, then set up an appointment with Telefilm's Festivals Bureau the following week. (Haig's previous experience was useful in negotiating the costs of the Cannes screening.) But when they asked Telefilm to cover the cost of blowing up the film from 16MM to 35MM for Cannes, "they said, 'You're on drugs. Go away.'" Raffé recalls. "Of course, there was no way we weren't going to go to Cannes because we didn't know who was going to pay for the blow-up." So the film was blown up, at a cost of about $40,000, without a committed sponsor.

When they returned from Cannes, Rozema and Raffé approached Telefilm again; again, the agency declined to pay for it, saying "we don't think it's a good idea. That's equity money." Instead, Telefilm suggested that Jan Rofekamp, who had earlier acquired foreign sales rights to the film for his Montreal company, Films Transit, absorb the cost of the blow-up and deduct it as an expense from the foreign sales revenues. On the basis of an initial handshake, Rofekamp readily agreed. At the time, he says, there was not yet "all this bullshit that Telefilm has now dumped on us, the pressure of minimum guarantees. It was much more casual, more on the level of people liking and respecting each other."

Inside his computer, Rofekamp stored a nine-page battle plan for Cannes—a detailed road map that covered everything from how many handbills to take to where to stay. For *Mermaids*, an entire promotional image had to be created, fast. Posters needed to be designed, and a press kit compiled. The script needed to be translated into French, and a subtitled

French print had to be made. Ads needed to be written and placed in *Variety* and other trade publications.

For some time, Rozema had the idea for the film's poster in her head, an oversized Magritte-like photograph of McCarthy's face, floating on water, disengaged from the world. She wanted a poster that would not only sell the film, but that would be aesthetically pleasing, so that people might later hang it in offices or homes. She discussed the idea with Toronto graphic artist Robbie Goulden, who did the assembly on spec—with promises of payment if the film sprouted legs. The actual photograph used was a family shot, taken by McCarthy's own father. The poster line taken from the movie, "Isn't life the strangest thing you've ever seen?", was suggested by Rozema. Rofekamp thought the poster extremely effective. "Everything in *Mermaids* is really unimportant except for the face of this woman. People liked it, and it worked." Eighty percent of all buyers of the film, he notes, used the same image in their promotional campaigns.

The film's selection to Cannes made *Variety*, prompting calls from American distributors. Rozema and Raffé had deliberately decided to retain U.S. rights—in part, says Raffé, "quite serendipitously," and in part because they were reluctant to "hand over everything to everyone else and have nothing to do." The interested American parties wanted private previews, a request the filmmakers denied. Raffé cannot remember why they made that decision, but "tactically," she says now, it was the right move. "We decided we wouldn't screen it for anybody. You would see it in the theatre with a big audience, and we would either win big or lose big."

CANNES Two Canadian films were selected for the Directors' Fortnight at the fortieth annual Cannes Film Festival in 1987—*Mermaids* and *Un Zoo La Nuit* (directed by Jean-Claude Lauzon). *Un Zoo* opened the competition on Friday night and, according to Bill House, "the French went nuts for it." The year before, Denys Arcand's *Le Déclin de l'Empire Américain* had opened to wildly appreciative audiences. "So it was back to back for Quebec," says House. "We thought we were dead—a tiny little movie, in English with subtitles, about art and women, and here's *Un Zoo*, this violent, extraordinarily elaborate, very visual movie, full of moving camera shots. We're dead." Raffé had the same instinct, calling *Un Zoo* "the first kind of grown-up film we've made in Canada." Compared to it, *Mermaids*, blown up from 16MM, looked like "a sea of dancing graves."

Mermaids was screened two nights later. House recalls waiting for the audience's reaction to a line of dialogue that occurs early in the film, where Polly describes herself as "organizationally impaired." How they laughed at that line, he knew, would be a good gauge of how they liked the film. "I'm very, very nervous at this point . . . and the film comes on. And the French laugh at that line. And the French went nuts. I mean, people said there hadn't been anything like that . . . ever. It went through the roof. An unbelievable standing ovation. It's something I'll remember my whole life." According to the late *Globe and Mail* film critic Jay Scott, the actual ovation lasted about six minutes, "an occurrence about as common in Cannes as a good buy."

There was another ovation on the way out. "It took us half an hour to get out of the theatre," Raffé recalls. The OFDC held a post-screening dinner at which she drank an entire bottle of wine before the food arrived—without any effect. Among the celebrants, of course, was Telefilm's Peter Pearson, who basked in the film's reflected limelight as if the struggle he had waged over production financing approvals had never occurred. In recognition of its critical acclaim, *Mermaids* won Cannes' Prix de la Jeunesse award, given to the festival's best film by a young filmmaker.

It was at Cannes that Rozema and Raffé negotiated the sale of U.S. rights, meeting with representatives of more than half a dozen major American distributors. Even before the festival, Miramax's Harvey Weinstein had been lobbying aggressively for the U.S. rights, sending daily messages and reminders of his interest. Various parties advised the filmmakers not to sign with Miramax; the company had spent most of its life in the rock concert promotion business, had dabbled in the distribution of soft-porn films and was just getting started as a distributor of more respectable mainstream and specialty art films. On the other hand, it was precisely their newness, says Rofekamp, that made them the right choice. "Miramax needed *Mermaids* as much as *Mermaids* needed them." Besides, says Rozema, "we figured that if they were half as aggressive with exhibitors as they were with us, then the film would sell."

During their first conversation with Miramax, Weinstein adopted his standard negotiating procedure. "The deal's $100,000 [US]," he said. "If you don't accept it right now, the deal is off the table. We leave the room and there's no offer."

Raffé and Rozema were prepared for that approach. "We thought, 'Fine. If you want it, you want it. And if you do, you'll come back with a bigger offer.' " Linda Beath, then head of production at Telefilm, advised them to pick a number and stick to it, "and don't have any regrets when everyone tells you after they would have given you more, because they weren't signing cheques." Although no fewer than seven American companies were bidding, including Orion Classics and Spectrafilm, both women liked the energy and enthusiasm of Weinstein and his colleague, Mark Silverman. Miramax, they felt, really wanted the film; "They'd seen it and they wanted it," says Raffé. "They hustled us. For every meeting we had with everyone else, we had three with Miramax." They were not simply bidding because it had become a hot property. Miramax kept coming back with higher numbers, always insisting that this was the final offer. Raffé and Rozema kept rejecting them. After one such rejection, they went for lunch with Sheila McCarthy on the beach, and a bottle of Dom Perignon appeared on the table, courtesy of Weinstein. Said Rozema: "I think they're still interested."

At about the third meeting with Weinstein in Cannes, Rozema and Raffé uttered the number $350,000. "It was the biggest number we could think of, " says Raffé. "The budget."

"Okay," he said. "Done."

"And both Patricia and I thought, 'That was too easy. Fuck it.' " So they then added, simultaneously: "U.S. dollars."

"Fine," said Weinstein.

So the U.S. distribution deal, converted to Canadian dollars, exceeded the entire cost of the picture. Rozema and Raffé took a 25 percent sales agents' fee from the transaction, and lived off the proceeds for the next six months. (Rozema was already writing the script for her next film, *White Room*.) Rofekamp assisted from the sidelines on the U.S. sales and helped draft the deal memo, but he was not around for the final negotiations with Miramax. It would have been nice, he concedes, to have earned a 25 percent commission on the sale, but "you can't have it all." The producers did, however, give him seven percent of their own commission, in recognition of his work. A more significant consequence of the Miramax deal was that, thereafter, many producers asked him to exempt the lucrative U.S. market from his contract, insisting they would do it themselves.

The OFDC's Bill House and Jonathon Barker later objected to the producers' taking the sales agent's fee. "I don't understand," Raffé asked. "Somebody's got to get the commission. And the OFDC is going to get its entire investment back within 15 months, and you've got a problem?" "Fuck 'em," Rofekamp said. "If they don't agree, I'll take the commission and pay you." In the end, the agency consented to the fee, but only on the minimum guarantee, not an any overages.

Beyond the U.S, Rofekamp, Don Haig and others had urged Rozema and Raffé to do a deal within 24 hours because after that, the buyers would have a new favourite to pursue. Atypically, it did not happen that way. Rofekamp and the producers were busy for an entire week. "I think I had an average of 20 to 25 meetings a day for eight days," Rofekamp recalls. "My agenda book was completely black. Five interested buyers from France. Six from the U.K. Nine or ten from Germany." In the case of England, a TV sale to Channel 4 was already "in the can for 60,000 pounds," a floor price that allowed him "to squeeze the other distributors." About 20 smaller countries, including Norway, Greece, Singapore and South Africa, were also interested, as were TV stations in several eastern European countries. It was, says Rofekamp, "completely ridiculous." By the time Cannes ended, they had made sales to 32 countries, and earned advances on royalties worth $1.1 million. Some of those five-year term contracts are now expiring, raising the possibility of resale. In fact, in the fall of 1992, Rofekamp made a sale to French TV worth $45,000.

Of course, Rofekamp has also ridden the down elevator at Cannes. A year later, he went back to the Festival with a smaller Quebec film that bombed.

"Instead of total triumph, we had a shocked and crying filmmaker to take care of." Being selected to Cannes or Berlin is not enough; the film still has to perform. "You can go these festivals and spend $100,000 and your film can go down the drain and you know it five minutes after the screening," he says. "It happens before your eyes."

Despite the sales, both producers returned to Canada largely broke and debt-ridden. Raffé assumed they would go back to chasing jobs as assistant directors and production managers. "We had no knowledge that our lives had just changed. You seldom sit at a crossroads and know it's a crossroads. But from the ovation afterward, my life was not going to be the same."

FESTIVAL OF FESTIVALS After the intense, unexpected hoopla of Cannes, it was perhaps inevitable that the screening of *Mermaids* at Toronto's Festival of Festivals—even as the Opening Gala—would be something of an anticlimax. Certainly, the principals felt a letdown. Part of it was that that the engines of hype had been working overtime in the summer after Cannes, and had built expectations to unrealistic levels. Raffé herself began to grow slightly weary of the "constant press Cinderella story. I mean, it's a smaller film. Its success was to do with context—expectations going in, and the charm, and coming out and feeling moved in a way you really didn't expect."

As a result, the audience that saw it in Toronto in September at the Ryerson Theatre had a certain, 'Is that all there is?' reaction; the film simply could not deliver the extravagant promises that had been made, implicitly, on its behalf. Bill House concurs. Blown up to 35MM, he says, the movie looked quite grainy. "It barely filled the screen. The first night audience in tuxedos, I think they were disappointed."

So was distributor Andre Bennett, charged with the cost of the post-premiere party celebrating the film's Festival appearance. Bennett felt pressure to "treat the film like a regular film that needs a lots of dollars spent on marketing," a premise he did not accept. "It cost me something like $30,000 for the privilege of opening the god-damned Festival of Festivals," Bennett complains. "We could have lived without that, couldn't we? That was money Alex didn't receive, Patricia didn't receive, I didn't receive. And that was just for the party. Not to mention all the newspaper display advertising." House rejects the argument, noting that Bennett was not compelled to position the film as the Opening Gala. Having accepted the invitation, there was no choice. No film, says House, can open the F of F without throwing a reception, "whatever the film is. You can't just sit there and have a little ad in the newspaper." If the issue is cost, says House, "then I don't blame anyone except Andre for not having partners in the costs." Others note that Bennett was swept up in the euphoria surrounding the film, and of his own volition bought a four-colour advertisement in *Time*.

DISTRIBUTION The status acquired at Cannes made *Mermaids* a hot property in Canada as well. Andre Bennett was wined and dined by a variety of distributors who had previously spurned rights to the film. Northstar in English Canada and Cinema Plus in Quebec, he recalls, were particularly aggressive, offering to buy him out for a generous multiple of his investment, or help him release the film for a commission. Bennett declined the offers.

With the front door firmly locked, competitors resorted to the back door, applying pressure on Rozema and Raffé to change distributors. Producer/distributor Robert Lantos offered to pay off Bennett and take the film; the offer was declined. "Patricia felt very strongly that you don't do that to people who have stuck by you," says Raffé, particularly since Lantos—and everyone except Cinephile—had earlier rejected the rights. There would have been no *film* without Andre, if he had not put himself on the line. It was inconceivable to then turn around and say, 'this is bigger than anything we've ever had before, so we'll take it away from you.' " For that position, they had solid suport from Linda Beath at Telefilm; she told Raffé at Cannes that the agency's investment in *Mermaids* was nothi compared to the promotional value the film had returned to Canada, and that they would not be pressured to make distribution decisions they did not want to make.

Initially, both Famous Players and Cineplex–Odeon wanted to secure exhibition rights to *Mermaids*. Bennett chose Cineplex, largely because it had supported him in the past and because it owned Toronto's Carlton Cinema, "the only decent art house owned by a chain in North America." Despite *Mermaid's* success at Cannes, the bookers at Cineplex–Odeon were not overly impressed by its commercial prospects. "They told me, 'Andre, take the film and put it in the Bloor Cinema,' " a small, run-down, mid-town Toronto repertory house. "I said, 'What about all the stuff that happened at Cannes?' And they said, 'Ah, it's not going to work here.' "

At first, Bennett tried to negotiate a two-screen opening, and met resistance. But after a week or two Cineplex called back with a change of heart, persuaded—Bennett remains convinced—only by the enthusiasm of the Montreal office. "Cineplex in Montreal wanted the film. They needed it. And so they got it for Montreal, and Cineplex Toronto changed its mind." But Bennett considered the American release strategy mimicked by the Canadian chains, with full-page newspaper ads on the opening weekend, absurd. "Of course, advertise," he says. "But advertise appropriately. Keep costs down." From Bennett's point of view—and he was then being asked to share 25–50 percent of the exhibitor's advertising costs—it made no sense to spend thousands of dollars promoting a film, particularly when the film had already generated thousands of dollars in free publicity and been warmly reviewed. "You don't create half-page ads when you have a hit. It's wasted money. It's a mindless commitment to the moronic, American commercial model." He voices the same complaint about video distribution, insisting that Northstar, which later acquired Canadian video rights to *Mermaids*, used the American release model and ended up with "a disaster." Under that model, art films—whatever their country of origin—automatically become defined as foreign films, an area of the store into which most buyers and renters of movies seldom venture.

A far more sensible approach, he says, is to look at the film, decide who the audience will be, and then figure out how to reach that audience without spending huge sums of money. "You have to spend some dollars," Bennett allows, "but the dollars shouldn't become the necessary condition for getting the audience." If he were doing *Mermaids* over again, Bennett says he would have tried to persuade the independent theatres across Canada to book an open run of the film, avoiding the chains altogether.

THEATRICAL RELEASE After a successful screening at Colorado's prestigious Telluride Festival on Labour Day weekend 1987, *Mermaids* opened its theatrical run in New York City at the 68th St. Playhouse on Friday, September 11, playing to enthusiastic and near-record audiences and accompanied by a $25,000 full-age ad in the *New York Times*. The box office grosses for the opening weekend were $26,000, until that time, the second biggest weekend in the theatre's history. In its first two weeks in New York, *Mermaids* earned more than $70,000. After four weeks, the film was bumped, not because of sagging grosses, but because another film had already been lock-dated.

Reviewing the film in the *Times*, critic Vincent Canby offered a mixed salad of reaction. After 40 minutes, he said, "Polly's innocence loses its charm and watching the movie is like being cornered by a whimsical, 500-lb. elf." He called Sheila McCarthy, however, "a find." *Time* was even tougher, calling the film "a fairy-tale for feminist pre-teens . . . a desperate audition for endearment." Others were far more positive, including Judith Crist and Roger Ebert. There was unanimous praise for McCarthy. "Sheila McCarthy is not just in the movie," said then Toronto *Star* critic Ron Base. "She is the movie." In the *Globe and Mail*, Jay Scott said McCarthy's performance was "almost too good—too magnetic, too funny, too much—to be believable as a nerdette."

The New York release provided a positive kick-off to a national roll-out, Miramax adding two or three cities each week. At one point, there were about 25 prints in circulation, and the film eventually played in some 50 U.S. cities. Commercially, the film performed best in cities with strong art-house audiences—Boston, Washington, Oakland. Overall, says Raffé, *Mermaids* grossed about $2.5 million in the United States, and made number 17 in *Variety*—"the biggest excitement of my entire life. There is nothing to equal seeing your film on the *Variety* billboard."

Later, there were questions about Miramax's "inscrutable bookkeeping methods," concedes Raffé. "I don't know if they have their full complement of toes and fingers because they count differently than me." Raffé had "enormous difficulty" getting data from the distributor; it was more than a year before the first written report was filed, and it reduced Miramax's expenses to a single line item. Raffé immediately asked for an expense break-down; that took several months more. Later, she learned second-hand that Miramax had made an unreported sale of *Mermaids* to a cable TV channel in New Jersey. She questioned it in writing; the sale turned up on the next report.

On the other hand, she says now, "I don't think the wastage was any worse there than anywhere else. And the greed is within a margin of tolerance that is the norm. It's not so offensive that you interfere and go through the cost of interfering. We're not dissatified with Miramax. We're wary, but we feel we got enough out of it, that we're not ripped off." The hard truth, says Raffé, is that American distributors "are disinclined to share the wealth when it happens, from the studios on down. We always assumed that the maximum we'd make was the sales advance—a pretty smart assumption to make as a general rule."

Overall, Raffé believes that the film benefitted from its association with Miramax, which was sold in 1992 to the Disney Studios. Its launch coincided with the relaunch of Miramax as a distributor of quality films, so that the top marketing people, including Mark Lipsky, were involved. "It was just a perfect combination of circumstances. What was good for us was good for them; what was good for them was good for us. But these are big boys. If you turn your back, you'll end up being roasted for breakfast."

Mermaids opened simultaneously in Canada at Toronto's multi-plexed Carlton, Market Square and Canada Square theatres, and at a rep house in Ottawa, earning more than $70,000 in its first 10 days. In Ottawa, it played more than three months. Later, it played in most major Canadian cities, and became one of the few movies made in English Canada to finish in the top 10 in gross revenues among Canadian-financed films in Quebec in 1987. Overall, says Raffé, Cinephile "did a beautiful job of the release, and a very cost effective job." Like almost everything else about *Mermaids*, that sort of accolade to the distributor is not a traditional part of most producers' retrospectives.

For Bennett, the problem for *Mermaids* as for other Canadian films was never distribution, but exhibition—and not just in theatres, but on TV and in home video. With 98 percent of all theatres controlled by American majors, the opportunities for Canadian producers to exhibit their films are strictly curtailed. "The Canadian public doesn't have access to the films. I couldn't get *Mermaids* screened in Sarnia, for example, Patricia's home town, because there were no independent cinemas. It was either Cineplex or Famous Players and they prefer American schlock. The film was out-grossing a lot of stuff in Toronto; Sarnia wouldn't play it. Multiply that by all the other smaller towns and cities across the country, and it's very frustrating."

Still, *Mermaids* performed better for Cinephile in Canada than almost every other Canadian film it has distributed.

By May 1992, *Mermaids* had earned domestic revenues of $644,000. That figure broke down as follows:

Theatrical: $264,965 (net, with an average of 40 percent to the distributor)

Non-theatrical: . . . .$11,223 (net)
Pay Television: . . . .$177,000 (gross)
Free television: . . . .$150,200 (gross)
Video: . . . . $41,000 (gross)

Cinephile's expenses to the same date totalled $207,000, including:

Prints/Lab: $34,000
Shipping: $2,900
Advertising Materials: $25,200
Publicity: . . (includes $30,000 for Festival of Festivals) $51,000
Censor fees: $1,100
Co-op Advertising: $88,200
Sundry: $2,800

The film's net position was therefore $437,000, of which Cinephile's distributor's share was $151,000, The balance accrued to Vos Productions. And for once, both Telefilm and the OFDC not only recouped their investments; they actually made money.

FINAL TAKES Bill House: "It worked, on all the levels that films work. It made you laugh, it made you cry. You feel the emotion of the Polly character and you are with the movie every step of the way. It made money simply because it cost so little. But it was a moment in time, all of these things coming together—Patricia's talent and Alex's talent and the creation of the funds at the OFDC and Telefilm and their desire to succeed, and the fluky selection to Cannes. That's the magic of movies."

Alex Raffé: "The harsh and scary morality tale to the whole thing is, had *Mermaids* been made for a million dollars, we would not yet have broken even. Or maybe just."

Don Haig: "If we only had the money Telefilm spent on films like *Bethune*, we could have made 47 *Mermaids*.

Patricia Rozema: "I told myself over and over again, do it for its images, for the pleasure you get out of it. Do it for your friends. If you get more, that's a bonus."

Donna Wong Juliani: "Above all, trust your instincts. Surround yourself with expertise and people whose judgement you respect, but keep to your course."

2
An Afternoon in the Mad House

The Outside Chance of Maximilian Glick

DIRECTOR:
Allan Goldstein
PRODUCER:
Stephen Foster
CO-PRODUCER:
Richard Davis
WRITER:
Phil Savath, from a
novel by Morley
Torgov
DIRECTOR OF PHOTOGRAPHY:
Ian Elkin
SOUND:
Leon Johnson
EDITOR:
Richard Martin
ACTORS:
Saul Rubinek,
Noam Zylberman,

Fairuza Balk,
Jan Rubes
DISTRIBUTOR:
ALLIANCE RELEASING
(Canada); SOUTH
GATE ENTERTAINMENT
(USA)
RELEASE DATE:
March 10, 1989
RUNNING TIME:
95 minutes
BUDGET:
$2,354,900

"For a producer, film is a series of love affairs. You have a love affair with your writer, and then in production you drop him. You have a love affair with your director, and then in post-production you drop him. And you stop returning their calls. And they're like jilted lovers. They fall apart on you. And cry all over you. And you say, 'Oh, go away. We're not doing that anymore.' And they're never going to talk to you. And rightly. I mean, I understand it." — Stephen Foster, producer

"One of the great difficulties of metaphors where one indulges in them is that they often tell more about one's self and one's life than they do about the subject at hand."
— Richard Davis, producer

SYNOPSIS Max Glick, a 13-year-old Jewish boy in the small town of Beausejour, Manitoba, comes to terms with his bar mitzvah, his family's prejudice, his infatuation with his Polish piano partner, and life, guided by the town's unconventional rabbi, who dreams of being a stand-up comedian.

ORIGINS Stephen Foster is something of a restless spirit. Every year, he goes travelling, devoting two months or more to exploring some distant and challenging corner of the earth—one year, Malaysia, the next, the Amazon. His professional life has been equally quixotic—an actor in Toronto, a student of biology and neuro-psychology at the University of Victoria, a house renovator, a cab driver, a labourer in the high Arctic and, from 1986–88, the driving force behind *The Outside Chance of Maximilian Glick*.

In 1985, an old friend of Foster, a transplanted Torontonian named Alan Morinis, invited him to join his new, Vancouver-based company, Meta Communications. Morinis, a Rhodes scholar and college professor, had learned how to ride the exhilarating crest of the decade's money wave, floating public companies on the Vancouver Stock Exchange. A few years earlier, he had launched a mining company and managed to make several people, including himself, quite rich. The general idea behind Meta was to raise private capital to make feature films—an attractive concept, as difficult to execute then as now. But Foster, with his background in theatre and his facile gift for salesmanship, seemed a good asset to have on board. And so accepting Morinis' offer, he flew back from Yellowknife on a Friday, rented an apartment the same day, bought a car the next, and on Monday morning started work at Northern Lights Media Corp., the production arm of Meta, as vice president of development.

The reality of Northern Lights, however, was as intangible as the astronomical phenomenon for which the company was named. A few respected documentary filmmakers were attached to the firm, including Jack Silberman (*Island of Whales*), but no one seemed to have any understanding of how to produce a feature film. There were "big ideas" to parlay the company's documentary strength into something more grandiose, but "no intelligent ideas I could relate to," Foster says. He did not feel particularly productive—and was made to feel even less so by his partners. "I'd go in every day. They'd say, 'what are you doing here?' " The company, he firmly believes, became a classic victim of its own mythology. "They'd hear that Orion was in trouble and think maybe they could buy it. We spent an entire day on that."

Foster spent his own time scouting for potential film properties, seeking a vessel that could successfully navigate the treacherous shoals of film financing in Canada. Among other things, he was convinced that to raise money for films, he needed a story that was quintessentially Canadian and not overly ambitious. Foster cannot now remember how he first learned about *The Outside Chance of Maximilian Glick*, a short novel by Toronto writer and lawyer Morley Torgov that had won the 1983 Stephen Leacock Award for Humour. He does recall tracking the book down, reading it, and knowing immediately "there was a film there." He knew it because of "one magic moment" in the novel in which the character of Rabbi Kalman Teitleman appears on television as a stand-up comic and, while delivering his spiel, speaks in a kind of code to Max Glick, the young boy who lies at the centre of the story. The incident was narrated differently in the book than it is in the film, but Foster saw it "as a moment outside of reality," with the potential for "classic filmmaking." Foster then asked his Toronto lawyer, Steve Levitan, to negotiate the film rights from Torgov's agent. After some predictable bargaining, Torgov agreed to sell a two-year option worth $2,500 a year, as an advance against a total purchase price of $25,000; additional

percentages were payable if the film were ever made.

At the time, Foster also wanted to spend what he calls a few hundred dollars more to acquire television rights. His partners in Northern Lights refused, claiming that it was at once unnecessary and too costly. "What do we need TV rights for," they said. "It's never going to be a TV series." Foster persisted, instructed Levitan to negotiate the deal with Torgov's agent, and helped turn *Glick* into a popular CBC–TV series that ran for two years. Levitan later left the practice of law to become his partner in the deal— a lucrative one for both producers.

Even after *Glick* gained momentum, Foster's relationship with his partners remained tenuous. The company "never believed for the longest time that this project would happen," he says. "Not a cent of public money raised to launch Northern Lights was invested in the production. I used to rant and rave. It was clear I was out of step." Morinis, who left Meta in 1988, confirms that "a healthy skepticism" surrounded the formative stages of the *Glick* project, but nothing more than most unproven producers would normally encounter. The film's co-producer, Richard Davis, offers a slightly different take on the role of Northern Lights—that its corporate distance from *Glick*, early and late, was occasioned as much by Foster's insistence on control as by anyone's lack of interest. Logically, Davis says, Northern Lights would have been interested, because "they desperately needed something to make the company credible and viable. Steven was extremely protective, and possibly rightly so, because he found the picture, developed it and brought it to where it was. It was his picture."

Foster readily concedes the point. Northern Lights, he claims, had raised somewhere in excess of $1.5 million and managed to spend it within a year. As the ensuing chaos "reduced its possibilities, and as my film increased in stature, they needed it more." By then, he was not inclined to share it. By then, "the best thing for me to do was protect the film, to keep it as far away as possible." Inevitably, there was resentment, especially after *Glick* was well received and Northern Lights was acknowledged, if at all, as a peripheral player.

DEVELOPMENT With the film rights secured, Foster began to search for a writer to adapt the book for the screen. Among the leading candidates was Joe Weisenfeld, a native Winnipegger who had written the teleplay for the immensely popular CBC special, *Anne of Green Gables*. Weisenfeld, however, was already committed to another project. Foster held talks with writer/director Paul Shapiro (*The Truth about Alex*), but he was looking for a feature film project; *Glick* was then conceived as a TV movie.

Then, in June 1986, Foster asked his friend and softball teammate, Phil Savath, to read the Torgov novel and to decide if he was interested in pursuing it. A native New Yorker, Savath had already written several screenplays, including *Fast Company*, which David Cronenberg had directed, *Big Meateater*, a rock 'n roll horror film, and *Samuel Lount*, an historical drama. Savath read the book and told Foster bluntly, "I don't think there's a movie here." According to Savath, there were two problems with the proposal. One was pragmatic. "Steven hadn't done anything. His company was fairly new. And the project didn't look like it had a lot of drive to the screen." The second consideration was creative. As Savath read it, Torgov's book was "about a rabbi who wanted to be a stand-up comic. It was about a family that was really messed up and never redeemed itself. So while it was a sweet family religious story, for that market, it was really anti-family and anti-religious. It seemed to be cutting its own throat as a film." Given this judgement, Savath's only question to Foster was the mercenary one: "Do you have any money?"

By the end of that summer, Foster had raised enough money to finance a treatment. Savath wrote it in two weeks, and indicated he would be prepared to write a first draft if Foster managed to raise development funding. In quest of funds, Foster then took the project to all the obvious suspects, government agencies and private-sector broadcasters. Because of the novel's Jewish content, Foster was confident that Vancouver's Jewish community, some of whose members were prominent in the local film industry, would back the project. He was disappointed. By and large, they either denigrated the book as too identifiably Jewish, or dismissed Torgov as the poor man's Phillip Roth.

Others, however, seemed to respond more favourably, finding the story at once simple, charming and universal. Among the early supporters was Don Smith at BCTV, the local CTV affiliate. Having read the Torgov novel, Smith immediately contributed $1,000 towards the initial treatment, several thousands more for development of the script, and ultimately took a small ($11,000) equity position in the production financing. Foster also approached Telefilm Canada's Western office, then headed by Wayne Sterloff, which agreed to inject about $5,000. Sterloff, who would later become CEO of the B.C. Film Fund and another equity investor in *Glick*, says he was impressed that Foster, although a neophyte, had assembled a solid team and had developed an entertaining property at a time when very little humour was being produced. He also liked Foster's attitude. "He listened. He didn't

come in with any expectation that he deserved funding."

The treatment Savath produced for *Glick* was essentially a sales document, not an outline designed to resolve every plot twist. In fact, according to Foster, "whenever we hit something in the story we couldn't solve, we just wrote it down in a way that made it the sexiest and most attractive. We realized then what was really important. It's not, 'here's our story, take it or leave it.' It's, 'okay, you've read it, you want to read more? Put some money in.' " In Winnipeg, where Foster flew to seek funds and to investigate the city as a possible location for the shoot, both the CBC's regional director Marv Terhoch and Jimy Silden, general manager of the province's newly-formed Cultural Industries Development Office (CIDO) expressed an early interest.

By this time, Foster was seeking a full-bodied development budget of $50,000–60,000. He was counting on Telefilm to deliver about half of that amount, and hoped to patch together the remainder. Through the fall of 1986, he lobbied actively for support—and succeeded. On the strength of the Torgov novel, a saleable treatment, Phil Savath's name attached as the screenwriter, his own energy, and a loose commitment to film in Manitoba, Foster ultimately won the support of the CBC, BCTV and Telefilm. CIDO declined to invest development dollars in a B.C.–produced project, but later became a crucial component in Foster's production financing.

Savath, convinced that Foster would never actually find money for development, let alone production, was at once shocked and horrified when Foster called to tell him to start work on the screenplay. Foster still remembers Savath's flat response to the news that the last development money had been raised: "Hmm . . . Great. I guess that means I have to write it now."

THE SCRIPT Phil Savath started work on the *Glick* screenplay in November 1986. One of his earliest creative decisions proved the most critical—to tell the entire story through the eyes of Max Glick himself. "The only way the events of the story would seem important enough dramatically would be if you were seeing them from inside the kid's head,"

Savath explains. To do that, he decided to rely on a technique widely discredited at the time—voice-over narration. Finding that mechanism was what Savath calls "the crack" in the creative process. Max "would narrate the film, but it would turn out that he wasn't narrating; he was making his bar mitzvah speech. And at the end, you would understand that the movie was his speech, where his parents were a captive audience and would have to listen to his point of view and would see that he was right and they were wrong." The first draft of the screenplay was written in six weeks. Savath worked closely with Foster, talking through the story line as well as individual scenes; only after they had found a mutually agreeable path did Savath begin to write. In this process, he made extensive use of note cards that described specific ideas for scenes or pieces of dialogue. Much of it was written in his head before it was put in the computer. Some of it was tried out on his wife and children and neighbourhood milkmen—in effect, the film's first focus group. For Savath, the writing process is at once mechanical and instinctual—mechanical in building the screenplay's structure, looking for natural act breaks, for scenes that adhere to each other, for seeds planted in one scene that germinate in another. The instinct operates on another plane. "I can smell it," Savath says. "I'm mining a vein and I know it's rich. Something is there. You get to a scene and you go, 'I know there's a joke here.' It's like sculpting. I just have to chip away at it."

In February 1987, Foster began circulating the first draft to friends and colleagues in the industry, soliciting comment. It was uniformly positive—in part, Savath believes, because his writing style "panders to the fact that it's going to be read. It reads well even without actors. It's consciously trying to create an emotional response in the reading of it. Because the clearer you can make them feel, the more likely the reader is to get it right. It's a fictional prose document in that sense." Aspiring screenwriters, Savath notes, must use every weapon in their arsenal to make their scripts stand out. "I try to make mine stand out by making you feel." The other reason why readers found the *Glick* script so appealing was that virtually everyone could identify with it, and see it as their own story. "It really wasn't my story, or Stephen's, or Richard's," Savath says. "But we all thought it was, and that happened to audiences too, whether they were Jewish or not." What remained uncertain was what to call the film. Neither Foster nor Savath was especially enamoured of the book's title, but their own alternatives were less than inspired. Among the other candidates were Red River Rabbi, Bar Mitzvah Boy (a British film had already claimed that title) and Maximilian Glick and the Master of the Universe. "Nothing else really worked," says Savath, so *Outside Chance* "sort of won by default."

Even before Savath had finished writing, Foster began to consider a budget for the film. Not knowing much about the process, he suggested to Richard Davis—a producer who had recently arrived from Australia and taken an office at Northern Lights—that he draft a preliminary budget, in the vicinity

Rabbi Teitleman (Saul Rubinek) advises Max (Noam Zylberman) on the mysteries of life in **The Outside Chance of Maximilian Glick.**

of $1.5 million. That figure was largely a guess, based in part on watching Sandy Wilson's *My American Cousin*, a film Foster thought comparable in scale to his vision of *Glick*. "I really had no idea whether it would cost that much," he says, "But it was a way of telling everybody what size and scale the film as I imagined it would be. I learned right off the bat that it's very important to have a set of answers, even if the answers don't have anything to do with reality." To find those answers, Foster knew that he needed some help. He knew it because, on his own, he could not satisfy the funding agencies that he was capable of making the film. And if they were not insisting on his hiring an executive producer, they were hinting it strongly. Choosing Davis as a co-producer, says Foster, was basically an inspired hunch.

By any standard, Davis was an unconventional character. Physically, he looked like he had just descended from 20 years of meditation on a Himalayan mountain top—tall, with a long mane of grey-white hair, a woolly grey beard and piercing blue eyes. On his hands, he wore silver rings and bracelets from New Mexico, and he was accustomed to coming to work in beach clothes and bare feet. Born in Britain, Davis had emigrated to Australia as a young man and had been, by turns, a writer, poet, cowboy, political advisor to prime minister Gough Whitlam, press secretary to a premier of New South Wales and head of the state's film commission when it backed *My Brilliant Career* and *Phar Lap*. He had moved to Canada for personal reasons, with Montreal as his destination, but stopped in Vancouver, fell in love with the city and stayed. In six months of circulating his resume to production companies, Davis managed to win just three interviews, and became so frustrated that he decided to produce movies on his own. That was how he ended up independently attached to Northern Lights, and how he gravitated within the orbit of *Glick*.

From the start, however, the relationship between Foster and Davis was uneasy. As a partnership, it worked well enough, but the undercurrents were always ominous. Whatever the source of these tensions, to outsiders they remained a credible team — Foster for his youthful exuberance and energy (he was 36 at the time), Davis, then 47, for his seasoning, and the inspiring (to investors at least) air of confidence with which he manipulated what they considered the single most important part of the movie, its budget.

In their approach to the various agencies, Foster was always the front man—charming, attentive, a bit of a firebrand, a quick reader of political winds. "Stephen presents well," Davis concedes. "He's very articulate, very adept at manoeuvring." Thwarted or crossed, however, Foster was also capable of strategic temper tantrums. On those occasions, Davis would be summoned to play the good cop, the calming, dispassionate voice of experience.

The long-accepted premise of *Glick*'s development, of course, was that it was to be a made-for-television movie. Foster had early on contemplated making a feature, but knew instinctively that a TV movie, shot in 16MM, would be in every respect a far simpler enterprise to launch, particularly for a novice producer. Courting senior CBC executives in charge of drama, he was given a mixed reception. Marv Terhoch in Winnipeg had been supportive, but his colleague Jim Burt in Toronto told Foster, "We've done Torgov. We've done Jewish. You probably won't have much of a chance." Foster was nothing if not tenacious. Indeed, for anyone interested in making films, sheer, unrelenting tenacity is probably the single most important requirement. Talent is useful. Brains are a bonus. A firm handshake is always nice. But unless these are accompanied by a steel-belted determination to make it happen, to do everything humanly possible to ensure that it does happen, it won't. All the better if, as in Foster's case, the tenacity arrives with a winning smile and a good set of teeth, a will of iron gloved in velvet.

Foster himself was the very antithesis of defeatism. It was one of the characteristics he decried in Canadians. "We have to stop making excuses in this country for why we can't do things," he says. "We have to stop having this dialogue with failure. Everywhere along the way you see people living in a state of compromise, whining about why it can't be done. There's a psychological assumption that we won't be able to do it. You can't have that in a creative process. You've got to dream the impossible." And so despite Burt's initial reservations, Foster could not afford to give up on the CBC; it was, he knew, "my ticket on that film. It was all going to come down to one meeting, a simple yes or no," that would either push *Glick* into production or stop it cold. "It always comes down to these critical moments. One meeting that may be where two years of my life dies. And it has to be yes. It can't be no. I have to do everything I can to make sure it's yes."

In fact, there were several critical meetings. One came at Banff in May 1987, where Foster had gone to pre-sell the broadcast license to the CBC for its maximum half a million dollars. With a broadcast guarantee, he could then apply to Telefilm Canada's Broadcast Fund for 49 percent of the budget (about $725,000) and find the remainder, he hoped, through provincial agencies and perhaps BCTV. Several CBC executives had read the script and liked it, including Rudy Carter, the head of independent production. But the Corporation wanted a second draft before committing to a broadcast license, and Foster was reluctant. "I was campaigning to get the message up the ladder, 'C'mon in, if you like it. We're going to write a second draft anyway. It'll only get better from here.' "

On a sunny spring day, on the lawn outside the Banff Park Lodge, Foster met with John Kennedy, the CBC's head of drama. Kennedy had read the script and liked it, but had several questions, central among them: who did Foster have in mind to direct? At the time, Foster had in mind Sheldon Larry, a Canadian living in Los Angeles, who had already directed several movies for American networks. In fact, he had held numerous conversations with Larry about attaching a star American actor to the project. (Robin Williams and Jeff Goldblum were among their choices for the role of Rabbi Teitleman.) This was, in effect, a two-track strategy, and Foster "was prepared to go with basically whatever came first. My priority always was the quickest deal. I didn't have big visions for stuff. I was going with the deal that was happening."

The Canadian track was a TV movie, with Telefilm, the CBC, the provinces and "we scam it together." The second track was to find a name American actor to give it instant credibility, a bigger budget and a potentially lucrative U.S. release, probably through HBO. The problem with track two, however, was that Telefilm would not commit as much money to a movie with an American star. Foster thought the policy was slightly perverse—as soon as a producer signed a star with proven box-office appeal, Telefilm cut back its investment so that "you couldn't make the film." Alternatively, he might have filled the shortfall with American money, but then been forced to make script changes that would alter the basic character of the film.

The 15-minute discussion with Kennedy was positive. In return for rights to the film's first window, he committed the CBC to come in for $500,000, conditional on a second draft and on the subsequent approval of Rudy Carter. That approval immediately allowed Foster to apply to Telefilm's Broadcast Fund for another $725,000; as a result, he was only $250,000 away from producing his first movie. Moreover, by delaying a script rewrite until the CBC had committed in principle, Foster managed to avoid producing a third draft, effecting savings of both time and money. All of the changes Savath needed to make could be accommodated in the second draft. The remaining $250,000, however, was not easily pinned down. Negotiations with CIDO dragged on for months. And in the end, he says, there was disappointment; the agency declined to invest what CIDO's guidelines said it could invest— $300,000—leaving Glick about $75,000 short of the amount needed.

Silden insists that CIDO did inject its maximum. In fact, she says, its final commitment of $245,000 was actually more than the maximum allowable under the locations program, the category under which the film qualified. But the agency's regulations did stipulate that participation could rise to $300,000 if the applicants demonstrated "significant benefits to target groups [francophones, native people and women]." Of course, at CIDO and elsewhere, maximum contributions are almost always discretionary, determined by a range of factors, often political. In the case of Glick, Manitoba's culture-crats—under fire for funding what the local film community regarded as an outside production—found it politically expedient to strike a compromise, giving Foster and Davis something less than the maximum, but something more than, on points, they contractually deserved. Foster continued to harangue Silden right through production, because every dollar he failed to wring from CIDO was a dollar he would have to defer.

The financing pieces for the *Glick*-as-TV-movie jigsaw had no sooner been arranged when the film began its strange odyssey into the realm of theatrical feature. Foster had flown to Toronto in the spring of 1987 for a meeting with Linda Beath, then head of production at Telefilm. Beath, in turn, wanted Foster to meet with Peter O'Brian, an independent producer (*The Grey Fox, My American Cousin*), with a view towards making him executive producer. There was, Foster could see, an enormous amount of interest in the project, much of it, he says, of the incredulous variety—as in, "who is this schmuck Foster and how did he come up with this amazing script?" Indeed, he soon concluded that while O'Brian appeared to be offering him help with the movie, he was in fact proposing to take it over. To Foster, it smelled like "a set-up," and he quickly rebuffed O'Brian's overtures. O'Brian says he simply told Foster that it was not his custom to get involved in projects unless he had a major role in decision-making and, since he had already made half a dozen movies, and Foster had made none, a reporting structure in which he answered to Foster seemed somehow inappropriate. But "you don't really need me," O'Brian recalls telling him. "Why don't you just do it yourself?"

With O'Brian or without, however, Linda Beath was urging Foster to turn his movie-of-the-week into a full-fledged feature film. Again, he was initially reluctant, arguing that he would never be able to raise enough money to make a feature. Beath complained that Foster lacked vision. "No," he demurred, "I'm just more practical than you. My priority is to get it made. I can make another good script after this one. This isn't where the world stops." What Foster did not then know, and what the CBC would soon discover to its horror, was that a newly-created Telefilm–National Film Board feature film fund was eagerly seeking projects, and that senior officials at both agencies had identified *Glick* as a prime candidate. All Foster knew was that he seemed to be facing a choice between not making the movie at all for at least another year, because Telefilm's Broadcast Fund was out of money, or trying to raise more money to make a feature; he readily chose the latter.

That choice had several critical consequences. One was that the film would need to be shot in 35MM instead of 16MM, a far more ambitious undertaking that would ultimately push the budget from $1.5 million to $2,354,900, and require Foster to find new investors. A second was that Foster immediately needed to find a Canadian distributor for the film, without which Telefilm could not participate. And a third result was that the CBC, having committed half a million dollars on the assumption of exclusivity and first broadcast rights, was furious about the change in the direction and ready to pull out entirely.

Finding most of the additional money for production proved less complicated than might have been expected. That, of course, was largely the result of the 1985 Telefilm–National Film Board accord, which funnelled money through the federal Department of Communications, expressly to finance private sector co-productions in the regions—outside Ontario and Quebec. The NFB's then head of production, Peter Katadotis, liked the *Glick* project and actively championed its cause. "It was almost a call to arms on his part," recalls Ches Yetman, the Board's executive producer for Manitoba. "I was a little amazed." The NFB ultimately committed $456,811 to the financing budget. And Wayne Sterloff's B.C. Film Fund pledged another $170,000 of production financing. Of that amount, however, Sterloff was able to reduce the agency's risk by selling half of its equity to the Beacon Group, a Vancouver–based venture capital firm; Beacon was essentially buying tax write-offs.

The distribution issue was addressed—at least temporarily—by shopping the project to various distributors and seeking the best minimum guarantee. Foster's first choice was Northstar, which was then being run by an old friend, Danny Weinzweig. But when Weinzweig read the script, he concluded that it would work best as a TV movie, not as a feature. Foster explained that Telefilm was urging him to make *Glick* a feature because no money was left in the Broadcast Fund. "I still don't think it's a theatrical movie," Weinzweig said bluntly. To which Foster replied: "I couldn't agree with you more."

Other Canadian distributors, including Astral, were equally underwhelmed. But one unlikely candidate did voice an interest—Montreal-based Malofilm. Foster quickly signed a letter of agreement accepting an offer from its president, René Malo—a $250,000 advance for Canadian rights only. That accord left Northern Lights with control of the potentially lucrative U.S. and foreign territories. In a production that already involved B.C. producers intending to shoot a film in Manitoba with the participation of two provincial agencies, Telefilm Canada, the CBC and the NFB, the addition of a Quebec-based distributor made *Glick* even more national in scope and, Foster hoped, that much more difficult to derail.

Indeed, on paper, the entire project now seemed simply irresistible. It had a script that almost everyone found amusing. It had a theme that trumpeted the motherhood virtues of ethnic tolerance and understanding. It had a budget that was within the bounds of rationality. It had a production team that combined Foster's energy with Davis' savvy, a blend of skills to hearten the most skeptical of bureaucrats. And, more important than anything else, it fulfilled the cultural/political mandates of its several sponsors—to make films and breed talent in places other than southern Ontario and Quebec. *Glick*, in short, was as perfectly and politically correct a product as anyone could ever have concocted. Astutely and unabashedly, Stephen Foster wrapped himself in this flag. "I must have said it a million times," he says. "If this film can't get made in this country, no film can ever get made in this country."

The key to all of it, Foster believed, was Savath's script, which even "pinheads and cretins could get, could see the film you were trying to make." He traded on that response even more after the second draft, which consensus said was more focussed and streamlined, with stronger female characterizations, and a more energized role for "Max" himself. The importance of the script is not misstated. Quality feature film scripts, even television scripts masquerading as feature films, are so rare in this country— rare in any country, for that matter—that the mere sight of one truly intelligent, amusing and artfully constructed screenplay is enough to send industry pulse rates soaring.

The producers' sole cause for concern was the CBC, where Ivan Fecan had succeeded John Kennedy as the czar of programming. According to Foster, Fecan was uninterested in quaint, rural, evocative, family-type movies. What Fecan wanted was hard-hitting, contemporary and urban. Yet later, it became clear that Fecan, too, loved the *Glick* script—so much so that he commissioned the TV series that followed the film. But Fecan's mindset was irrelevant. The issue here had nothing to do with genre, and everything to do with ownership of the property, on which the CBC believed it held the only valid deed.

By then, Foster had already sublet space from the National Film Board and set up a pre-production office in Winnipeg. When he called the CBC's Rudy Carter to announce that the TV movie the Corporation had helped develop had suddenly been turned into a theatrical feature, he knew that the CBC would be incensed and, more critically, that his $500,000 broadcast guarantee would be instantly in jeopardy. Foster immediately arranged an appointment to see Fecan. The day before the scheduled meeting, Carter called to say that Fecan had cancelled. "I'm coming anyway," Foster told Carter. "And I'm going to sit outside his office until he sees me. I'm going to phone the press. I'm going to phone everybody, just to let them know I'm sitting there, because I've got nowhere else to be." The meeting was held at 11 A.M. the next day.

"Everybody just tore at me," Foster recalls. " 'You fucking kid! You don't know what you're doing.' It was that sort of fury about the whole thing." And normally I would be tense, but I was loose. It had gone from the sublime to the ridiculous." Foster could afford to be loose because the anger was not directed at him, but at Telefilm's Linda Beath and the NFB's Peter Katadotis, the perceived co-conspirators. "Stephen," Carter agrees, "was just the meat in the sandwich." Fecan's attitude was, "why do I need to buy your picture now? I don't have to commit half a million dollars. If you're going to do a feature film, I'll wait until it's done, and look at it; then I'll make an offer. Why does everyone want me to play my hand? Let's see them [Telefilm] play their hand," he added, alluding to the agency's failure to sign a real contract with Foster. "It's the colour of money, baby."

Foster's counter-argument—lame, but the only one available—was that the CBC had a cultural obligation to support Canadian films, particularly a film like *Glick*. It was only natural that as producer, he would take the biggest opportunity and the biggest budget; anybody in his situation would have done the same. Unfortunately, as a consequence, the CBC would be losing a broadcast window and the chance to include the film in next year's programming line-up.

Fecan's reservations, of course, were as much political as pragmatic. According to Carter, "Ivan was livid" that the project had effectively been hijacked by Telefilm and the Film Board. In fact, it was worse than that. The takeover had been conducted in total secrecy, without consultation. Fecan had been handed a fait accompli. And more than *Glick* was potentially involved; Carter says the Telefilm-NFB accord had targetted a whole package of CBC-developed TV movies. Thus, in an industry driven by cultural priorities, the heart-warming *Glick* project had become first prize in a nasty, institutional tug-of-war. From Foster's perspective it was "like everyone wants to make this film so much, they're going to kill each other trying to do it, and we'll never get it made."

Indeed, while virtually everyone was theoretically committed, virtually no one had signed. The CBC advance was now in limbo. The only piece of paper Foster had from his distributor, René Malo, was a one-page letter of intent; discussions about the details were proving contentious. CIDO's money was always conditional on Telefilm involvement. And the Telefilm money itself was in grave doubt. Although the agency had given the project an unofficial green light, it had not yet formally approved the project. Worse, there were persistent rumours that Telefilm had exceeded its budget by a reported $40 million and was on the brink of closing its doors for the rest of the fiscal year, leaving *Glick* and several other scheduled productions in jeopardy. In the interim, the agency was demanding reassurance of the CBC's financial commitment now that the film had become a theatrical feature—a demand Fecan and Carter greeted with their sarcastic "After you, Alfonse."

Eventually, the CBC acquiesced, but slashed its $500,000 first window fee to a $250,000 second window license. The subsequent $250,000 gap made Telefilm's dollars even more crucial. It was Linda Beath who had urged Foster to think 'feature,' Beath who had assured him that financing could be arranged. Now, that assurance looked in doubt.

There were problems as well with the National Film Board, which, in return for its money, wanted to be named lead producer. Foster was determined not "to let it do that. This wasn't an in-house thing for them. They weren't producing the film. We had a big fight because I said, 'Look, you're coming in at the very end with money. You don't get the right to claim top credit.'" Yetman stood firm; the NFB, he said, would need to have a lead credit or there would simply be no film. "Stephen realized I was rigid about that." In the end, they compromised, giving the Film Board the credit line, "in association with," instead of its more customary and preferred "in co-production with." And so as the summer of 1987 gave way to fall, and Foster and Davis went into pre-production, the producers "had no idea what the financing was," and *The Outside Chance of Maximilian Glick* was looking chancier by the day.

It was about to get worse. Two crises at Telefilm separately threatened to scuttle the *Glick* enterprise. Foster and Davis at this point were deeply into pre-production and running out of money. Telefilm had announced a freeze on all payments until its books had been sorted out. Without an immediate infusion of about $50,000, the production would be forced to suspend operations. Foster looked everywhere for interim or bridge financing—from CIDO, from Northern Lights—but everyone "danced away." On a Friday evening in October, Foster received a call from the CBC's Rudy Carter, who was attending the Vancouver International Film Festival. Carter invited him to have a beer.

"I'll tell you, Rudy," Foster said. "It's not a beer that I need."

"Oh?," said Carter, "What do you need?"

"I need $50,000 to buy me some time while Telefilm sorts things out, and I don't think I can do it."

Carter tried to be encouraging. "You've got to do it. You've got to hang in there."

"Fine," said Foster. "Then give me $50,000."

"When do you need it," Carter inquired.

The money was approved by Ivan Fecan the following Monday—an accelerated partial payment of the CBC's broadcast license fee. Foster was later told that no cheque had ever moved with more speed through the CBC system. Looking back on that moment, Foster now sees it as one of a series of remarkable events that conspired, at key points, to sustain the project. But that was only the first hurdle. The second, which came a few weeks later, proved to be an even larger challenge. This time, it was not an interim payment from Telefilm that was being delayed. This time, the agency was in the throes of fiscal anarchy. It had over-committed its feature film fund and was pulling back from projects that had been conditionally green-lighted. Its entire commitment to *Glick* hung in the balance. Again, Foster was within hours of shutting down production, possibly forever.

Inevitably, perhaps, there are now many claimants to the title of saviour of *Max Glick*. Jimy Silden, for example, believes that it was the Manitobans— CIDO, as well as the regional director for the Department of Communications in Ottawa, Roger Collet—who ultimately managed to save the project. The Manitoban argument was that Telefilm's own bureaucratic delays had caused *Glick* to get caught in the snares of the agency's financial shortfall; the first major feature film in the province did not deserve to be victimized by administrative negligence.

The NFB's Ches Yetman remembers anguished calls to Peter Katadotis and to François Macerola, the Film Board's president. Katadotis was convinced that nothing could salvage the *Glick* production. Macerola, who held a seat on Telefilm's board, was more optimistic. Later, Foster received a call from Jean Sirois, then chairman of Telefilm Canada, who seldom talked directly to producers. Sirois told him to "sit tight," and assured him that "things were being taken care of."

The central question was not whether to save *Glick*; there was more than enough political weight behind the project to do that. The question was how, since the whole Telefilm financing structure was essentially in limbo. The answer was bridge financing, the unlikely financiers being B.C. Film Commission ($295,000) and the NFB itself (a larger amount that, amazingly, no one seems able to remember). That provided enough money to last until Telefilm's new fiscal year kicked in. The final financing arrangement, almost wholly dependent on the public purse, later earned Foster some friendly derision from colleagues in the industry. But in a year in which many other projects were either delayed or cancelled outright, Foster's pan-Canadian approach gave him the last laugh. In fact, by the time it played at Toronto's Festival of Festivals in 1988, *Glick* was being hailed as the new model of film financing.

Eventually, the production was fully financed, except for about $75,000–100,000—the proverbial shortfall that affects virtually every Canadian film. Inevitably, there were now hints that the producers should bridge the gap by deferring some of their fees. Foster says he "hit the roof" when the D word was used. and threatened to walk away from the project. "I said, 'No. If I'm doing a deferral, it all goes down,' " Foster recollects. "As far as I was concerned, it was not on—period. Fuck them all!" If that was a bluff, no one was prepared to call it. Too much work had been done, and by then, *Glick* was no longer simply Stephen Foster's film; it was Linda Beath's film, Peter Katadotis' film, Ches Yetman's film and Jimy Silden's film, among others.

In the end, after an enormous wrangle with Telefilm, Foster did agree to a small deferral. It became an equity investment in the film and was "grandfathered," so that it was eligible for the 100 percent Capital Cost Allowance write-off. (The CCA regime, in place until the late 1980s, provided tax incentives to investments in Canadian film.) Foster then sold the write-off to the Beacon Group, which, he noted ironically, was then able to call itself an investor in a film that was already made and in which it had taken no risk. Northern Lights also agreed to defer a portion of its production company fee, but was given a first tier in recoupment. Total deferrals amounted to $68,188.

In retrospect, Foster sees the deferral issue as "a terrible fight," but an important one for producers. It may have been easy for the agencies to say to him, 'you own the film. You have the most potentially to gain. Therefore, take some risk up front by deferring your fee.' But the awful truth of

Canadian cinema is that very few films have any realistic hope of profit at the back end. And what producers are deferring is not so much their profit, but their livelihood. In the end, Foster earned $70,000, making himself on a per-hour basis, "the lowest-paid person on that show." But the money, Foster insists, was incidental, "because it was my entry-level film and I was there for the ride." Davis was paid $50,000.

The final financing picture was as follows:

Telefilm:	$1,153,000
NFB:	$456,811
B.C. Film:	$170,000
CIDO:	$245,000
CBC:	$250,000
Deferrals:	$68,188
BCTV:	$11,000

FINDING A DIRECTOR Back when *Glick* was still a TV movie, Stephen Foster had approached Paul Shapiro as a possible writer/director. Shapiro turned it down, explaining that he wanted to make feature films. Foster then talked to Sandy Wilson who had a conflict, and to Emmy-award-winning television and film director George Bloomfield, who was also unavailable. Later, Foster "hung on almost too long" for Sheldon Larry, thinking he would eventually accept. Davis judged the whole romance with Larry doomed because neither Jeff Goldblum nor any other Hollywood star was likely to work on such a small film. In the end, Foster believes, Larry "got nervous, career-wise. It wasn't a big enough picture for him. He just couldn't make the leap."

Late in the process, Foster sent Allan Goldstein a copy of Torgov's novel. A native of Montreal, Goldstein was living in New York, directing TV movies. He liked the book and asked to read Savath's adaptation. Later, while shooting a mini-series for American Playhouse in Toronto, Goldstein arranged to meet Foster for lunch at the Peter Pan restaurant. It was there that they reached an agreement. The director's fee: $100,000. For Goldstein, Glick was "my story." The son of militant trade unionists (his grandfather was a founder of the United Textile Workers of America), Goldstein grew up in the working-class, Catholic, east end of Montreal. "So all the stuff that little boy was going through, I went through. Falling in love with a Catholic girl. The whole thing. I really responded to that. A lot of screenplays lose something in translation from a book. Phil only made it better."

Just as writers must write what they know best, directors, Goldstein believes, must work with material that speaks to them, something that resonates "like a piece of fine crystal. When you hear that lovely sound," he advises, "pursue it. Be dogged, be determined, do not stop for anything or anybody." That, certainly, was his attitude on the set of *Glick*, and it was one that won him a goodly number of enemies. Goldstein is not especially perturbed by that legacy. "As long as you get through it, everyone will be happy in the end. They'll have a movie they'll think about for the rest of their careers and go 'Geez, it was a bitch to make, but it was a great picture.'"

CASTING As a first-time producer, Stephen Foster readily acknowledged his ignorance of many areas of film production. Casting was not one of them. As a former actor, Foster felt he understood both the craft and the kinds of talent he needed to successfully translate the Savath script to film. His handicap was budget, but he was convinced that good actors (like directors) were always hungry for good material and would sacrifice major-league fees for a chance to play a part rich in character.

Having drafted a tentative list of actors he wanted, Foster approached the largest casting agency in Toronto. When the agency heard his proposed budget, they told him he would never be able to sign those actors. Foster insisted he would, and soon hired an independent casting agent, Arlene Berman, to work for the film. "I am," he says, "a firm believer in [Hollywood screenwriter] William Goldman's first and only law of filmmaking, which is that nobody knows anything. My approach was: I will listen and at a certain point it shuts down, and then I make my decision and I live with the consequences." With two exceptions, every one of the actors on Foster's original list said yes, including Jan and Susan Rubes, and Fairuza Balk.

Because the core of the movie is the character of Max Glick, Foster knew that it "lived or died" on the choice of "that kid. I had to deliver there, or there was no film." Dozens of child actors were auditioned. Foster rejected them all. The right kid, in Foster's opinion, was Seth Green, the child actor who had appeared in Woody Allen's *Radio Days*. Because he was American, however, none of the agencies would allow him to be hired. Eventually, but not without reservations, the largely inexperienced Noam Zylberman was hired for the role.

For the part of Rabbi Teitleman, Foster had early on considered Saul Rubinek, one of the country's leading character actors. But on the written page, the character was imbued with a mystical, almost Chagallian soul, floating off the ground. In Foster's mind, Rubinek was too earthy an actr to play that part, and perhaps too old. As a result, Foster auditioned se other candidates before he decided to send the script to Rubinek. Ev he instructed Rubinek to read it for the role of Max's father. T' was exactly what Foster had expected—a stream of phone ca' from Rubinek insisting that he had to have the Teitleman actor could do justice to it. Foster says he "deliberate' calls for a couple of days. I just let it fester." Thi' give Foster negotiating leverage, so that he c' financial and creative, that the producer dicta. $25,000, less than the actor could have elsewhere

THE OUTSIDE CHANCE OF M

demands were simply the theatrical convention when Telefilm could tell you otherwise was to leave itself exposed—and lost the film as a result. And he remains convinced that Malo "was happy to see it go. If he had really wanted it, he would have sorted it out." (René Malo himself declined to recount his own chronicle of events.) Thus, with Telefilm's tacit blessing, Foster allowed a signing deadline to pass, and announced that the deal was off. When Malo then said it was prepared to reopen talks, Foster declined.

THE FESTIVAL OF FESTIVALS Stephen Foster does not believe in the focus group school of filmmaking. As a result, he had deliberately kept advance screenings of the film to a bare minimum. Festival organizers had of course looked at it. But Foster does not mind admitting that he "really didn't want people to see it. In the end, you're making your own film. How much do you need to listen to what people think? I really wanted to control how the film went out there."

Glick's appearance at the F of F, therefore, was very much a premiere. And critically, it was probably the film's high-water mark. An overflow crowd turned up for the gala event. For Foster, seeing the line-up snaking round the Varsity Cinema was "of all the moments, the best moment. Half the people I've met in my life were there." And contrary to every expectation, the film won the festival's best Canadian film award, trumping the front-runner, David Cronenberg's Dead Ringers, and pocketing $25,000. A few days later, Foster met with Alliance's Victor Loewy and sold the film's Canadian rights to Alliance for a $250,000 minimum guarantee, plus what he calls favourable terms on producer's percentages past the recoupment of Alliance's costs. And it was there, too, that the CBC first broached the tantalizing possibility of Glick as a TV series.

THE CAMPAIGN The poster chosen for the Canadian release of Glick—a last-minute substitution, made after Alliance's Victor Loewy rejected an earlier choice—showed the backs of Max and his Polish girlfriend, holding hands, seated at the piano. It carried the tag line, 'Some people have all the luck.' (In Yiddish, glick means luck.) Davis thought the shot was out of focus—and it was. Alliance's director of marketing, Mary-Pat Gleeson, confirms that it was the one slide from the unit photography shoot that could be made to work, and even it "had to be air-brushed like crazy." Foster approved the poster design, but later concluded that a less interesting poster would have been hard to find. Goldstein thought "it made absolutely no sense. My movie is not about the backs of two kids staring at a piano. My movie is a comedy. It's meant to be irreverent and funny." The poster designed for the U.S. release was at once savvier and more compelling; a collage, it showed a baseball glove, a piano and Max's family. It also had a very clever tag line: "When Max was born, they cut off his . . . Thirteen years later, they're still at it." And the American distributor (South Gate

Entertainment), Goldstein observes, had even less money for the one-sheet than Alliance.

In Gleeson's mind, the primary audience for Glick was 12–24 year-olds. But it was a tough sell because after the age of 15, teenagers "don't want to see this. Then you go for the moms and dads and people who want a nice little story." The Jewish community was an obvious target, but Alliance was fearful of focussing the film too narrowly. To Gleeson, it was just "a sweet, gentle love story about two little kids. Jewish, Polish, Irish, English, it wouldn't have mattered." In total, she estimates that Alliance poured about $100,000 into the film's prints and ads campaign, including about $10,000 for a trailer.

Foster thinks Alliance's campaign was as good as it could be, given its limitations. From a promotional standpoint, it was understaffed. Advertising was expensive. And there was no expectation of profit. Still, he is not without criticism. Not enough posters were actually put up in theatres. Alliance simply wrote off Quebec. And while he liked the trailer—"too bad they didn't show it. I went to every theatre. I never saw it, not once." It was, he concluded, the classic Canadian denouement.

THE OPENING *Glick* premiered in Winnipeg on March 3, 1989, almost six months after its appearance at the Toronto Festival of Festivals. Part of the delay was occasioned by the making of the trailer, and part by the unsuccessful attempt to find a U.S. distributor and piggy-back the Canadian release. Alliance's Victor Loewy had been reluctant to open in Winnipeg— he considered it too small—but Foster felt it was the logical choice. The results were disappointing. "All the politicians and everybody" came to the premiere, Foster recalls, but "they were the deadest audience, and the run was completely a dead run. I don't know if they had all moved to Miami for the winter."

The film opened in Toronto and Vancouver on March 10, 1989 to mixed reviews. "Stereotypes never get out of the box in this slight, small-town comedy," said *Variety*. "Director Allan Goldstein seems incapable of keeping others from stereotypical mugging and he doesn't sustain the action. Theatrical potential dim." In the *Globe and Mail*, Rick Groen called the film a "sweetly comic ode to the virtues of middle class life . . . a little precious, a little awkward, but with a bright and shiny moral clearly conveyed." Rubinek, Groen said, was the comic pulse of the film and its main source of energy. *Maclean's* Brian D. Johnson described *Glick* as a "Jewish Walt Disney," full of "brotherhood themes too cutely portrayed."

In Toronto, Foster says, Cineplex "promised us a couple of theatres but we only got one," Canada Square for six weeks and then the Carlton. A more logical choice would have been the Promenade multiplex, in the heart of the city's northern Jewish neighbourhood. In Vancouver, the film was originally booked at the downtown multiplexed Royal Centre, where Foster was convinced it would die an early death. "I got in and bitched and moaned, and had it moved to the Oakridge," in the city's Jewish district. In Montreal, *Glick* opened on May 19, 1989 at the Alexis Nihon Plaza, opposite the Montreal Forum, on the night of a playoff hockey game. "You wouldn't put any good film in there," Foster contends. "We were dumped in there." Nevertheless, it grossed a respectable $40,106 during its Montreal run.

Altogether *Glick* ran 12 weeks in Toronto, six weeks in Vancouver and 10 weeks in Montreal. Still, Foster felt that Cineplex, the exhibitor, "let us down. We got the back of the bus. We were not given more than one theatre in each town." In total, the film grossed $179,981 in Canada—better, says Alliance's Gleeson, than had been expected. She takes Foster's criticism as the standard bleat. "I've never seen a producer who wasn't disappointed with the gross," she says. "Stephen thought he had a wunderkind. It was a nice little film, but it wasn't the greatest film we've ever seen."

Sterloff, from his Vancouver vantage point, thought Alliance's efforts were typical of the day. "The film wasn't mistreated," he says. "It was just victimized by the normal method of operation. There was very little in the way of marketing and promotion. That was what happened to indigenous films that didn't have American stars in them." Davis is equally accepting of the distributor's dilemma. When a company is promoting films with no stars and only three percent of Canada's screen time available for exhibition, it's comparable to "running downhill with a very large boulder getting closer and closer. That's not conducive to people either taking risks or going all out." Within the constraints, he says, Alliance "did a good job."

THE U.S. RELEASE After the film was complete, Foster hired Linda Beath, who had been fired from Telefilm, to shop the film to U.S. distributors. Foster's account of these discussions is vague. He "danced with the Americans for a while," and held out hope that Samuel Goldwyn would buy the film, given its reputation for the successful handling of smaller pictures. He and Beath "worked our way down the list." In the end, the Americans just "weren't putting up the kind of money we wanted to get. And you're left having to do the best deal you can do." In this case, however, the best deal was no deal at all. By 1989, Foster had set up his own company, Fosterfilm, leaving *Glick*'s foreign rights to Northern Lights, by then under the operating control of Richard Davis.

The very clear lesson here is closure. If a film does well at a major festival, says Wayne Sterloff, the producers have 24 hours to nail down a good deal. "You don't have seven days or two weeks, because by then it's on to the next festival and the next potential hit." That, he concedes, represents an investor's opinion. The investor has taken the financial risk, supported emerging talent and now wants to recoup as fast as possible. "Sure, there may be a chance of doing something better, but we've had our long shot, thank you very much. It's time now to get a little more pragmatic and start covering our butt." *Glick*, Sterloff notes, was doing very well at festivals. "Some very nice deals should have been signed that weren't signed. I think they did as well as they could for a team of under-capitalized neophytes, but in retrospect that's where the blip was. We didn't exploit the American opportunities."

Goldstein agrees. "There's no question in my mind that Richard and Stephen dropped the ball on the U.S. release." Goldstein recalls 12 or 13 separate offers for the film after its screening at the Festival of Festivals. "New Line, Goldwyn, Orion Classics, everybody wanted to distribute this picture. I said 'Stephen, this is not *Robocop*. This is not *Gone With the Wind*. This is a little movie. Go with them.'" Like Sterloff, Goldstein maintained that *Glick* had a very narrow window of opportunity to exploit. "We were the flavour of the week. And I told him, "either take advantage now or we're long forgotten.'"

The foreign rights to *Glick* were eventually acquired by the International Movie Group when it took over Northern Lights in 1989. Davis acknowledges that the funding agencies were not amused at the fact that the rights had been transferred for no advance. But his position is that he deserved some credit just for getting the film, "which had been around the block for a year," into the hands of a distributor. "What are you going to do? Let the picture die? Or are you going to get the picture out. It may well have been a mistake," Davis admits. "But I would rather have the picture I was associated with seen, than have it sit on a shelf."

IMG, in turn, sold U.S. (and Israeli) rights to South Gate Entertainment. According to Foster, South Gate, too, initially had "great hopes" for the film, despite a poor reception in San Francisco, where it was test-marketed. The American release strategy was platforming—opening in Florida and the southeastern corridor and then building on that success as it moved into other regions. For a family-oriented film with no exploitation, no car crashes, no mayhem, no murders and no sex, the platforming route made the most marketing sense.

Sterloff, among others, thought its obvious appeal to Jewish filmgoers would give it legs in large American cities—long theatrical runs that would translate into healthy video and pay–television sales. But South Gate ran into problems booking suitable theatres. And the company was under-capitalized—it has since filed for protection from its creditors under Chapter 11 of the U.S. bankruptcy laws—and decided to move *Glick* quickly into video to recover some of its expenses. Foster says *Glick* was beaten in the U.S. by a combination of bad luck and bad management. Producers, he insists, must navigate their film through distribution, just as they do through the actual shoot. Otherwise, "you're competing with 20 or 30 other films, and there's no reason for them to push any harder on one than another."

Sterloff considers the U.S. theatrical release of *Glick* the most disappointing aspect of the film's history. Had it been promoted by a company that understood regional platform releasing, it would, he insists, have done much better. He points out, of course, that the movie was governed by now obsolete release strategies. "Six months pay windows, six months theatrical windows—that was the standard thinking three years ago," says Sterloff. "Now it's a joke. As soon as the theatrical window closes, you move, either into video or into pay-TV. If you've got a free [TV] deal, then move into free, and as soon as the broadcaster has his shot, get it out into video or pay-per-view. But for God's sake compress—so that you're maximizing the earning potential."

Nevertheless, the film did perform well in isolated markets, particularly the Miami/Fort Lauderdale area where it played some 22 weeks and won the best film award at the Fort Lauderdale Film Festival. *Glick* was also nominated for (but did not win any of) five Genie awards, including Best Picture, Best Actor (Rubinek), Best Supporting Actress (Susan Rubes), Best Adapted Screenplay and Best Costume Design. But perhaps the best compliment it received was the CBC's decision to turn it into a half-hour TV series.

Davis was furious that Foster had negotiated the ownership of the TV rights while still working at Northern Lights. "Stephen had part ownership of Northern Lights, the movie was developed at Northern Lights, and just because the contract didn't include TV rights, it was fairly fast footwork to set up a deal with somebody else and then announce that you were leaving and doing the series." Foster says the company had had its chance to buy the rights and refused. But he did — on Davis' insistence—agree to pay a token fee on each TV episode to Northern Lights.

To some extent, Foster maintains, the controversy that swirled around the film is symptomatic of structural flaws that still exist in the Canadian film industry. The agendas of the financing agencies are driven largely by politics and culture, not by commercial considerations. As a result, mainstream films made in Canada tend to solve a series of political and cultural problems, without reference to market standards. The more government agencies involved, the more political the issues. "It's the tail wagging the dog," Foster insists, "over and over again. It's why most of our films are not very interesting. We pretend we've got a bona fide, complete film industry when we don't. It's just an artificially constructed, government-financed hobby." Others disagree, noting that Foster's 'hobby' creates thousands of full-time jobs and that, in the absence of private-sector involvement, governments represent the only financing vehicle still moving.

FINAL TAKES Richard Davis: "The real danger for producers is that because you are in the rare position of being God, it's very hard to keep a sense of proportion. Because you're never really the conductor. You're always maybe the first violin. And so every time you take the stand and say, 'I'm in charge here,' somebody pulls the chain from somewhere else. Essentially, producers are neurotic control freaks, but then so are most of the people on the picture. It's an afternoon in the madhouse."

Stephen Foster: "Film is a team effort, and because there are so many variables, you're always compromising. But given an allowable amount of compromise, I do feel that the film we set out to make, and the film we ended up making, were as close as you could get."

3
Hanging On
To The Horses

A Rustling of
Leaves: Inside the
Philippine
Revolution

Nettie Wild
PRODUCER:
Nettie Wild
EXECUTIVE PRODUCER:
Chris Pinney
ASSOCIATE PRODUCER:
Peter Wintonick
CINEMATOGRAPHY:
Kirk Tougas
SOUND:
Gary Marcuse
EDITOR:
Peter Wintonick
DISTRIBUTOR:
KALASIKAS
PRODUCTIONS
(Canada); THE
EMPOWERMENT

PROJECT (USA); FILMS
TRANSIT (world)
RELEASE DATE:
April 21, 1989
RUNNING TIME:
112 minutes
BUDGET:
$500,000

"There's a policy and there's a reality. And as an independent producer, you just cannot afford to take 'No' for an answer." — Nettie Wild

SYNOPSIS *A Rustling of Leaves* explores the bloody landscape of the modern Philippines by focussing on three separate parties to the conflict— the legal left, as represented by Senate candidate (and former rebel) Bernabe (Dante) Buscayno; the illegal left (the underground New People's Army and Sparrow assassins); and the right-wing vigilantes (the Alsa Masa and radio DJ and propagandist, Jun Pala). Their interwoven stories illuminate the difficult political choices that confront reform-minded Filipinos.

ORIGINS In the early 1980s, a young, politically-charged actress named Nettie Barry Canada Wild directed *Right to Fight*, a video documenting the relationship between housing and profit—specifically a long and bitter struggle between the residents of Kitsilano, a Vancouver neighbourhood, and a group of real estate developers. Eventually, the developers went bankrupt, and the government was persuaded to build more affordable housing. It is a measure of Wild's fierce political convictions that she now lives on that very site, occupying a small apartment in a 42-unit housing co-operative. The co-op is designed, she says, "for single parents and wacko artists." Where that leaves Wild is not exactly clear; she has no children and, while her cinematic art has been described in many ways, sometimes even pejorative ways, wacko is not one of them.

Tall, lean and angular, Nettie Wild is like an Annie Hall who has

Nettie Wild, producer and director, **A Rustling of Leaves.**

discovered politics, at once insouciant and totally committed. She projects an inner gaiety and yet, in common with those filmmakers who actually manage to cross the great chasm between conception and execution in film, she is never at rest. The daughter of a journeyman journalist and a Metropolitan Opera singer, Wild studied theatre at the University of British Columbia, and then acted in several community-based and avant-garde theatre groups. One show, "Under the Gun—A Disarming Review" (1983)—skewered what it saw as Canada's duplicitous role in support of military dictatorships; the story involved a fictitious weapons company executive who travels to the Philippines. Wild played Pierre Elliott Trudeau.

Among her audiences were members of Canada's expatriate Filipino community, who urged her to visit their homeland. Nothing if not resourceful, Wild then managed to parlay her interest in the Philippines into an $8,000 Canada Council theatre grant to study the country's popular theatre, and a smaller "investigate" grant from the National Film Board to consider making a film on indigenous Filipino theatre. So, in 1985, she embarked on what she calls "this very extraordinary adventure, in this incredible zoo that was the Philippines." She attended a popular theatre festival in Manila and then, using a code name ("Mandy," her dog's name) and in high secrecy, trekked with a Filipino translator, Inday, into the mountains of Mindanao—stronghold of the rebel New Peoples Army (NPA)—to work with a nascent theatre group. It was on Mindanao, where art was politics by another name, that she met for the first time the committed NPA commanders and disciples who would later figure prominently in *A Rustling of Leaves.*

By the time she returned to Canada five months later, she had heard and seen enough to know that the NPA would make an ideal subject for a documentary film. She had no real experience in direction or production, and no money. But she had something more important—privileged access to the NPA and to Raoul, commander of the unit that had been her host on Mindanao. Before she left, she typed up an agreement under which she would be permitted to film three specific scenes: a gathering of the people's revolutionary court; the Sparrows (the NPA's urban assassins); and a tactical raid by the NPA regular forces. Like many such agreements, a pragmatic symbiosis was at work. For the NPA, the documentary offered a chance to spread its political message beyond the Philippine archipelago. For Wild, it provided an opportunity to put herself on the map of Canadian filmmaking.

DEVELOPMENT Back in Vancouver, Wild suggested to a friend, Chris Pinney, a local film distributor, that they draft proposals for two small TV films—one 30-minute film exploring Filipino street theatre; the other, a more straightforward, 60-minute journalistic documentary on the NPA. Versions of the two treatments were duly written, tailored to specific audiences and sent everywhere—CBC, CTV, PBS, the Canada Council, the National Film Board and all the commercial networks in the U.S. The NPA treatment, about 30 pages of single-spaced copy, generated more interest than did street theatre and was immediately promoted to the front burner. The working title was *Kalasikas*, which means "a rustling of leaves" in the Tagalog language. Only in post-production did Wild decide to adopt the translation as the title, "because nobody could pronounce it." She used Kalasikas as the name of her production company.

Pinney agreed to produce but, owing to his work with Vancouver–based IDERA Films and its connections to the field of international development, he deemed it politically prudent to adopt a pseudonym—Chris James; Wild would direct. They tentatively decided to begin filming in early 1986—assuming they could raise production financing. It was a generous assumption. The Canadian networks were completely unresponsive to her proposal. CTV declined to see her. TV Ontario voiced interest, but offered no money. And at the CBC, one official told her flatly, "Canadians aren't interested in little brown people on the other side of the world." The Americans, on the other hand, were interested. Wild had something no American news correspondent could match: exclusive access to the NPA. Not surprisingly, however, they were interested on their terms only. Flown to New York to meet NBC's head of current affairs, Wild realized that her own role in any network production would be minimal. NBC would provide the crew, the on–camera journalist, the producer, the executive producer.

"And where would I fit in?" Wild asked. "Well, we could call you the associate producer," said the NBC executive. "It would be your project, but we would of course retain final edit control." It did not take her long to conclude that "I was there to open the door for them. So I opened the door, and walked out."

From New York, she went to Boston to meet PBS, which was preparing a three-part series on the Philippines. For a time, there was talk of making Wild's film the fourth installment, but structurally it was a poor fit, and Wild felt the PBS journalist was "not into taking the left seriously, anyway." The next—and final—stop was Montreal, and the Film Board. Pinney had worked at the NFB for several years and knew the key players, among them Peter Katadotis, head of English-language production. Pinney had actually sat on the committee that hired Katadotis. Driving out to see him on a rainy afternoon, Wild recalls thinking that this meeting "was an all or nothing thing." With the exception of a small Canada Council Explorations grant ($15,000), no agency seemed willing to fund production. If the NFB said no, the project would be dead. "I was so scared that it was going to be no," Wild recalls. "I had been up all night. Chris had to pour three Grand Marniers down my throat to get me to shut up. So we walked into Katadotis' office, and he was kind of bunkered in at that point. He looked like a Sandinista general. He sat down and said, "Well, I've read both your proposals. And I'm going to do everything I can to get them made.""

FINANCING Like virtually everyone who manages to make a film in Canada, Nettie Wild needed a principal patron. Peter Katadotis became hers. It is Wild's conviction that Katadotis used his considerable leverage to push *Leaves* through the NFB system—even though it would never earn recognition as an official Film Board production—because "politically, he thought the film should be made." In fact, it is well known that during his years at the NFB, Katadotis was, in Wild's words, "driving pet projects through the system no matter whose feathers were ruffled," an operating style that prompted critics to refer to Katadotis as Studio K. Without him, she believes, the NFB's financial and services support would have been far more limited, and her film forced to find a Canadian context—some priest from Alberta preaching liberation theology in the jungles of the Philippines—in order to qualify for funding. With Katadotis, a novice was able to parlay an initial $10,000 grant from the Program to Assist Filmmakers in the Private Sector (PAFPS) into more than $260,000 in NFB money, services, film stock and equipment. Wild herself concedes that it was "a huge scam, just humungous, but I had to do it." It is a safe assumption that Katadotis and others inside the Film Board knew it was being done and sanctioned it.

Katadotis, however, now head of production and development at Telefilm Canada, spurns the Godfather role. "I liked her idea," he says. "I thought it was interesting, going into the mountains with the NPA. I thought it was courageous. She wasn't asking for any big cash from me. We had a program to help people like that. So I said sure. The hardest thing," he says, "was persuading the NFB's camera department to give up their cameras." It was especially hard because Wild ultimately retained custody of the equipment for eight months, and was often incommunicado. Later, Pinney took the proposal to Channel 4 in London, and met Rod Stoneman, commissioning editor for the station's Eleventh Hour public-affairs show. Stoneman, on his way to Paris, read the proposal en route, immediately called Pinney, and

Wild spent eight weeks living with and filming the NPA at its jungle stronghold for her documentary, **A Rustling of Leaves.**

offered to buy U.K. television rights for $50,000, payable in three installments. The original agreement called for delivery of the one-hour film by the end of 1986.

It was hardly a fortune, but with Channel 4's commitment, $15,000 from the Canada Council and the NFB's stock and equipment, Nettie Wild, in the late fall of 1985, was finally ready to begin pre-production. Her initial crew consisted of two respected names in Canadian film, Martin Duckworth as cinematographer and Aerlyn Weissman as sound recordist. Because of the subject's political sensitivity, Wild went to elaborate lengths to keep the shoot's preparations secret. Worried about eavesdroppers at both ends of the trans-oceanic cable—the secret service in the Philippines and the Canadian Security & Intelligence Service (CSIS) in Canada—she spoke in code and often used the telephones of friends in the housing co-op, instead of her own.

The paranoia was not entirely misplaced. One day, Wild received a 5 A.M. phone call from Katadotis in Montreal; he instructed her to go to another telephone and immediately call him back at another number. When she did, Katadotis told her that he had been contacted by a high-ranking Department of Communications official who had been approached by a CSIS agent, demanding that the NFB turn over every file connected with Nettie Wild—proposals, correspondence, etc.—"because I was a threat to national security." The spy agency apparently made a similar demand of the Canada Council. In fact, a still unsolved break-in at the Council's Ottawa offices was later reported, in which documents pertaining to *Leaves* were taken. "Normally, I just tell these people to fuck off," Katadotis said to Wild. "But this is coming from a fairly high place, and I can't do that."

Wild then went to see Vancouver human rights lawyer Craig Patterson. Pinney, ash-white, was already there, convinced that his career in international development was about to be summarily terminated. Hearing the story, Patterson opened his windows overlooking Granville Street and yelled out: "Here she is! Canada's number one threat to national security! Come and get her!" More soberly, Patterson advised them not to stop work on the film—that was precisely CSIS's objective—and wrote a letter to the agency suggesting that if it had any further questions about Wild's professional career, he would be pleased to answer them. There was no reply.

PRE-PRODUCTION 1 Shooting was originally scheduled to begin in February 1986—the same month the tottering regime of Ferdinand Marcos had called a national presidential election. But Wild's plans were soon overtaken by events—the stunning election victory of Cory Aquino and the ensuing coup that finally toppled Marcos. The triumph of people power in the Philippines sparked an immediate avalanche of press attention. The American networks arrived en masse, complete with helicopters, Mercedes-Benzes, cellular phones. ABC and NBC, says Wild, had 14 crews apiece, a small army of news-obsessed journalists.

Amid that outbreak of media hysteria, Wild postponed her shoot. Aquino was the political miracle of the year. The euphoria that followed her election inevitably put the revolutionary left on the defensive. Wild was convinced that the Aquino bubble would eventually burst and the media would move on to the next trouble spot; in the meantime, she had no ability to compete with every other TV network on the planet, and very little interest in doing so. She did cover Aquino's release of left-wing political prisoners for CBC Radio (Sunday Morning and As It Happens), which gave her access to figures later interviewed in her film. But the heart of her story was still the NPA, and the NPA was, for the time being, in disarray. A political movement in disarray never acts; it just holds meetings. And meetings, Wild was convinced, would not a documentary make. "Basically," explains Chris Pinney, "we lost a year because of the coup."

They also lost the crew, which had other projects to work on. Wild spent the next several months living with members of the underground. She observed a training session for political officers on the island of Luzon. And she directed an NPA–scripted play that carefully put the left's spin on Cory Aquino—that she was essentially the same American puppet that Marcos had been. Eventually, Wild returned to Vancouver, $8,000 poorer. "It was not a good situation at all," she recalls. "It was really taut."

In search of another crew, Wild went to Toronto and New York, seeking people who "would have enough sense of adventure to compensate for the fact that they weren't going to get paid much and that their lives would be on the line." The pickings were slim. Arriving in New York, with $200 borrowed from filmmaker Peter Raymont, Wild accidently left her wallet in a phone booth at Grand Central Station. She soon discovered the loss, and raced back to the terminal; the wallet was gone. But when she went to report the loss, she found an officer counting out her money. "It's mine," she said. "I'm a filmmaker and it's my last two hundred dollars." "Lady," he said, "I've been here 14 years and nobody's ever turned in a wallet with money before. Somebody must want you to make that film real bad."

She was less successful finding a crew. One cinematographer told her he might do it for his best friend, but "I hardly know you." At that point, Wild returned home convinced that only people who knew her could be persuaded to sign on. Her first choice was Kirk Tougas. A friend since university, Tougas had studied theatre and film at the University of British Columbia; then, in 1971, in collaboration with the National Film Board and the Vancouver Art Gallery, he founded the Pacific Cinematheque, where he worked for the next eight years. Later, he gravitated into film production, sometimes as director or producer, sometimes as cinematographer. In fact, Tougas had shot the video on the Kitsilano controversy.

Tougas agreed to shoot Wild's film, but was prepared to go only so far in the life-risking business. "I'll do anything I can to help you get the film made," he told her. "But I will not go up into the mountains to get killed. That's my bottom line." A sound recordist proved harder to find; Pinney and Tougas hired Gary Marcuse only after Wild had already returned to Manila to resume pre-production. A second Canadian crew was subsequently retained, at higher rates of pay, for the planned Mindanao shoot.

Before leaving, Wild managed to raise another $7,000 by pitching her proposal and her experiences to gatherings of lawyers and human rights activists in the Vancouver area. A charitable foundation was set up to receive the money, which issued tax-deductible receipts. No one, Wild assured her audiences, should nurture any illusions about making money from the venture. The United Church of Canada also invested about $8,000.

To earn some money for herself, Wild prepared a series of letters to Peter Gzowski's CBC radio show, Morningside, based on her Mindanao guerrilla stories. The downside of this endeavour was that the CBC insisted on Wild using her real name, and she feared that, once back in Manila, she might be followed and inadvertently lead the enemy to her underground contacts. As a result, she legally changed her name, was issued a new passport, and to this day travels under this new, stage name.

PRE-PRODUCTION 2 At the end of 1986, Wild returned to the Philippines to begin pre-production for a new shooting schedule. By then, the New People's Army had embraced ceasefire negotiations with the Aquino government. The talks would later collapse, but in the interlude, once-faceless rebels had been forced to show their public face. Assuming she could reconfirm permission to shoot, Wild knew she would have a much more interesting film. In the middle of negotiations, Wild accompanied Saturo Ocampo, chairman of the National Democratic Front, on a trip to meet revolutionary units in Mindanao, and became reacquainted with friends she had made during her 1985 visit, including Raoul, the rebel commander.

The past year, Raoul told her, had been a nightmare. Pro-Marcos infiltrators had successfully stirred paranoia within the ranks of the guerrilla armies. It had started with NPA soldiers being shot in the back during battles, and quickly escalated. Commanding officers went on witch hunts, putting suspected traitors, sometimes as many as 30 people, into cages. Kangaroo courts dispensed summary justice; dozens were executed on grounds only of suspicion. It was, says Wild, "Heart of Darkness stuff." The revolutionaries had essentially turned their venom on themselves. The killings ended only after the restitution of a more legitimate people's court. Raoul, who later changed his name to Ka Oris, then trapped his two senior underlings; they were tried, found guilty and executed. At the end of this account, Raoul turned to Wild and said: "What do you think of me now?"

"My honest response was . . . I couldn't believe that I was saying it . . . was that I understood. I didn't understand everything, but I thought I could see, in a way that very few westerners could, the context of it. The tragedy of it was not that he and the others were demonic. But that they were human and humans do buckle. When put in an inhuman situation, they become inhuman."

That's why Raoul had pushed for acceptance of Cory Aquino's ceasefire proposal. The revolution had nearly collapsed, consumed by its own passions. Raoul requested that the national NPA leadership demote him; the request was refused.

Now, with the ceasefire still holding, he at last agreed to let Wild and her crew trek into the mountain strongholds. But no sooner had she returned to Manila than she again lost contact with her friends on Mindanao. She had the firm impression that urban members of the guerrilla underground had another agenda; they did not want her filming in the mountains. Convinced, however, that Raoul had meant what he had said, Wild decided to act unilaterally and made arrangements for Tougas and Marcuse to fly from Canada, bringing the treasure trove of NFB equipment, and to begin shooting in cities and the government-controlled countryside.

To get the cameras released, the production needed insurance. Several prospective insurers rejected the business as altogether too risky. Finally, an agent in Vancouver agreed to insure the entire package for $5,000—a bargain war-zone price. Eight months later, minus a boom pole and with algae growing inside a few lenses, Pinney went to file a claim for about $8,000. But the agent who had sold him the policy had moved on, and the parent company only agreed to cover $1,500. Apparently, the former agent had never had the policy approved at head office. In effect, he had pocketed the production's $5,000. So $100,000 of NFB equipment had been dragged through the jungles of the Philippines for eight months, uninsured. Wild's lawyer, Rhys Davies, was later able to have the former agent's wages garnisheed until $5,000 had been recovered.

Wild had booked the crew rooms in an apartment hotel in Manila; within days, it had been transformed into a kind of safe house for the underground. There were endless meetings to discuss the shoot; then, when the crew left for meals, other meetings were held with "all sorts of people, speaking languages we didn't understand; we had no idea who they were." In the middle of these discussions, sound recorder Marcuse announced that he was a pacifist, and did not wish to be put in a position in which he was a de facto supporter of armed resistance. "You're a *pacifist*?" Wild asked, incredulous. On other grounds, Kirk Tougas had already tabled objections to shooting in the mountains. It would be hard enough filming and sleeping in 90-degree heat, he knew, coddled by the available comforts of lodging and diet in the cities. But he was not prepared to risk the countryside's "general exposure to disease" or other hazards to health. It was therefore agreed that the first shoot would focus on the legal left in Manila and on sugar workers on the island of Negros, people who might be working underground, but not, in Wild's words, "people with guns coming out of their noses." Nevertheless, Wild did intend to film the Sparrows—the covert team of urban assassins who worked on the NPA's behalf. Marcuse agreed, reluctantly.

PRODUCTION Because they were covertly filming a covert operation, Wild and the crew spent a lot of time waiting—waiting for meetings to be held, decisions to be made, calls to be returned. At times, she thought, the entire production seemed to hinge on a single telephone call. On their behalf, the underground had hired a jeep driver and translator for the Negros shoot; the latter turned out to be a born-again Christian and the sister of one of the Sparrows. She had not seen her brother for several years and considered him an agent of the devil; because he was a relative, the revolutionary movement had assumed her politics were in sync. One day, out in the sugar cane fields, the crew's jeep was suddenly surrounded by Sparrows, all armed with M-16 rifles. One of them was the brother.

After the introductions, it became clear that the Sparrows intended to attach themselves to the crew. The ensuing episodes were at once comic and surreal. All of them slept together on the floor of a peasant's house, the pacifist Marcuse cheek-by-jowl with a group of teenagers carrying grenades, assault rifles and M-16s. Tougas, a self-styled gourmet chef, cooked a goat with the head Sparrow, another self-styled gourmet. Wild was given private sleeping quarters with the only other woman, the God-fearing translator. One night, the woman asked Wild whether she believed in the Father, Son and Holy Ghost; Nettie answered honestly, saying she believed in some sort of God, but was not too enthusiastic about the church. "You, too, are Satan," the translator told her.

The first shoot lasted about 30 days, from late January to late February, although some of that time, Wild concedes, was spent trying to "figure out what the hell was happening next." Next it was back to Manila, where mysterious people continued to hold whispered conversations in exotic languages in their rented living room. One day, Wild learned from a source that the ceasefire negotiations were about to break off. The same day, a major demonstration by farmers was planned outside the palace gates in Manila, demanding land reform. Cinematically, the choice seemed obvious—protest demonstrations almost always deliver better visuals than a set of closed doors

But Wild was handicapped by her Filipino minders—production managers, assistants, translators, each of whom had to be vetted by if not actually affiliated with the underground. "You couldn't just hire somebody because he had a good eye," she says. "He had to be politically correct as well." The Filipinos wanted to film every opposition political faction at the demonstration. Wild was more interested in finding symbolic representatives, but faced resistance; the production people were concerned about cultural appropriation of their revolution. In the end, therefore, she chose to cover the ceasefire talks, instead of the rally—"a big mistake." The negotiations collapsed as predicted, but the rally, as she later heard on the radio, erupted into a bloody massacre—38 people were killed. By the time she reached the palace, it was over. (She later managed to buy some extraordinary half-inch video footage from a Filipino cameraman.)

When Tougas and Marcuse returned to Canada, taking the exposed film with them, Wild began preparations for her Mindanao mountain expedition. Courtesy of a sympathetic PBS correspondent, she parked her NFB equipment and unexposed film stock inside the posh Manila Hotel—the political nexus of the Philippines—and moved into the back room of a tiny tailor shop at a cost of $5 per week; seamstresses slept on the floor beneath their sewing machines. The underground cadres in the capital had at last given their tentative blessing to the NPA mountain shoot, but warned her that somebody from the movement would have to join her in the editing suite. Wild balked, insisting that while she would be happy to accept their comments at various stages of the edit, she had to retain final control. The revolutionaries were equally adamant; they wanted a hand-picked emissary to accompany the shoot, and a movement-approved editor.

Afterward, Wild concluded that the movement itself was torn by indecision about how to treat her, uncertain whether to make artistic concessions to allow their story to reach the outside world, or whether to insist on total control. Finally, Wild agreed to allow an agent from Manila central to accompany the crew, and prepared to fly with her to Mindanao to set up. Meanwhile, Chris Pinney in Vancouver had found a crew willing to undertake the mission; its baggage was packed and they were due in from

Vancouver two days later. Then, only an hour before Wild's plane was scheduled for takeoff, the NPA's agent took her outside, sat her down on the curb and informed her that the shoot had been cancelled. "If we have no editorial control," she told Wild, "you have absolutely no access to the underground."

Wild's essential problem was that she was dealing with two quite separate strands of the New People's Army. One group—those who knew her from her days as a documentarian of indigenous theatre—was quite supportive. The other, says Tougas, was "critical, wary, dismissive or contemptuous of her." Like most clandestine organizations, it instinctively distrusted outsiders, especially artists, because artists always carried non-conforming agendas. They were afraid, he says, that Wild "wouldn't tell the story their way. It wouldn't be their line, their specific description of reality. And they were right—it wasn't."

But at that point, there were also two Nettie Wilds. One of them was deeply and understandably depressed. "I had changed my name. I was living in a sweat shop. I couldn't turn around and whine to someone that the underground had dumped me. I was a third of the way through the film. There was no going back. I was really a basket case." Completely unhinged, this Nettie Wild called Pinney from the tailor shop and instructed him not to put the new crew on the plane. He, in turn, advised her to get some sleep and call back the next day with a new movie.

The other Nettie Wild was more lucid and more determined. She refused to relinquish the idea of filming the NPA. "I'm going to try again," she thought. "I'm going to appeal. I'm going to do whatever it takes." In the meantime, she would redouble her energies on the legal side of the political equation. "Promise me you won't block that," she demanded of her NPA friend at the airport curb. The woman agreed. "I had to move really fast to make sure that plan B wasn't blocked," Wild says, "even though I hadn't really thought through plan B."

In retrospect, Wild believes that the NPA was spooked chiefly by security issues, by not being able to control the situation. Allowing a filmmaker into a base camp for six or eight weeks was not the same as inviting a *Newsweek* photographer or *New York Times* correspondent in for a few hours. Wild could see it from their point of view. "Their lives were on the line. At any step, I could have betrayed them. I didn't have a working relationship with the people in Manila, so there was no trust, as there was with the people in the mountains. And you can't invent that currency overnight, even if you have the right political credentials on paper."

But Wild also knew what would happen to her film if she acquiesced to their demands for editorial control—a pat little story on the NPA vision of land reform that might be lucky to play in a few church basements in Canada. She would be perceived as a mere propagandist, and her reputation as a filmmaker would suffer accordingly. Still, her commitment to her own vision, she sees now, "rattled the shit out of people whose lives were on the line. I can say with confidence that I totally blew it in terms of not really understanding the degree of what they were going through." By the same token, her political sitters in Manila showed little appreciation for her own dedication to the project or for what she had sacrificed on its behalf. It was, she says, a classic cultural clash.

The next day, Wild pitched Pinney the new concept, a broadened film about the legal and illegal left, with some voices on the right thrown in as well. She also called Katadotis at the NFB and Rod Stoneman at Channel 4 in London and, without telling either of them that she had been frozen out by the movement, now argued that "it would be naive to do a film only on the New People's Army." Both of them agreed. Later, she wrote Katadotis asking him to ship another 50 rolls of film; he immediately did. In Vancouver, Pinney paid off the crew, forfeiting several thousand dollars in unrecoverable plane fares. For him, the production seemed to be sliding out of control. While "Nettie was freaking out over there," he was forced to attend to other developments, including an ailing mother, back home. The role he had hoped to play, as producer, was now too large for the time he had available, forcing Wild to don more hats than she then knew how to wear.

Even with the implicit sanction of her sponsors, Wild remained deeply distressed. She recalls walking the streets of Manila, staring at her feet, bemoaning her plight and thinking that insanity was the only sane response to her situation. "But this little voice said, 'Net, if you go nuts, you'll die, because nobody cares.'" Her self-delivered sermon "jerked her back to her senses." She then began to interview the characters who were to become central figures in the new documentary—Kumander Dante Buscayno, the founder of the NPA who had been released by Aquino after 10 years in prison and was pondering a run for the Philippine Senate; Father Ed de la Torre, Manila's revolutionary artist/priest who would become the film's de facto host; and Jun Pala, a right-wing radio DJ and anti-Communist crusader in Davao, with a chilling fascination for Goebbels. That whole process, Wild says, resurrected her interest. "It was like lining up horses," she says, "You just fly out of the gate with all the horses and just hang on. That's really what *A Rustling of Leaves* was all about. It was riding on the backs of Dante and Ed and wacky old Jun Pala and Inday and Raoul and all that crowd." By the end of March, Kirk Tougas had returned for the second shoot.

For Wild, Tougas was another source of long-distance solace. "I received many telephone calls at very weird hours from Manila or God knows where," he recalls. "Nettie was going through real soul-searching because events had changed. In documentaries, one is dealing with life, and one cannot control life. One cannot write the script, or get the actors to do what you want them to do. One has to intuit what's going on, and sense when the elements in front of one are indeed part of history." Working against the broad and always shifting panorama of Philippine politics, the task was even more delicate. Dante Buscayno, campaigning for the Senate, was constantly under threat of assassination. Armed right-wing vigilantes, probably linked to the armed forces, waged a zealous war on communists and other left-wing organizations. The menacing Jun Pala used his radio slot to broadcast names of suspected rebels; within days, the named targets had been killed.

The crew's base camp in Davao was a sprawling five-room apartment on the second floor of a three-storey cinder block building. Again, the flat played host to a colourful cast of characters, interpreters, NPA functionaries, foreign journalists, all trying to understand the political events of the day, and generally failing. The building boasted a bizarre menagerie of other tenants—on the crew's floor, straight-laced Japanese businessmen living with Filipino housemaids; downstairs, a half-dozen very young Filipino prostitutes; and upstairs, a group of muscled young men in well-pressed blue jeans, laundered white shirts and designer sunglasses. Evidently a unit of someone's private army, they cleaned M–16 assault rifles on the balcony and drove around town in open-air jeeps with sound systems blaring. Outside, at night, strange men with walkie-talkies patrolled the alleyways.

The only phone in the building was located in a small courtyard canteen, run by three generations of a Filipino family. At various times, the canteen's tables would be occupied by prostitutes doing their nails, and by the muscle men and their friends drinking gin and tonics. Then, recalls Tougas, "the phone would ring and it would be for Nettie under her code name, and Nettie would come down and take the phone and suddenly everything would go dead quiet, everyone straining to hear what she was saying." Wild would then try to arrange meetings, set up shoots and elicit information—in code—without disclosing details to her unwanted audience. "Yes, of course I'll bring the six buckets of dried fish," Wild might say. "Where would you like them? The market?"

Technically, Tougas had to rely during the second shoot on largely untrained Filipinos as camera assistants, sound recordists and lighting technicians. The results were disappointing. "There was a lot of stuff that a good sound recordist would have done brilliantly that we barely got. The sound editors, he says, later did "an awesome job of recreating the sound, giving it depth and coherence."

Back in Manila, Wild finally received a call from Inday on Mindanao; late May had been set for her trip to join the NPA. She hung up the telephone and turned to Tougas. "We can go."

"You can go," he said.

"It's the last leg of the film," she pleaded.

"You knew from the start I wasn't going up there."

Tougas encouraged Wild and a young Filipino still photographer, JoJo Sescon, who had assisted him during the Davao shoot, to go to Mindanao themselves. To that end, he spent the next three days teaching them the rudiments of cinematography—loading, unloading, cleaning, taking apart lenses, reassembly—a crash course. But even as she accompanied Tougas to the airport, Wild was hoping he would change his mind.

"Like, do me a favour, Kirk. It's my birthday coming up. There's still a movie to shoot. I've never shot a movie." Tougas was unmoved. "I have a plane to catch," he said.

He walked through customs, turned around, smiled and said, "Don't forget to change the filter."

So Wild, Sescon and Jeanne Marie Hallacy, an American still photographer recruited to help out with sound, flew to Mindanao, bought supplies and transferred the equipment into backpacks. In an area crawling with armed forces personnel, Wild told anyone who asked that she had come to film a documentary about women in rural areas (she gave her mother the same cover story). The next day, they were met by NPA insurgents and hiked five hours into the hills, eventually reaching the fortified guerrilla base camp, commanded by her old friend Raoul. They planned to stay three weeks; they stayed eight.

The NPA universe had its own special rhythms and routines—cooking, walking, carrying messages, organizing, teaching—often disrupted by rain or rumours of approaching army units. A basic rule of rebel life (and of Wild's agreement with Raoul) was that they had to be able to flee at a moment's notice; this required her to spend 40 minutes every evening burying the NFB's not very portable Aaton camera, lenses and unexposed stock, always in a different place. Just in case, Wild and Sescon slept at night (on hammocks made from rice sacks) with sound kits and wind-up Bolexes beside them, the latter loaded with only 100 feet of film.

About four weeks into their stay, Raoul learned that a 19-year-old recruit named Batman had disappeared from camp. Soon, he was spotted at army checkpoints, helping soldiers identify NPA sympathizers coming out of the hills. The rebels were vulnerable. A plan was drafted to recapture Batman and have him tried by a people's court. Raoul allowed Wild to film the trial, in part perhaps because he assumed the community would be lenient; the film would therefore show the benevolent face of the revolution. To his surprise, the court—after a lengthy deliberation—called for Batman's execution, arguing that exile, the only other option, would put their lives at continued risk. At that point, rebel priest Father Frank Navarro suggested taking the verdict back to the NPA for ratification. The community denied Navarro that opportunity; this is our court, they said, and this is our final judgement. Still, Navarro, Raoul and other camp leaders debated the decision, and concluded that the execution would have to proceed. "And don't think you're going to film that," Raoul exclaimed, turning on Wild. "Don't think we're going to let you make sensational headlines out if this."

In more measured tones, he argued that if she showed the execution, its context would be irrelevant. The mere image of it would forever paint the

NPA as savage and ruthless—the very antithesis of the profile it wanted to project. Wild lobbied to film everything she thought was necessary, up to, but not including, the actual execution, agreeing that "it wasn't necessary to shatter what remained of Batman's human dignity by actually filming his life being taken away."

Later, there would be sharp debate about Wild's decision. In a documentary already tilted heavily in favour of Marxist–Leninist ideology, some maintained, she had agreed to self-censor a scene that depicted the ugly underside of the revolution. Others thought it would have been immoral to have photographed the death. Tougas, for one, is not prepared to judge the correctness of Wild's action. Very rarely, he says, are people forced to make a choice that profound. Talking about it and making it "out in the field" are two different things. "No one, other than Nettie, will ever be exactly in that place and able to compare all of the things she was juggling in her spirit when she came to that conclusion."

Wild herself insists there are no rules, no definite ethical lines for such delicate situations; each one requires "you to re-draw it so that you can live with yourself. The night before the actual execution was the most harrowing of my life." The next morning, they filmed Occoy, a United Church minister turned guerrilla, breaking the news to Batman, and Batman's poignant response: "They kept me alive. Now I'll die." In the middle of this drama came another. Cameraman Sescon decided to keep the camera rolling as Occoy placed a bandana over Batman's eyes and the NPA assassins moved into position. Wild put her hand on Sescon's shoulder, and said "cut," but he ignored her. Every instinct in his body, Wild knew, said "agreement, schmeement. Shoot it, then decide what to do." But in her own mind, Wild was thinking, "I've been given the trust of this agreement and if I break it I will not only feel badly, but it will be the end." Realizing that Sescon would not stop, Wild pushed the camera lens away just as the bullets went off.

As edited, the sequence shows Occoy beginning to read the court's decision to Batman, then cuts to his coffin being presented to the boy's father. Wild did not want to excuse the execution, but did want to present its context. That was part of why she insisted on full editorial control. And it was why she felt the film needed in the end to run at something close to two hours, regardless of its impact on financial revenues. "I had to be true to the context."

In the middle of July, Wild finally made her way back to Manila. She immediately wrote to the National Film Board, apologized for keeping its equipment for seven months, and explained why she needed it for just one more shoot. Kumander Dante had been wounded in a post-election assassination attempt. Two of his aides had been killed. Wild wanted to see whether he would now say on camera what he had only said off-camera before—that armed struggle was not the only answer for the Filipino left. He did. It would be another month before Nettie Wild finally decided that she had enough footage to make her movie. On August 21, with 64,000 feet of film in the can, she returned to Canada.

POST-PRODUCTION Eight months later, after editing, only 4,000 feet would remain. Making celluloid sense of the material, she knew, required an editor with experience and the right political sensitivity. On the advice of friends, she called Peter Wintonick, a Montreal editor and producer. Wintonick was quite agreeable, although he scarcely thought at the time that the eight weeks he was committing to would turn into 28.

Owing to her own inexperience—and the challenge of shooting in the middle of a tactical offensive—Wild had been convinced that three-quarters of her footage would be out of focus and useless. "It's going to be a saving job," she told Wintonick bluntly. "And I'm only going to apologize once. It was the best we could do at the time. I gave everything I could for it. I don't want to be auditioned by an editor. What's there is there, and what isn't we'll have to make up for. Either take it and run with it, with all its warts, or don't." Wintonick did. When Wild contacted him, he had been editing and producing films for more than 10 years and was looking for another interesting project. *Leaves* passed the test; no less critically, he in turn passed through Wild's filter of political sympathies. In going to Vancouver, he would, he knew, be entering a land with too many New Age joggers. "But I'm a self-abusive person," Wintonick explains. "I'm an editor."

He arrived in Vancouver in November 1987. Wild says he was "the wackiest, weirdest person" she had ever met, totally eccentric, with a great mane of hair that looked like he had been standing too close to a Van de Graaff generator. Or, as a friend of hers described him: "He looks like a portrait that jumped off the wall of the National Gallery." According to Wild, Wintonick bicycled over to the NFB building in downtown Vancouver in a driving rainstorm, took off his shoes and socks, and started working in his bare feet.

There was no money left, of course, to pay for the edit, so even before hiring Wintonick, Wild had begun making calls. She went first to the Canada Council, submitting three unedited rolls of film only fifteen minutes before the deadline. The jury saw enough to be convinced of its merit and gave Wild the full grant—$35,000—to pay for the edit. (The Council would later add another $15,000.) Overall, says Wintonick, his relationship with Wild was excellent. A novitiate at the cutting table, she seems to have given him a wide berth, wider certainly than he might have been given by a more experienced director. "Nettie left me alone with my imagination," he concedes.

Like most documentary films, *Leaves* was recreated in the editing room. "That's where the sparks start flying," Wintonick says. "It's like sculpting in plastic, a dream state entered into." The editor's job is to crystallize the director's vision, a job that cannot commence until he or she has a full understanding of exactly what that vision is. Wintonick and Wild thus spent many preliminary hours just screening the raw footage and holding what he calls "a long Socratic dialogue" about its meaning. The Batman sequence posed a particularly tough dilemma. A life-long pacifist, Wintonick viewed the material "as a challenge to myself, to figure out my own limitations and, despite my objections to the use of force in conflict resolution, as a way to try to understand the daily life issues in the Third World." Later, in editing the sequence, he was guided by the less-is-more principle; the more oblique or referential the juxtaposition of shots, the more cinematic power it delivered.

Pinney took the view that the entire Batman episode was overblown, and "not germane to the film." It was part of his larger critique about length, a critique over which he and Wild would ultimately part company. "My whole concern was to get the film seen. That was my interest in film, as a tool for empowerment, to raise consciousness." By implication, the more people who saw *Leaves*, the more people who would have a better understanding of Filipino politics. At its final 112-minute length, Pinney believed then and now that instead of the mass audience it might have reached had it been cut, "it had been condemned to the alternate film festival circuit."

Technically, the major editing problem was syncing the sound to the images; much of it had been poorly recorded on a Sony Walkman. And there were miles of recorded sound that had to be categorized. The film's music was recorded in Wild's own living room, where the chief scorer, Filipino rock 'n roll musician Joey Ayala, had installed an 8-track studio. Wintonick had been cutting the film to the music of David Byrne's Talking Heads, and liked the rhythms it engendered. So Wild wrote to Byrne, offering him a chance to co-score the film. Byrne was otherwise engaged, but gave his blessing to the use of his music without charge, unless *Leaves* ever went into profit. Later, the Bee Gees did the same. Ayala was paid $1,000, plus his return air fare to Davao.

Wild herself was earning no money, but managed to live on a $1,000 a month grant from the Laidlaw Foundation (a private foundation sponsored by the late philanthropist Nick Laidlaw). Her housing cooperative forgave her four months' rent, and a friend provided her favourite form of transportation—a bicycle. But she was still short about $12,000 to finance the film's sound mix, as well as its marriage of picture to sound. Her first avenue of appeal was the NFB's then Vancouver director Barbara Janes. Janes had seen a rough cut and liked it, but wanted to clarify exactly how much money the Film Board had already spent in goods and services, in the production. The next day, she summoned Wild to her office.

"Do you know how much the Film Board has invested," Janes asked her.

"I guess about $175,000," Wild said.

"It's $261,000," Janes replied. "Do you know how hard it is to get even

$10,000 for this studio? Two hundred and sixty-one thousand dollars! Now, I'm not blaming you," Janes added. "If somebody had turned on the tap of water, I'd just keep drinking, too."

But under the circumstances, it was impossible for Janes to sanction any further expenditure on *Leaves*. Wild's next stop was the Laidlaw Foundation, which after viewing the film, wanted to invest $12,000 and take an equity position. After discussing the idea with Pinney, Wild suggested that the Foundation would be wiser to donate the money, since profits were unlikely and since it would then at least reap the tax benefit. After some deliberation, the Foundation agreed. Indeed, it ultimately injected a total of $24,000.

Even with the extra money, Wild was still short for the lab bill at Alpha Cine. The lab was prepared to do the mix, charge a flat fee of $3,500 (although the cost of the work was, she believes, at least five or six times that amount) and give Wild a year to pay it. She then approached the B.C. Film Fund, an agency "allergic to the word grant," and ultimately persuaded it to invest $10,000 on a last-in, first-out basis. (First-out, after the repayment of deferred wages to Wild and the crew.)

Then she went back to Telefilm Canada, where Peter Katadotis had been recently installed as head of development and production. Since no broadcaster had been willing to buy a TV license, and no distributor "would touch us with a thousand-foot pole," Wild was encouraged to apply for funds under something called the Regular Fund, a small residue of money that had been left over from the era of Telefilm's predecessor, the Canadian Film Development Corporation (CFDC). The agency then invested $60,000, which was delivered after the film was complete and which went to repay its debts and union-scale back wages to the crew. In fact, the total amount of deferred fees was $172,000, so even with the Telefilm, B.C. Film Fund and Canada Council investments, it did not add up. By the autumn of 1993, the crew still had only been paid about 65 percent of what was owing to them. "Everybody," says Wild, "is still waiting in line."

A "firm believer" in test screenings, Wild held several, at various stages of post-production. The screenings helped her regain a perspective on the film that had been lost in the editing suite. There were screenings of the rushes for people who had been involved in the shoot and, later, screenings of the five-hour rough-cut assembly, for which the audience was more carefully selected. A detailed shot list was printed up and distributed, to help viewers pinpoint problem areas. Generally, says Wild, the reactions of people tended to reinforce her own instincts. When people criticized the film's length or the left-wing slant of its narration, she "didn't even pay attention, because that's my movie, not their movie." When the fine-cut was finished, Wild organized several screenings with audiences composed for specific purposes—to judge the pacing or the political content or some other aspect of the film.

A *Rustling of Leaves* was mixed through August and early September 1988, with a view towards being entered in Montreal's World Film Festival or Toronto's Festival of Festivals. However, officials of both organizations who saw rough cuts of the film rejected it outright—Wild says because they simply did not like it or because "they hated the narration." She felt "just really horrible" about the snub, but was encouraged when Alan Franey, organizer of the Vancouver International Film Festival, saw the same rough cut and wanted it.

FESTIVALS *Leaves* premiered at the Vancouver Festival in October 1988. Franey had proposed holding the Festival screenings in the 800-seat Ridge Theatre—exactly what Wild did not want. Planning to open three weeks later at the Vancouver East Cinema for a limited theatrical run, she wanted the festival showings to be held in the Pacific Cinematheque, which seats less than 200. "As much as I support the Vancouver Film Festival," she says, "I wanted the dollar. Two showings at the Ridge would have been 1,600 people that we don't see a dime for." Wild won that argument, sold out the Cinematheque and handed out flyers to those turned away advising them of its later opening at the Van East. She also tried to conserve her free media publicity and not "blow too much" on the festival. At the Van East, the film was scheduled for a 10 P.M. screening, following *Hour of the Furnaces*, a heavy, three-hour documentary on Central America. That night, Wild recalls, "there was a Manila kind of monsoon rain just lashing down." Still, she had to turn people away.

Globe and Mail arts writer Liam Lacey called it "dynamic and disturbing," a film that documented not only a political revolution but the filmmaker's own political odyssey. *Maclean's* film critic Brian D. Johnson, who reviewed it the following April, said Wild had managed to survive "the crossfire between romance and realism." And *Variety* said, in its characteristic shotgun prose, that "given the conditions under which pic was shot, quality of image is remarkable and cutting effective."

Having been rejected by both the Toronto and Montreal festivals, Wild was thrilled that organizers of the Berlin Film Festival accepted the film for screening the following February in the Forum of Young Cinema. Resorting to various sleights of hand, she managed to negotiate free airfare for seven members of the crew and smuggled them all into one single room at the Savoy, one of the city's premier hotels. To ensure that critics, buyers, distributors and TV programmers actually saw the film, Wintonick and Tougas drafted a plan committing all of them to finding five people to attend one of the three screenings. The group was so busy putting up posters and distributing handbills, they barely had time to see any of the festival's other films. The work paid off. *Leaves* played to packed houses and was voted the festival's most popular film in the Forum of Young Cinema category. Later that year, it also garnered a Genie nomination for best feature-length documentary in Canada, won Grand Prize at the Houston International

Festival and a Red Ribbon at the American Film Festival in Chicago. Tougas received a Best Cinematographer's Award from the Canadian Society of Cinematographers.

At Berlin, Wild also signed two new distribution agreements—one for German-speaking countries and one with Switzerland's Film Cooperativo, which paid for a French translation and brought in the revolutionary priest Father Ed de la Torre, then living in Holland, to launch the opening. For Wild, as for most documentarians, there was no additional advance money attached to these contracts; it was sufficient that distributors "with integrity" had picked up the rights and would guarantee a release in new markets.

DISTRIBUTION Returning to Canada, Wild began to look in earnest for a theatrical distributor. At Cineplex–Odeon, she had already talked to Jeff Sackman, who liked the film and was considering whether to book it into the Carlton. But the Carlton had recently taken a financial scrubbing on Ron Mann's *Comic Book Confidential*, another feature-length documentary, and was less than eager to repeat the experience. She also conferred with Andre Bennett at Cinephile, but feared his organization was in too much chaos to successfully promote the film. Shut out of the commercial chains, Wild tried to re-interest the Canadian TV networks in showing it. She had two meetings with a CBC executive, who suggested that by taking "a little bit here and a little bit there," she could cut the film from 112 minutes to 57, the length needed to fit a TV hour—a preposterous suggestion that Wild quickly rejected.

It was Alan Franey who finally suggested she distribute the film herself. "It will kill you," Franey said. "But there's no way a distributor will get this in to the theatres. You're the only one who can do it." The film needed a community-activist approach to distribution, a kind of distribution, Franey said, "that is not in place in this country." Taking his advice, Wild joined forces with the Canada Asia Working Group, a grass-roots lobby, and began to strike deals with independent cinemas across the country. She fixed Toronto as the logical launch city, because it was the home of the national press. "I figured if I could spend two months getting them all pumped up, that would feed everyone else."

The film opened at Toronto's Bloor Cinema rep house on April 21, 1989. Ed de la Torre flew in for that event as well. The Bloor, too, had bet against the film's theatrical potential, opting to strike a four-wall agreement with Wild—accepting a flat fee for rental of the house and taking no share of the box-office revenue. It was a bad bet; in five days, the film grossed $14,000.

The follow-up release strategy was to open in a new major city every 10 days or more, working west across the country to Ottawa, Winnipeg, Calgary, Edmonton and Vancouver. Wild saved Montreal for last, entering the film in the National Film Board's Documentaire Sa Fête, a 10-day retrospective in June 1989, and winning the $5,000 Prix du Public award. A few days later, *Leaves* opened a week-long run at Montreal's Le Cinema Parallele, a small, 100-seat theatre that Wild considered ideal. In a cineplexed environment, she knew, the week's lowest-grossing film was typically jettisoned for a new product. At a theatre like Le Parallele, the film could nearly fill the house at both evening shows, sell enough high mark-up café au lait to please the exhibitor, and stay long enough to generate favourable word of mouth, the elusive elixir of the back-end.

Wild's campaign for recognition of her film was waged not only with the exhibitors and their thirst for Hollywood product, but with the printed and electronic media. By 1989, the care and feeding of the continent's movie critics had become an industry unto itself—regular junkets to Los Angeles, one-on-one interviews with the stars, plus the full battery of stills and electronic press kits. The entertainment pages of Canadian newspapers and the entertainment segments of TV newscasts had become de facto cogs in the promotion wheel, a symbiotic union which spawned the phenomenon of 'info-tainment.' When it came to movies, info-tainment was essentially a euphemism for hype.

Certainly, not many film critics were interested even in reviewing a $500,000, two-hour documentary, shot in 16MM, about doctrinaire Marxist guerrillas in the Philippines, let alone producing a feature article on the subject. Wild therefore took a different tack, trying to generate interest among the editorial or political staff at major dailies, seeking op-ed pieces or human rights features. She also managed to win many columns of press from the alternate, tabloid press.

The film did well enough in its first Vancouver appearance to merit a second run at the Van East Cinema. Wild herself was present to field questions after the screenings, a tactic used promotionally in other cities as well. The audience filled between half to two-thirds of the house, divided about 60 percent non-Filipinos and 40 percent Filipinos. Overall, *Leaves* did better theatrically than many or most Canadian dramatic features. One study claimed it outperformed eight of 10 Canadian feature-length films. The box office numbers indicated not only a continuing appetite for documentary films—a trend confirmed in 1991 when five feature-length documentaries were given theatrical release—but the fundamental importance of strategic, target-marketing. Altogether, the film had 100 theatrical playdates in Canada and grossed $58,675.

Internationally, *Leaves'* release was initially handled by Jan Rofekamp's Films Transit. Indeed, it was Rofekamp who had introduced the Berlin Festival's Erlich Gregore to the film and helped secure its screening there. But Rofekamp and Wild were at loggerheads over the film's length. For marketing purposes, Rofekamp was convinced that the film had to be cut to an hour—advice that was constantly on Wild's mind in the editing. Her editor, Peter Wintonick, told her then that all sorts of options were available—two-hour, one-hour, 20-minute or even 30-second versions. She just had to decided which film she wanted to make. Documentary films, Wintonick explains, have a natural length, but those lengths rarely coincide with commercial television's definition of an hour. In the end, he suggests, the length of a film "will depend on how honest the filmmmaker is to the material" or how submissive he or she is to the constraints of the market-place.

Nettie Wild was not familiar with the notion of submission. The one-hour version had never tempted her, because it would have meant taking the guerrillas entirely out of the movie, and breaking a bond of trust she felt obliged to keep intact. Even later, when Rofekamp serenaded her about the impracticality of marketing a 112-minute film in territories increasingly wedded to 57-minute formats, Wild says "there was never a day when I thought I had made the wrong decision." Rofekamp continues to believe that Wild's obduracy victimized her own film. "I am convinced that the story Nettie tells can be told in one hour," he says. "I had a whole list of clients who would have bought it at one hour"—Wild disputes this contention—"yet she wouldn't move. She's an impossible woman. I thought it was incredibly stupid, because she has an important story to tell. Why make it so difficult for people to see this film? It's not even a question of taste. It's time and place, slots on the air, slots of hours. It's almost arithmetic." Wintonick, while respecting Wild's convictions, agrees with Rofekamp. "It's a very good film," he insists, "and I'm quite proud of it. But it's a shame it didn't reach more people. It's important to get the message out. If that means cutting the film to an hour, I'd do it. It has to reach the masses." To make his own 1992 film, *Manufacturing Consent*, more accessible, Wintonick produced several versions. As for Rofekamp, he ultimately resigned the *Leaves* account in frustration and returned the rights to Wild. Its total gross from world sales and rentals: $9,020.

ANCILLARY SALES Later, Wild managed to get a videotaped copy of the film to Trina McQueen, who had recently moved into a senior CBC position in news and current affairs. Wild was prepared for the usual too-long, too-political reaction—several other CBC executives had already rejected the film on precisely those grounds—but instead was treated to a warm cup of tea and a blunt, "I like your film and want to buy it." Wild says she "just about fell off the side of my chair." McQueen said she thought the film was more evenly balanced than it had been portrayed in the press. The CBC bought the film for its new, prime-time summer series of documentaries, Witness, paying $80,000.

The CBC agreement called for the film to be shown uncut. At the eleventh hour, McQueen discovered a major gap in the contract: the CBC had always intended to run a panel discussion on the Philippines afterward, an impossibility at *Leaves'* 112-minute length. Wild had no objection to the panel, but suggested they simply run the discussion in The Journal, following the national news. McQueen could not do that. Wild's options at that point were either to cut the film to accommodate the panel or forfeit the prestigious CBC window. She therefore agreed to make the cuts, at her discretion, and did "a squeeze" of the videotape. That technical manoeuvre saved the needed time but badly distorted the film's sound track. However, because the CBC was contractually bound to air the full-length film, Wild also managed to squeeze some additional money out of McQueen for her next project.

The actual broadcast of *Leaves* in June 1990 was interrupted at its climax—Batman learning that he must die—by a CBC special news update on the First Ministers' Meech Lake constitutional crisis. Wild was in California, "thank God, or I would have thrown the TV set through the window." Wintonick thought the incident the paradigmatic irony—in the middle of a film about how the Third World attempted to resolve its national conflicts, a little reminder about how Canada tried to solve its own. Wild also sold it to TV Cinq in Quebec for $15,000, although she ended up with less than $3,000 because of the high cost of dubbing the French version and sub-titling. Most of the costs of sub-titling ($26,000) were covered by Telefilm Canada.

In the U.S., there was a $5,000 sale to New York's PBS station, WNET, with a contract clause prohibiting any showing before November 1, 1990—a provision that gave Wild a two-month window for a theatrical release. Later, she discovered that WNET had scheduled an August broadcast. The station was duly reminded of its legal obligations, but for Wild the incident was somehow typical of her encounters with the alien universe of distributors and exhibitors. "There hasn't been one contract we've signed that's been held to," she says. "I don't think it's necessarily diddling. I think it's people moving really, really, fast." The distinction is certainly subtle, and arguably non-existent.

THE U.S. RELEASE In search of a U.S. theatrical release, Wild had first taken the film to the American independent film and video market in New York in September 1989. Most major U.S. distributors saw the film, although few were seriously interested in acquiring it. Among those who expressed some early interest was Mitch Block's Direct Cinema. Block sat on the jury that chose feature documentaries for the Academy Award nominations and had somehow managed to acquire distribution rights to five of the 10 Oscar-winning films in that category between 1980 and 1990. But Wild's interest in Block was not reciprocated. He voiced concern that Filipinos would make and circulate pirate copies of the *Leaves* videotape, which would seriously erode the video market's potential revenue. And Direct Cinema only rarely ventured into the black hole Wild was determined to explore—theatrical distribution.

The original U.S. release strategy was to platform in New York City and move it west in major American markets. That plan was hinged on the hope that Karen Cooper, chief programmer for the prestigious Film Forum in New York, would accept the film. A booking at the Film Forum is worth an estimated $20,000 in free publicity, reviews by all the serious critics, plus feature stories in the *New York Times*. Cooper, however, rejected *Leaves*— explaining in one conversation with Wild that she simply did not like it, and thought the narration too conventional, and in another that she did not have any openings.

Again, therefore, Wild was left with plan B—to open the film in California, heartland of the expatriate Filipino community, and roll it out, eastward, across the U.S, building up reviews and, it was hoped, box office grosses. It was Mitch Block who suggested that Wild contact the Santa Monica–based Empowerment Project, a media resource centre for independent filmmakers with a progressive bias. The EP had by that time also produced two documentaries of its own, including *Cover Up*, a 1988 film dealing with the Iran–Contra scandal that was released in 80 cinemas across the U.S. In 1993, the organization also won an Oscar for its film, *The Panama Deception*.

After a series of discussions, Wild decided to "team up with" the Empowerment people. To some extent, it was a choice made by default. She was convinced by then that no major or even minor specialty film distributors in the U.S. "were going to pick us up," a precise echo of her experience in Canada. And the educational distributors would not commit to giving the film what Wild wanted—a decent shot at a theatrical run. So Wild—over the objections of Kirk Tougas, who thought the contract was stacked against her—resolved to unite her own muscle and limited financial resources with the community contacts of the Empowerment Project. "The alternative," Wild insists, "was a standard distribution agreement that I knew wasn't going to go anywhere." She had been able to make it work in Canada because "I knew Canada. I didn't have those kind of contacts in the States. So it made real sense." It made sense in part because the EP, as a result of releasing *Cover Up*, had compiled an exhaustive 'blue book' of contacts in cities across the United States—community organizers, exhibitors, donors, film reviewers, all with telephone numbers and addresses—an amazing resource for any distributor. But recipes alone are never enough. Making the formula work requires time, energy, willpower, resources—in effect, the same kind of machinery that creates Hollywood product, at one-one-thousandth of the cost.

The EP, however, had very little interest in film as an art form. For it, as for Chris Pinney, film was a political tool, a way to motivate people to act for social change. Making money on theatrical release was not a prime objective; what was important was finding a target audience that could be persuaded that lobbying could make a genuine difference on a specific issue. To that end, the EP sought to distribute films that ran 80 minutes or less—leaving enough time after the screening to conduct what amounted to training seminars in community action. Among the problems it encountered with Wild, says Barbara Trent, the EP's co-founder and co-director, was that *Leaves* ran too long, encroaching on the real agenda—social empowerment. Trent expresses sincere respect for Wild's energy and dedication. But during negotiations on the distribution agreement, she became persuaded that Wild had "unrealistic expectations" of the film's theatrical performance. "I don't think she comprehended the sacrifices required to do a political film in the United States." Eventually, however, they agreed on a 50–50 split of box office and other revenues, after expenses. In consultation with Wild, the EP developed a poster, ad slicks, programs for hand-out in theatres, flyers and a video box. Wild was put on salary—paid out of the film's revenues—given rent-free accommodation in a coach-house garage in Venice Beach and a bicycle for transportation.

Another focus of dispute was the U.S. poster design, which featured four armed guerrillas against a backdrop that included three helicopter gunships and a towering image of Corazon Aquino. "I hated it," says Wild. "I thought it was stupid. It was just a saccharine Hollywood rip-off. It kind of re-creates Vietnam. I was very unhappy, mostly with myself for not holding my ground." Occasionally, Wild felt compelled to have a little talk with herself. 'Come on, Net,' she'd say, 'you're in partnership with an American distributor because you said you didn't know the States. This is the way the Americans do things, and it works. You have to make a decision here. Either you go along, or you do it totally on your own and you call the shots.'

The Canadian release materials had been based on two central images. One was a black-and-white poster featuring a smiling, scarf-wrapped Wild, holding a raised still camera, and standing behind a guerrilla with a machine gun; only his eyes were visible. The shot itself is arresting, but Wild's broad smile effectively undercuts its power; it looks like a staged moment, which it is, instead of a real moment. The second, four-colour one-sheet showed a Filipino couple, holding guns and again smiling. For Wild, the latter Canadian image was "much more together. But then I had total control over it." With a little effort, she was even able to have it put up in church foyers, as well as in more conventional locales. The money for the posters and other costs of the Canadian distribution—$10,000—was taken from Telefilm funds originally allocated to the production. It was part of Kalasikas' $60,000 contract with the agency. Wild recommends that documentarians try to negotiate similar arrangements in their contracts with funding institutions— "a small nut that is specifically to buy the time and materials with which to sell the film."

However well these images might have worked in Canada, the EP people insisted that they would not sell in American markets. "They thought these designs were really boring," Wild says, "because they didn't have Mrs. Aquino's face all over it." Barbara Trent says the Canadian posters said "absolutely nothing about what the film was about," and were therefore ineffective. Aquino's role in the film was minor, but at least she was a known commodity, "one of the few recognizable symbols of the Philippines."

THE U.S. OPENING *Leaves* opened at the Monica 4-Plex in Santa Monica, California on May 24, 1990. It played for 10 days to solid audiences and briefly outsold the four other movies then showing in the theatre. The film moved on to the Roxie in San Francisco and did well there, and then played (with Wild's presence) in Berkeley, San Diego, Portland, Seattle, Denver and finally Chicago. According to Trent, Wild at that point announced that she was returning to Canada to work on a new film project. *Leaves* continued to play, appearing in half a dozen other centres after Wild's return—a situation Trent found "acceptable, but certainly not preferable," since the appearance of the filmmaker is a major drawing card. "We really needed her to drive the film, do the interviews. Losing Nettie was a watershed event." Had she stayed with the project, Trent maintains, *Leaves* might easily have played in 50 U.S. markets, instead of 12–15. Altogther, it had some 124 American screenings.

In some cities, the film failed to rally support from traditional constituencies, including Quakers and Unitarians. "We did not anticipate," concedes Trent, "the extent to which *Leaves* was perceived as supporting armed resistance." There was tremendous interest, predictably, from Filipino expatriates, but "we were not able to cross over into the rest of the community." In many ways, the tour was an exercise in guerrilla film distribution. At each stop, post-screening political discussions, often quite heated, were conducted. Wild and Empowerment used these occasions to market the film in video format and raise funds to take it on to the next U.S. city. "We'd have 350 people shouting at each other and having a great discussion about U.S. involvement in the Third World," she recalls. Then, they would explain how they needed to raise $7,000 to open in, say, Chicago, for airfare, overhead, flyers and newspaper ads. "And somebody would come up with a hundred dollars and you'd get them on a roll and in three minutes you could wind up with about two and a half thousand dollars." The proceeds doubled the film's box office revenues.

The crass commercialism of the video sales pitch troubled Wild, but "there's enough of a hustler in me." That, and the terror of needing to find the money for the next opening. The pitch part was one of a series of aggressive, alternative marketing ideas proposed by the Empowerment Project. Wild endured some tense and frustrating moments with her erstwhile colleagues at the EP. Most of it, she says now, was personality conflict, but she found that the marketing genius of the American way carried a very rough edge. "I didn't like the way I was treated as a human being at all. I'd do it alone, rather than do it with them again."

The Americans voice similar reservations about Wild. After her return to

Canada, says Trent, Nettie "chose to revisit the contract. She insisted on arrangements that would have given her a flat percentage of the revenue grosses, without allowing for the costs of advertising or flyers." In effect, says Trent, Wild was "leaving nothing to trust or faith or honesty. She wanted a simple method of calculating her share of the box office." That proposal, says Kirk Tougas, was the only solution to the fact that the EP was charging all kinds of expenses against *Leaves*.

Now, the mixed agendas of the two parties became glaringly apparent. Trent was prepared to spend all of the available money "driving the film," using theatrical simply as a platform for television, video and tertiary markets—and community organization. "If we broke even, that would have been enough. You can't make these kind of films for money, because they'll fail." Wild had no interest in money, either; she simply wanted to get the film seen. She had devoted almost four years of her life to the Philippines. There were new projects in Canada she wanted to pursue. And she was exhausted. Part of the film's failure to do better, Wild believes, was the result of basic burn-out. By the time she returned home in July 1990, Wild had resolved to take only the summer off. "Six months later, I woke up." It wasn't until the spring of 1992, she points out, that she found the energy to tackle a direct-mail promotion to American colleges and universities, a market she should have targetted two years earlier.

In the meantime, the new contract demands eventually turned ugly. At one point, there was a tense confrontation in Santa Monica between Tougas, whom Wild had asked to intervene, and the EP people. "I couldn't sit in the same room," says Trent. "I couldn't understand why someone [Tougas] would speak to me in so offensive a tone. There were lives at stake in the Philippines. If people can't even tell their friends from their enemies, they're in trouble." Wild says Trent's account is only half-right. The problem, she says, is "that there were too many ways for the EP to build in overhead, and not enough other projects to charge it against. My film was carrying too much of their burden." Everything Tougas had warned her against had come to pass. "They weren't crooks," she says. "They weren't diddling the numbers. But Kirk thought I was getting screwed, and said so."

Tougas himself noted that EP had risked no dollars in the theatrical release. "All the money, about $8,600, was Nettie's." Ostensibly, Trent's contribution was the community networks, but these groups had not coalesced around Filipino politics and in some cities, says Tougas, "were worth zip."

The gulf was unbridgeable. The saga ended in a flurry of harsh lawyer's letters and the return of U.S. rights to Wild. Trent calls it a lose–lose situation. "The film lost. We lost. She lost. And the American people lost. I'd like to think if Nettie were doing this again, she wouldn't make the same decision." Altogether, the film earned revenues in America of $42,475; Kalasikas' share ($20,101) almost matched its share of expenses ($24,835).

FINAL TAKES Nettie Wild: "The gatekeepers tell us the films have to be an hour, television being the axis around which everything moves, and people don't have a mind that can hang on to something for longer. And so I was lucky with *Leaves*. Because I realized it could be done; you could make a two-hour film that had those complexities and people would watch it, and choose it over *Rambo* in a theatrical cinema, and it would play on TV, on a national network to boot, without ads. And so all of those 'it can't be dones' weren't true. The only thing we didn't do was make a lot of money. It did extraordinarily well for what it was, but we never got into real profit."

4
Star Power

━━━━━━━━━━━━━━

Les Noces de Papier
(Paper Wedding)

DIRECTOR:
Michel Brault
EXECUTIVE PRODUCER:
Aimée Danis/LES
PRODUCTIONS DU
VERSEAU
ASSOCIATE PRODUCER:
Danièle Bussy
WRITERS:
Jefferson Lewis &
Andrée Pelletier
DIRECTOR OF PHOTOGRAHY:
Sylvain Brault
SOUND:
Dominique Chartrand
EDITOR:
Jacques Gagné
ACTORS:
Geneviève Bujold,

Manuel Aranguiz,
Dorothée Berryman,
Jean Mathieu
DISTRIBUTORS:
MAX Films (Canada);
CAPITOL
ENTERTAINMENT
(USA); FILMS TRANSIT
(world)
RELEASE DATE:
October 29, 1989
RUNNING TIME:
86 minutes
BUDGET:
$889,000

━━━━━━━━━━━━━━

"Success always surprises me, because you never know until you've put it together whether it will work. You have all these good little things, but will they fit together? Then you see a rough cut, and you see what you can fix and what you can add, and then Berlin wants it, but will the audience like it or the critics? It's a very gradual process. It never hits you suddenly." — Michel Brault, director

SYNOPSIS Trapped in a dead-end relationship with a married man, Claire, a fortyish professor of literature, agrees to marry a Latin American refugee, Pablo, and help him escape deportation from Canada. Immigration authorities, convinced that the wedding is fraudulent, continue to monitor the couple. To demonstrate its legitimacy, Claire and Pablo begin to live together and in time come to love each other.

ORIGINS Given the increasing desire of distributors to shuffle films out of the money-losing realm of theatrical exhibition into the recoupment worlds of television and video, a movie that goes the other way—appears first on television and only then is shown in commercial theatres—is almost unthinkable. Yet such is the amazing history of *Les Noces de Papier*, a film made expressly for Quebec television which subsequently enjoyed modest theatrical success in North America and considerable box-office appeal in more than 30 countries around the world. Its performance would doubtless have been even more remarkable but for an untimely coincidence—the nearly-simultaneous release in North America of *Green Card*, an inferior Hollywood movie directed by Peter Weir (*Witness*), starring French

cinematic powerhouse Gérard Dépardieu and Andie McDowell, which was based on exactly the same story line. Indeed, while *Les Noces* was written and made first, the similarities between the two films are so uncanny that a number of people are still tempted to concoct an elaborate conspiracy theory. Peter Weir himself does not figure in the speculation, since he has reportedly said on several occasions that had he seen Michel Brault's film, he would never have agreed to direct *Green Card*. Still, the theory remains.

But the crucial question to be asked is not whether some enterprising Hollywood producer quietly arranged for a rewrite of a film script by an unknown Canadian writer. The crucial question is: why was *Les Noces* special? Why, among all the films made for television in Canada that year (or in any year), was it selected to go, after its television screening in Quebec, to the Berlin Film Festival—and from there to its extraordinary career on the theatrical circuit? There are, of course, several possible answers. But the most persuasive one seems to be the movie's leading lady—Geneviève Bujold, a certified, bankable Hollywood star. Since moving to Los Angeles in the 1970s, Bujold had been featured in many films, playing Anne Boleyn in *Anne of a Thousand Days*, opposite the late Richard Burton; in David Cronenberg's *Dead Ringers*, opposite Jeremy Irons; in *Coma*, opposite Michael Douglas; in Louis Malle's *The Thief of Paris*; and in Phillipe de Broca's *King of Hearts*. She agreed to star in *Les Noces* for $50,000, a fraction of her normal fee, and by the drawing power of her name alone was able to give the film a degree of respect it might not otherwise have received.

The original idea for *Les Noces* came inevitably from real life. Montreal screenwriter Jeff Lewis had heard a story from his sister's roommate about a woman who had married a Frenchman without knowing him in order to let him stay in the country. The couple had subsequently fallen in love. Lewis knew immediately that the concept had film potential, but he had never written a feature before and, busy with other projects, put it aside. A former journalist (Ottawa *Citizen*, Southam News and the CBC), he was best known as the writer and producer of documentary films, including a profile of abortion crusader Dr. Henry Morgantaler, *Democracy on Trial*, which had won a prize at the prestigious Berlin Film Festival; and a biography of pioneering brain surgeon Wilder Penfield. His only venture into fiction had been to write a few episodes of *Mount Royal*, the ill-fated prime-time soap, which lasted one season. Eventually, after three or four years, Lewis returned to the 'paper wedding' idea and wrote a 20-page film treatment. He submitted it to Quebec's SOGIC, (Société Générale des Industries Culturelle), and, on the strength of it, was awarded $8,000 to write a first draft.

About the same time, he received a call from Aimée Danis, executive producer of Montreal's Les Productions du Verseau. Founded by Danis and her former husband Guy Fournier, Verseau had been making features, TV films and commercials for more than 15 years. (It would later be responsible for *Léolo*, one of the country's major film successes of the past decade.) In 1986, Verseau became a partner in Les Producteurs TV Films Associés—a joint-venture agreement, funded by Telefilm Canada, SOGIC and Radio-Québec, to produce made-for-TV movies with three other Montreal producers and the Quebec branch of the National Film Board. The agreement had yielded seven or eight TV movies in 1987, all of them pre-financed for about $850,000. The fees were fixed: writers earned $34,000, directors were paid $40,000 and so on. All the films were shot in 16MM, edited on video and aired for broadcast with no expectation of theatrical release. "It was a good program," Lewis says. "Things actually went quite quickly. Instead of the interminable delays from the agencies, Verseau said yes on the basis of a 20-page outline. It provided work for technicians. It gave new opportunities to writers and directors. And a lot of good films got made."

Looking for new material, Danis had called Lewis to ask if he had anything he wanted to do. "So I sent along two or three things, including this outline for *Les Noces*. We had a meeting, and she said, 'this is the one I want to do.'" Lewis readily agreed; he took his development contract from SOGIC, rolled it into a new agreement with Verseau, and sat down to write the first draft—in English. Danis already had decided who should play the lead role—Geneviève Bujold. The decision was not a fantasy. Bujold had recently completed another film for Verseau (*L'Emprise*), which was part fiction, part documentary, and had offered to make another film with them if Michel Brault was the director. Bujold had a long-standing professional relationship with Brault dating back to the late 1950s, when she was an aspiring teenage actress and he was a fixture at the NFB. According to Danis, it is safe to suggest that without Brault's participation, there would have been no Bujold; and without Bujold, there would have been no theatrical after-life to the history of *Les Noces*. Lewis agrees. "Other scripts in the series were well-written. They were well-acted and well-directed. But none had a Geneviève Bujold."

DEVELOPMENT At Verseau, Aimée Danis soon handed off the reins of authority to her associate, Danièle Bussy. Producing her first feature film, Bussy quickly encountered her first major problem: because Brault had declined to commit to the project, Danis had already agreed to retain the services of Claude Fournier, her ex-husband's brother, who had directed *The Tin Soldier*. Bussy told Danis that she wanted Brault to direct and would find a way to make it happen. Then, she called Fournier and, for "a very small amount of money," bought him out of his unsigned agreement, explaining that "Michel had been promised the film."

Brault's reluctance to make a firm directorial commitment may have been due to the fact that it had been almost 15 years since he had actually directed a feature film. That was the award-winning and highly acclaimed *Les Ordres*, a searing indictment of Pierre Trudeau's use of the *War Measures Act* during the 1972 October Crisis. In the intervening years, Brault had functioned as a director of photography for a number of prominent directors, American and European.

. The product of an aristocratic Montreal family—his great-grandfather, F. Gabriel Marchand, had been premier of Quebec—Brault first became interested in cinema as a teenager, while attending a private boarding school. A friend owned a small movie camera, with which Brault "discovered how marvelous it was to be able to record life on film." It was there, too, that he met and became friendly with Claude Jutra, who had arrived to shoot a film on boy scouts. (The son of a radiologist, Jutra himself became a doctor, although Brault maintains the only diagnosis he ever did came one day when Brault complained of abdominal pain on his right side. "Go to a hospital. Now," said Jutra. Brault's appendix was removed that night.)

It was Jutra who in the late 1950s facilitated Brault's return to the National Film Board—he had been there earlier as a summer intern, but had lost the job, he says, because he was so undisciplined. For the next 20 years, he worked on dozens of NFB documentaries, both as a director and as a cameraman. His versatility, he says, "gave me a certain freedom to be able to accept or refuse a project." That, too, helps explain the 15-year directorial gap between *Les Ordres* and *Les Noces*. "It wasn't that there weren't offers. It was that I wasn't interested in the scripts. I don't understand how directors earn a living if they are waiting for the good script to happen. There aren't that many good scripts."

While Brault considered his options, Lewis started writing. As part of his research, he interviewed an immigration adviser, Claire, a former federal official who had crossed to the other side and was now counselling refugees how to escape the grasp of the immigration laws. Pretending to be the adviser's assistant, Lewis attended a number of immigration hearings. The research confirmed his thesis: the arranged marriage was "still one of the great ways of getting into the country, because they basically have to prove

Pablo (Manuel Aranguiz) and Claire (Geneviève Bujold), whose fabricated marriage to fool immigration authorities leads to unintended romance in **Les Noces de Papier.**

that you didn't marry sincerely. That's a hard thing to prove." And the hearings suggested great material for a comedy, "especially when it turns out the two people have fallen in love and weren't supposed to fall in love." That was the premise from the beginning—that a well-paid, middle-class university professor would agree to marry a minimum-wage earning, lower-class, South American restaurant worker. The contrast could not be greater.

The first draft, entitled *Bye Bye, Love*, took Lewis about a month. He told the story to everyone he knew; when people's eyes started to glaze over, he knew he had hit a slow patch. When people suggested good plot wrinkles, he was quick to incorporate them. "I'll steal anyone's ideas," he laughs. By the time Michel Brault voiced serious interest in the project, Lewis had written two drafts of the script. The second was done in French. "I kept waiting for someone to yell fraud," he says. For assistance, he turned to his partner, actress Andrée Pelletier, who helped him polish the dialogue.

By the summer of 1988, Brault had agreed to direct the film. Inevitably, he brought his own sensibility to the material. Lewis had conceived "a comedy with a black edge to it." The version Brault directed tended to consist mostly of the darker edges, with a little bittersweet comedy thrown in. There was a particularly sharp difference of opinion about the Bujold character (Claire). In Lewis' script, Claire is a woman who has come to terms with her life. "She's hit 40. She's had lots of affairs, and she's decided that it's okay if she doesn't marry and doesn't have children. She's basically content. Brault, 25 years older than Lewis, had known more than one woman in precisely the same situation as Claire; and in his experience, they were anything but content. Indeed, one close friend of his was at that point carrying on an extra-marital affair with such a woman—also a university professor of literature—and was being pressured to leave the marriage. Such women, Brault argued, were not resigned to their fates. Recalls Lewis: "He kept pushing the line about this tragic woman who couldn't persuade her lover to leave his wife."

Brault also lobbied for changes in the basic story line. In the first draft, Bujold's sister (played in the film by Dorothée Berryman) is having an affair with her client, a Latin American immigrant. Anxious to keep him in the country, she persuades Bujold to marry him. This, Lewis concedes, made for a far more complicated plot—"too complicated for Michel to deal with, because he saw the story in terms of a woman torn between her married lover and her new love interest . . . I basically deferred to most of what he suggested, partly because I had so little experience at that point," and partly because Lewis' own partner [co-writer Andrée Pelletier] "was eight months pregnant. My mind was not fully focussed on the screenplay."

Still, Lewis says, "we arm-wrestled for three or four weeks over just about everything." For Brault, the character of Pablo—a man who has been tortured in South America—could never be anything other than a tragic figure. "Whereas," says Lewis, "I would argue that you don't stop laughing just because you've lived through horrible experiences. It changes the way you laugh perhaps, but life goes on, you fall in love, and all kinds of things happen. Michel had a very hard time with that. He wanted to make it darker, more like an unrelieved tragedy. Michel is a very personal director. The last idea he's heard is always the best idea. And he doesn't really feel that scripts are anything but things you improvise from." Lewis found the process of negotiating line-by-line script changes with Brault debilitating. Or, as Verseau president Aimée Danis acknowledges: "It's not easy working with Michel Brault." Still, Lewis says the experience was "a piece of cake," compared to the tensions created by revisions to *Mon Ami Max*, another Lewis-scripted, Brault-directed, Verseau-produced feature film, which started shooting in March 1993.

Brault had a different view of this process. The nuances he was looking for, he says, were buried in the original script, but were undeveloped. "I wanted to go deeper. I always think that if you have an element, you should push it a little further, make it a little more evident, not just half something." Brault interviewed his professor friend and asked her what she did to combat loneliness. Her answers led Brault to add three specific elements of Claire's life—her cat, the telephone that follows her everywhere and her distinct way of shutting a door—stopping just before it closes in the vain hope that someone might be coming in. And he found the process of adapting the script somehow exhilirating. "It was wonderful to change things, to go around things and to accept that the script should be reworked and reworked until it's shot. Many scriptwriters think their script is sacred—my God. I know it's not easy," Brault concedes, "but you have to do it. A lot of unsuccessful films in this country get shot before they're ready because agencies have to spend money, distributors need to fill their quota and directors need a job. There's a lesson in that."

CASTING If Geneviève Bujold was an obvious choice for the role of Claire, finding the right actor to play the character of the haunted Pablo was anything but simple. In search of the right candidate, producer Danièle Bussy contacted several Latin American organizations in Montreal. Several actors emerged, but none seemed to fit the part. It was writer Lewis who in September 1988, only a few weeks before the scheduled start of production, finally discovered Chilean Manuel Aranguiz—introducing a Spanish-language TV documentary on El Salvador on late-night TV. Lewis only happened to be watching because of the erratic sleeping habits of his and Pelletier's newborn daughter. He then arranged for a tape of the documentary to be delivered to Bussy.

The son of an equipment repairman, Aranguiz had worked as an actor in theatre and television in his native Santiago. In February 1974, only five months after the coup d'état staged by Augustus Pinochet, Aranguiz came to Montreal; he was 28. Although he managed to find occasional work as an actor, there were relatively few opportunities for a man who spoke strongly-accented French. Eventually, he went back to university to earn a B.A. in languages, hoping to work as a translator. He had just graduated when Bussy called to invite him to audition for *Les Noces*.

After reading the script, Aranguiz was convinced that he could play the part. In the reign of terror that followed the coup, he had known people who had been arrested, imprisoned, tortured and even killed by the Pinochet regime. The survivors of that period lived with ghosts, a sense of hidden pain that Aranguiz communicated to Brault during their first encounter—a 45-minute conversation which Brault videotaped. Brault's objective was to take a reading of character. "He wanted to know who I was," Aranguiz recalls. "My relationship with politics in Chile, how I came to Canada, my acting experience. He wanted to know me as a human being." Ten days later, Brault summoned him to a second interview, but waited another week before awarding him the part. The day Bussy called him was his forty-third birthday. He was paid about $12,000.

But almost until the last moment, Brault remained ambivalent about his own participation in the film. He remembers standing in his bathroom at home and suddenly asking himself, 'What am I doing? I'm going to go somewhere else. I don't want to do this.' Once, he had read that the director of *On Golden Pond*, Bruce Beresford, had compared appearing on the set every day to walking into the spinning propeller of a airplane and being chopped into pieces. Brault sometimes felt the same terror. Even with a well-written script, he says, "you feel you have to create life, to make this little thing fly, and you feel like the Wright brothers—maybe it'll never get off the ground. And everybody is looking to you. 'Speak up, say something, tell me what I'm doing here, where's this, where's that?' Everybody's waiting for you to speak. You're not prepared for a thousand questions. And you realize that you're the one who has to lift the 747—every morning. It's terrifying, even when you're well-prepared."

PRODUCTION Although everyone connected with the production of *Les Noces* knew that the project was a television movie, there was, says Jeff Lewis, a tacit understanding "that we weren't making television. We said we're going to make a movie. It may only cost $850,000, but it's not going to be a TV movie, it's going to be a movie. Whatever happens afterward, we'll have made a movie."

Les Noces was shot on location during a 20-day period that began in late October 1988. The crew was union, but worked for TV, not feature film rates. Lewis credits producer Bussy with performing miracles to extract as much production value as was possible from the budget and dealing with the gigantic egos involved—no smaller for TV movies than for features. "In a three-week shoot, there's no time to indulge the egos," he says. "You're too busy with logistics. But the film looks a lot richer than it is." Some locations were in Lewis' own neighbourhood. In the morning, he would walk to his office and pass a dozen trucks all advertising the film he had written. It was, he says, "a quite pleasant feeling of power."

Although Brault frequently invited him to spend time on the set, Lewis was reluctant. "The truth is that it's a lousy place for a writer to be. When you're there, there's nothing you can do. You can get coffee for people. You can hang around and gossip with the crew. But you can't *do* anything." On the last day, however, he turned up with Andrée Pelletier and was accorded a standing ovation by cast and crew.

Aranguiz remembers the production as a very happy experience. "Michel is a very intelligent director. He knows how to talk to you. I was a little intimidated, working with Geneviève. I did not know how to cope with a big star, how to talk to her—not during the scenes, but during the breaks." At one point, Brault was filming in a Latin dance hall. It was the end of a long day, and everyone was exhausted. The scene required Aranguiz to dance with Bujold. To get the necessary close-ups of her, Brault placed the camera on the actor's shoulder. When it came time to shoot the same scene from Bujold's POV, Brault asked Aranguiz if he would mind dancing with a stand-in—Bujold was tired. Not at all, he said. "But then Geneviève came and danced with me. That was very nice."

For Brault, "the shoot went very fast." There were no nightmares, only an occasional dispute with Bujold, a brilliant actress who always brings her own concepts and interpretations to her work. "You have to give her a better reason to do it your way." By the end of October, the shoot was complete—$40,000 over its projected budget.

POST·PRODUCTION The film was edited by Jacques Gagné over the winter and spring of 1988–89. Brault's approach is to watch the rushes with the editor, "say what I have to say," and let him work on his own. As Lewis might have felt on the set, observing his script being turned into film, so Brault believes that the director has no real place in the editing suite. "If you're there all the time, you're just there as a watchdog," he says. "You're just watching what you tried to do. And you might not have succeeded. You end up trying to force it. You've got to let him see what he sees, and discover things about the material that you didn't even know."

DISTRIBUTION *Les Noces De Papier* was broadcast on Radio–Québec in October 1989, and drew an estimated 300,000 viewers. That—and subsequent rebroadcasts—might have been the end of its story but for Jan Rofekamp, president of Montreal–based Films Transit, who owned the international rights to the film (and to all the TV movies created by the companies working under Les Producteurs' umbrella). It was Rofekamp who, making his annual autumnal trek to the Cannes TV festival, took a little detour to attend the Nyon festival of documentary films in Switzerland, carrying a cassette of *Les Noces* with him. In Nyon, he went to lunch with Moritz de Hadeln, director of the Berlin Film Festival, told him *Les Noces* was the best Canadian film of the year and asked him to consider it for competition. If it were, Rofekamp said, he would arrange for the necessary blow-up to 35MM. Six weeks later, a week before Christmas, de Hadeln called Rofekamp at home to tell him the film had been accepted.

The blow-up proved to be more complicated than Rofekamp had anticipated. Because the original had been edited on video, the entire negative had to be re-edited—blown up, remixed for sound quality and then subtitled for English. Michel Brault here took what every director would doubtless have taken, the opportunity to reshoot one scene and cut a few others. The $120,000 operation was borne largely by SOGIC (as a subsidy, not an investment) and partly by Telefilm Canada.

As it has been for many Canadian films and filmmakers—among them, Ron Mann and *Comic Book Confidential*; Nettie Wild and *A Rustling of Leaves*—Berlin was an almost magical experience for the producers of *Les Noces*. Part of it was simply seeing a 16MM movie blown up to 35MM, and projected on a vast screen before 2,000 appreciative filmgoers. Brault took his bows afterward but, as is his habit with all of his films, refused to sit through the actual screenings. Part of it, too, was the sense of participating in history. Brault recalls crossing what was then the border between the Western sector and East Berlin one night in the rain and hearing the "chink chink" sound of hundreds of hammers chipping away pieces of the Wall.

For the film itself, simply to be entered in competition guaranteed a certain level of international buying interest. "Because it had Geneviève's name, people saw it, liked it and snapped it up all over the place," Lewis says. "I remember going to Rofekamp's booth and he had already sold it to 26 countries and he said, 'I'm not leaving here until I get to 30.' " He ultimately sold it to 43 countries—"which is quite good," Rofekamp says, because the maximum is really about 60. In fact, at the end of that year, Rofekamp says he wrote the largest cheque he had ever written—to Les Producteurs TV Films Associés, the parent company of which du Verseau was part. Much earlier, he says, he claims to have advised Aimée Danis to take Les Noces out of the package of 10 TV movies Les Producteurs was slated to produce, rather than be forced to share the dividends from international sales with her partners. "It was short- sighted, but du Verseau didn't listen," Rofekamp insists. "So all the revenue had to be split over 10 films, most of which were junk. The profits from Les Noces paid for the losses of the other films in the package." Aimée Danis admits that Verseau made nothing from its $30,000 investment in the film. "We recouped our investment, but nothing more," she says. "Rofekamp made the money. The distributors always make the money because their fees are off the top, and their expenses are high, and you, as the producer, have no control."

The response from audiences, critics and buyers to Les Noces in Berlin was so positive that for a time Lewis thought the film might actually win in competition. At a reception one night, he dared to voice his optimism to a festival insider. The man promptly took him aside and said, 'My friend, let me tell you how it works here. They have a deal here. Everyone knows about it. Every second year, like clockwork, they have to give the best movie award to an American film because if they don't, the Americans won't come. Last year, it was a foreign film, so this year it has to be an American movie. So don't even think about it.' " That year, The Music Box, a Hollywood movie, won Berlin's best film award.

It was also in Berlin that Pierre Latour, head of distribution at Roger Frappier's and Pierre Gendron's Max Films, saw the film for the first time. Afterward, he approached Danièle Bussy.

"We must release this commercially," he said.

"That's crazy." she said. "It's already been on TV in Quebec. Twice."

"I don't care," Latour replied. "It's such a great film. You already have a 35MM print. Let's do it.' "

In fact, Latour was not the first to make the suggestion. Shortly after it played on Radio-Québec, another distributor had approached Verseau about arranging a theatrical release; at the time, of course, no 35MM print had been struck. And in Berlin, now-defunct Cinema Plus also approached Danis about acquiring the rights. Danis ultimately agreed to go with Max Films.

BANFF In April of 1990—after Berlin—*Les Noces* was officially selected for competition at the Banff Television Festival. A few weeks before the festival began, Lewis received a call from a woman connected with the festival who asked him if he was planning to attend. The answer was no. At which point, Lewis recalls, "she said, 'well, you didn't hear this from me, but it's won the best film award, so maybe you should come.'" An additional incentive was that one of the jury members was an Australian producer who had expressed interest in buying the rights to *Les Noces* and making an English-language version. So Lewis "went out and bought the only full-fare ticket I've bought in my life, which I ended up getting stiffed for."

Michel Brault also flew to Banff. But when he arrived in the Calgary airport, no one met him and he did not quite know where Banff was, or how to get there. "I had to call back to Montreal, and ask, 'what do I do now?' So they suggested I take a taxi. I said, 'To Banff?' He ended up waiting for a bus. By the time he arrived, the prize had already been awarded. He rode back the next morning with Jan Rofekamp. "He had a rented Cadillac," Brault recalls, "rented on my hook!"

Lewis' negotiations with the Australian dragged on for months. "Bizarre contracts," he says, "went back and forth between the lawyers. They wanted intergalactic rights. It was the first time I'd actually seen the expression, 'and for the universe' in a contract. Finally, by the fall of 1989, everything was in place—Lewis was to receive $10,000 (US) for the option, and substantially more if the film were made. All that remained was to sign the contracts. Then, one day in late November, Lewis took a call from the producer. "I think we have a problem," she said. She had been invited to attend a pre-release screening of Peter Weir's *Green Card*, a film that sounded suspiciously like an English-language version of *Les Noces*. She called again the next day, having seen *Green Card*. "We're toast," she said. "I'll never be able to raise the money for this now."

CANADIAN DISTRIBUTION Pierre Latour's plan to release *Les Noces* theatrically in Canada almost ran into a roadblock—Radio-Québec. It owned the rights, and it had no intention of releasing them. When Verseau said it was thinking about mounting a theatrical campaign, the Quebec network told the producers to think again. The film was made for TV. It had a TV contract. It was not possible to change it. Fortunately, Latour knew one of the senior executives at Radio-Québec. "I called him and explained the situation," Latour recalls. "I knew it might not have a great box office, but I was convinced that it wouldn't lose money, and that it would enhance the reputation of the film and of the filmmakers. He said 'okay.'"

Max Films offered no minimum guarantee, but did spend between

$75,000–100,000 on prints and ads in English and French Canada. Because it had already appeared on television, Latour was skeptical of its prospects in Quebec. "I was never over-confident about Quebec," he says. "I was sure that the damage done by TV meant that it couldn't reach astronomical figures." Still, it did "quite well," running for about four weeks. Of course, what the distributor regards as quite well, the creators regard as disappointment. For Jeff Lewis, *Les Noces'* failure to last more than a month in Quebec theatres is evidence of Max Films' refusal to put any serious effort into the promotion. "There was no muscle," he says. "It closed after four weeks—a typical Canadian story. The best way to get a movie on the screen in Canada is to release it first elsewhere."

As they had been abroad, the reviewers were impressed. The *Globe and Mail's* Jay Scott called it "goodhearted, gentle, unassuming and mildly witty . . . . Despite the intermittent crudeness of the script, there is Bujold at every turn, charming, touching, sexy, intelligent, acerbic." In the *Edmonton Journal*, critic Marc Horton was struck by the *Green Card* parallels. He stopped short of suggesting that Peter Weir actually saw *Les Noces*, "but someone must have, because the echoes of *Paper Wedding* are deafening."

Bussy, who saw the American film on an airplane flight to France, found it all "very strange. I cannot believe Peter Weir saw *Les Noces de Papier* before he did *Green Card*. I think the early drafts for Weir were written before *Les Noces*. I think it's just a coincidence of life." And a recognition that the arranged marriage was a solid film concept. Indeed, there may have been a third film on the same theme. In October 1986, *Cinema Canada* reported that a Canadian-financed Chinese feature film was shooting in Edmonton. It was an action-comedy about the misadventures of a couple that had wed for immigration purposes. Its title: *Paper Marriage*.

Lewis tends to agree that the possibility of outright theft is remote. "You'd have to be a really wild conspiracy theorist to believe that they stole the film. But there is a theory, which is that Verseau sent the first English-language draft of the script to Bujold in Los Angeles in 1988, and that it somehow got into other hands." Lewis himself saw the Weir film with Pelletier and walked out before the end. "There were too many eerie similarities," he says. "Even bits of dialogue from the English version." And he felt strongly enough about the issue to consult a Montreal lawyer, who advised him that proving theft would be both expensive and, in the absence of a solid paper trail, difficult. "If I had been the producer," he says, "I would have rented a big theatre in Hollywood and advertised to the Los Angeles film community to come and decide which is the better movie. This one [*Green Card*] cost $10 million and this one [*Les Noces*] cost $900,000. The publicity alone would have been fabulous. But Verseau couldn't be bothered." Three years after its release, Latour believes that *Les Noces* "probably broke even on a global basis. It never performed in English Canada. Its total box office in Canada was about $200,000, which is very, very average. But it seemed to be very important to position the film at that [theatrical] level." Later, it was sold to the CBC for $75,000.

But the theatrical life of Les Noces was probably nowhere more successful than in France, where it played for several months and sold an estimated 100,000 tickets. The posters, Lewis says, "shamelessly played off" the previous success of another Quebec film. "In the land of The Decline of the American Empire," said the words on the one-sheet, "you don't play with marriages." The film also had extended runs in Latin America. In 1992, while Lewis was in Buenos Aires researching another project, Les Noces was still playing in theatres in the Argentine provinces. In Montevideo, he found it in a video store. "You can't even get it in a video store in Canada," he says. The Film Board distributes the video here, so you can get it only at an NFB office—if you can find one. They don't really want you to have the film."

Indeed, like many Canadian filmmakers, Lewis has a jaundiced view of the federal and provincial agencies that underwrite the industry. "We really punish success here," he maintains. "There is no pleasure taken in watching people succeed. Without getting unduly paranoid, I always feel the bureaucrats at SOGIC and Telefilm and the OFDC [Ontario Film Development Corp.] are waiting for me to fall on my ass. The meetings get harder, I get grilled more, there are more ultimatums. You might have thought that after Les Noces, people would look at the team assembled for Mon Ami, Max and say 'Wow, the same people are going to come back and do another movie. Isn't that great?' We had so much trouble. Only weeks before the film, Telefilm was still threatening to pull its money out. In Hollywood, even though it's half bullshit, there's a pleasure in making things happen. Here, the pleasure is in making things not happen." The benefit of the Canadian way, he says, is that "if you get through all of this, you can make movies that have a lot more integrity. You don't have a studio saying 'give it a happy ending.' "

U.S. RELEASE Ted Goldberg, president of Washington-based Capitol Entertainment, saw Les Noces for the first time at the Toronto Film Festival in September 1990. He contacted Rofekamp and arranged for a 15-city distribution deal, putting up only $20,000 as a minimum guarantee. He showcased it at the Washington, D.C. FilmFest in May 1991 (at the new Canadian embassy) to excellent reviews. Motion Picture Association President and film czar Jack Valenti came. Geneviève Bujold came. "I was flying high," Goldberg says. "I thought I had a hit." What he had not anticipated was the effect of Green Card on Les Noces. "If you've already seen Green Card," Goldberg says, why would you want to see Paper Wedding? In French, no less." To avoid comparisons with Green Card, newspaper ads in New York and elsewhere included a still photo of Bujold in wedding veil, ran three quotes from critics and the lines, 'They met, they married and then they Fell in Love.' There was no mention of the immigration theme.

The film opened commercially on June 21, 1991 at New York's Lincoln

Plaza theatre; it played six weeks, grossing $21,000. Film critic Janet Maislin, writing in the *New York Times*, called it "a more serious and less stylish version of *Green Card* . . . . It is simply directed and holds little surprise, but it is given considerable substance by the performance of Miss Bujold. Her Claire, fully formed yet also touchingly uncertain, is a lonely figure with a keen cynical intelligence." Maislin praised Lewis' script for avoiding the potential for cuteness.

But she, too, was struck by the uncanny parallels with *Green Card*. Both heroines, she noted, "are more or less scholarly types; both heroes are immigrants with restaurant jobs; each hero is more sensitive and distinguished than originally appears. Each heroine has a suspicious erstwhile beau who resents her new situation and is persistent. And each couple must go to elaborate lengths to hoodwink immigration authorities." Only the presence of Bujold was able to stir the interest of the *Village Voice*. "There's no reason to hie thyself to Michel Brault's humdrum, predictable [film], except to watch Geneviève Bujold . . . . Bujold plain is more interesting than seeing Jane Fonda or Cher fancy. It's a relief to find age frankly displayed."

Despite generally favourable reviews, *Les Noces'* record across the U.S. was spotty. It played six weeks at the Bridge Theatre in San Francisco and four weeks at the Fine Arts in Los Angeles, but died in Houston—a city with a large Hispanic population, where Goldberg had expected it to perform well. There was another good run in Boston (eight weeks at the West Newton), but disappointment in Washington, D.C. "It never really had legs," Goldberg says. Had it opened six months earlier, says Pierre Latour, the results might have been quite different. "But it was worse than Ted anticipated because nobody in the U.S. believed *Les Noces* was done prior to *Green Card*, so it therefore seemed like a copy, with less well-known actors."

The other problem with the film's box-office performance in the U.S., Goldberg says, was Bujold. "She was very nice on the phone, but she did not want to promote the film. I had a cover story arranged in *Parade*, a magazine supplement in millions of Sunday newspapers. That was the kind of publicity you cannot buy. She's sort of a recluse. It doesn't help the film if you don't get out there and sell it." Goldberg estimates the movie's total gross at $250,000 (US), and says both he and Telefilm Canada—which contributed launch funds—lost money. Its performance in video was even more dismal—with sales in two years of about 400 units.

Given the accolades heaped upon *Les Noces*, including six Gemeaux (Gemini) awards for Radio–Québec, Brault felt it only appropriate to enter it in SOGIC's annual best feature film award, which carried a $100,000 prize. To his surprise, the agency rejected the film from consideration, noting that it had been shown first on Radio–Québec and that the rules specifically stipulated that the primary market for entered films was to be commercial. Unwilling to accept that verdict, Brault rallied support from the province's filmmaking organizations and sought an injunction in Quebec Superior Court to force SOGIC to accept the film. Regardless of its appearance on television, the appeal argued, the primary market for the film had been theatrical. Mr. Justice Kenneth Mackay rejected the application, saying there had been no serious prejudice shown by the film agency and that no serious violation of law had occurred.

FINAL TAKES Jefferson Lewis: "It's the names that make the whole thing work. This is what we've got to do. Take a big name and put an unknown Canadian next to them and make heroes out of them. We need to make more Geneviève Bujolds. Let them go to Hollywood. I don't care where they live. As long as they come back and make movies from time to time."

Jan Rofekamp: "It's a story that proves that this whole notion of a TV movie and a theatrical film doesn't work any more. If the film is strong, if it gets critical acclaim, if it gets into a major festival, if it has some commercial elements in it, it can be theatrical—even if it's been made for $850,000. That's what's wrong with our system. We decide the future of the film before it's finished, slotting them into the TV Fund or the feature fund. You can only judge a film when it's done."

Michel Brault: "This confirmed for me that I could do something very different from *Les Ordres*. That could have been in doubt, especially after 15 years. But when a million and a half people see my film, on TV or in the theatres, that's more satisfying than any career. Even if only a million people are really paying attention, still—a million people. That's amazing. When I started making films, we were happy if two or three hundred people saw them."

5
If It's Not Working, Change It

Diplomatic Immunity

DIRECTOR:	Michael Hogan
Sturla Gunnarsson	**DISTRIBUTOR:**
PRODUCERS:	ASTRAL FILMS
Sturla Gunnarsson &	(Canada/French-
Steve Lucas	speaking Europe);
EXECUTIVE PRODUCERS:	ALLIANCE RELEASING
Michael Donovan &	(USA)
Lyn Goleby	**RELEASE DATE:**
WRITER:	October 4, 1991
Steve Lucas	**RUNNING TIME:**
DIRECTOR OF PHOTOGRAPHY:	93 minutes
Harald Ortenburger	**BUDGET:**
SOUND:	$2.68 million
Jose Garcia	
EDITOR:	
Jeff Warren	
ACTORS:	
Wendell Meldrum,	
Ofelia Medina,	

"Ted Kotcheff had a great line a few years ago. He said, 'You don't learn anything from one project to the next. You're always starting at zero.' This is one of the great problems. But it's also the way it is. What's different about this is that we went through our learning curve on one project." — Steve Lucas, writer

"See, what you're really doing in the Canadian market is you're really making TV movies and trying to release them theatrically. You can't do that in the U.S. and you certainly can't do it in Canada." — Wayne Case, distributor

SYNOPSIS A Canadian foreign service officer, Kim Dades, reluctantly accepts an assignment in El Salvador and discovers that a housing project built with Canadian aid dollars has been turned into a brothel for the Salvadorean military. The ensuing drama, and her developing friendship with a Salvadorean aid worker, force Dades to see the human face of foreign policy. Ultimately, she must confront the conflict between the army and the people—and choose sides.

ORIGINS Sturla Gunnarsson, an ambitious young filmmaker from Vancouver, was introduced to Steve Lucas, a hard-boiled copy writer at Cockfield Brown in Toronto, in 1978. They disliked each other at once. At the time, Gunnarsson had just moved to Toronto to finish work on *A Day Much Like the Others*, a four-minute experimental film that would later win a $10,000 Norman McLaren award and launch his career. Lucas was in the throes of extricating himself from the world of advertising, a universe he despised. He had never quite managed to suspend his disbelief, a prerequisite, it would seem, for anyone writing advertising copy. Eventually, Cockfield Brown decided to end Lucas' misery; it fired him.

It was that firing which led the two men to their first collaboration—they had by then managed to transcend first impressions—*After the Axe*, a 1980 docu-drama about a 40-year-old marketing executive who loses his job. A rare co-production of the National Film Board of Canada and the CBC, the film was later nominated for an Academy Award. Even before it was completed, Gunnarsson and Lucas had begun scouting around for a new project. During the 1980 Christmas holidays, Gunnarsson met a Chilean refugee in Vancouver who had been tortured by the Pinochet regime. The woman had been kept in a cell with a metal floor, wired for electricity. Guards left her food on one side of the cell and then switched on the circuits; her choice was to starve or risk electrocution.

Back in Toronto, Gunnarsson discovered a group of medical doctors who had established a downtown clinic to treat Latin American torture victims. Among them was a Salvadorean woman, whose story formed the core of the next Lucas–Gunnarsson film proposal, a documentary to be known as *Torture*. After more than two dozen scripts, the basic elements of her story would still be found in the film that became *Diplomatic Immunity*. The central questions then, says Gunnarsson, were: why are these things happening, and what do they have to do with us? Ten years later, the questions had not appreciably changed.

DEVELOPMENT In Hollywood, a film project often takes years to make it to the screen. Three to five years is probably the norm; 10 years is not uncommon. In Canada, however, a film that lingers in the waters of development for too long is apt to shrivel, losing whatever appeal it may have had to investors. *Immunity* is a rare exception. Nine years in what Gunnarsson calls "development hell," it died many deaths along the way, only to be resurrected by a variety of life-giving benefactors.

To research their proposed documentary, Gunnarsson and Lucas applied to the NFB for an "investigate," essentially a grant to examine the feasibility of making the film. The NFB's Ontario region gave them $3,000. Six months later, in June of 1981, they submitted an impassioned 90-page report, written, Lucas would later concede, "by a couple of angry young guys" convinced that Latin Americans suffered so that North Americans could prosper. That inflammatory thesis was bound to stir controversy at the NFB—and it did. The Ontario centre, backers of *After the Axe*, suddenly lost interest. "It was the same old story," Gunnarsson complains. "We financed your film. You've had your chance. Now we want somebody else. Like, why carry on with someone who's made a film that's succeeded?"

Spurned in Ontario, Gunnarsson and Lucas turned to the NFB's Studio B in Montreal. There, they won the support of two crucial patrons—Peter Katadotis, then head of English-language production and something of a

Latinophile; and Bob Verrall, the producer in charge of turning Timothy Findley's *The Wars* into an epic TV series. With their backing, Gunnarsson and Lucas were eventually given the green light—and more money ($20,000)—to do further research. That was the Film Board way—investigate feasibility, do the research and then, from the research, write the script. This time, however, they would be researching not a documentary, but a full-scale feature film.

Convinced that the real story could only be found *in situ*, the pair planned an extended trip to Mexico, the way station for refugees from Central and South America. In the end, Gunnarsson concedes, the trip "might have been a mistake. Because we could have made a movie here. There was a story here, this huge mass of people from Latin America trying to adjust. But we didn't want to do a psychological study. We felt this was a bigger story. We wanted to say, 'This is what's going on. This is what it's got to do with us. And we should be doing something about it.'" Owing to other commitments, Gunnarsson did not leave for Mexico City until February 1983, taking a bus to Buffalo to catch a cheap flight. The day he left, *After the Axe* was nominated for an Academy Award in the feature documentary category. The nomination would briefly make Gunnarsson and Lucas hot properties in Hollywood—a Warholian 15-minutes of fame—and would later provide another of the many side trips on the interminable voyage of *Immunity*.

Gunnarsson and Lucas spent four months in Mexico City. They took daily two-hour Spanish lessons, met exiles by the dozens, interviewed Salvadorean leaders of the FMLN, the left-wing guerrilla organization, were introduced to the powers who ran Cona Cite, one of the country's two major studios, and hobnobbed with journalists, intellectuals, diplomats. What made the Canadian project attractive to the Mexicans were the dollar signs, an opportunity to bring foreign currency and work into Mexico. "We had the Oscar nomination," says Gunnarsson. "We had the Film Board behind us. And we were Canadian—not American. And for Mexicans, that's a big thing." In turn, Gunnarsson and Lucas saw a chance to set the movie in an exotic but authentic locale and—given the declining value of the peso—to produce it more cheaply than it might otherwise be produced in Canada.

But they were still struggling with the story line for the script. The truth, says Gunnarsson, is that "we went to Mexico not really knowing what the hell we were going to do." In fact, until perhaps 1985, he says, their plot lines for the script were all "cooked up out of our imagination, not real stories. But we always had just enough momentum to keep it alive." Momentum was the key. There was no story, no script, no stars, no financiers. Gunnarsson had yet to direct his first dramatic movie. Lucas had never written one; his work had been confined to documentaries. All they really had was a vague concept, and the irrepressible enthusiasm of youth. It was not important that they did not know where they were going; what was important was that others believed they knew.

For a time, they considered setting the story in South America, then in Central America, then in a fictional country (Santa Esperanza "or something stupid like that," says Lucas). One consistent plot focus, however, was the diplomatic corps. After extensive discussions with the Department of External Affairs in Ottawa, Gunnarsson and Lucas were given access to the Canadian embassy in Mexico City to see how it worked. When Canada formally agreed to begin accepting refugees from El Salvador, the embassy's immigration officer, Claudette Deschenes, organized a field trip to the region.

The journey was a revelation. At once surreal and macabre, it delivered the first genuine hints of what their film might be about. Every afternoon, the monied class would gather poolside at the Camino Real, the city's luxury hotel, order lavish meals and, in Gunnarsson's words, "work like pigs to have fun." By dusk they were gone, and in the morning army patrols would prowl through the streets, collecting the night's ransom of corpses. Accompanying Deschenes, the filmmakers were struck by an odd dichotomy—the trauma of the refugees on the one hand, and Deschenes' necessarily disinterested response. "She's there to be Canada," Gunnarsson explains. "That's her job. She's not there to look after Salvadorans." Deschenes interviewed people, trying to determine which ones qualified as refugees. Did they have a legitimate fear of death? And if they did, did they hold radical political views that might incite trouble in Canada? Did they have survival skills, so they would not become a burden on the social system? "All very legitimate," Gunnarsson allows.

But at the same time, "refugees are sneaking into the hotel under cover of darkness to be interviewed, because there are corpses in the bloody street. There were these two worlds and they had nothing to do with each other." By the time they returned to Mexico, Gunnarsson and Lucas were convinced that their film lay in the gap between civilian terror and diplomatic sang-froid. Deschenes, they believed, had backed into El Salvador, her gaze fixed steadily on Ottawa. The mind-set was like an emotional flak-jacket.

"Out there," says Lucas, "you get affected, and it fucks you up. Which is why you get moved a round a lot."

Back in Mexico City, Gunnarsson and Lucas had tuxedoes made and flew to Los Angeles for the 1983 Academy Award ceremonies; they did not win. Still, the nomination opened doors—assuring them of at least one pitch meeting with every major studio. They had no idea how the L.A. system worked and no idea of how to put a deal together. They had no agent, no lawyer and no script. All they had was a short treatment—an outline. Even the outline, they knew, was feeble, so at every meeting they refused to leave it behind. "We had good pitches," says Lucas, "but no story." Two studios, however—Paramount and Columbia Triumph—offered development deals, in the range of $20,000–25,000. Gunnarsson says now that if they had accepted the offers, the film probably would have been made six years earlier, "and it would have been distributed." Lucas agrees, saying the decision to reject the offers was "a bit stupid." But for two self-professed Canadian nationalists, it seemed like the right decision at the time, in part because they knew Hollywood would have commercialized and Americanized the film. "Remember," Lucas said in 1991, "we were coming out of the Film Board. What's the Film Board about? Explaining Canada to Canadians."

By July of 1983, Gunnarsson and Lucas were back in Canada. They had spent about $40,000 in development money and still had nothing that inspired confidence in themselves, let alone their mentors. Among the first people they called was one of those mentors, the NFB's Bob Verrall, the man who wanted to executive produce *Immunity*. He was, Gunnarsson recalls, very subdued. And with good reason. *The Wars* had gone catastrophically over budget. The NFB was engulfed in a sea of overages. No money remained even for worthy in-house projects, let alone half-baked proposals from outside. Just how little interest remained was clear a week later when Gunnarsson called again. "Oh, didn't we tell you," the Film Board said, "Bob's in New Zealand. He'll be back in six months." Gunnarsson was stunned; his first mate had just abandoned ship. "The whole structure of the deal," he says, "at that point went to rat shit." Verrall's successor showed no particular interest in the project.

So in February 1984, Gunnarsson and Lucas became full-fledged independent producers, set up Metropolis Motion Pictures, hired lawyers and accountants, and bought the film back from the NFB. The price: one dollar, plus equity in the film—equal to the Board's investment to that date—if it were ever made. Of course, neither Lucas nor Gunnarsson had ever tried to raise money for a film before. Now, sailing out of the Film Board's cosy harbour, they were about to navigate the treacherous waters of independent financing.

In search of development money, Metropolis approached the Canadian Film Development Corp.'s Bob Linnell, and quickly sold him on their proposal. "We still didn't have a script," Gunnarsson says. "But we kept pushing on and people

A career diplomat, Kim Dades (Wendell Meldrum) is forced by circumstance to reevaluate the morality of her country's support for a Latin American dictatorship in **Diplomatic Immunity.**

kept believing in it. Why? I don't know. I guess the material was so interesting that everybody just kept thinking, 'Well, sooner or later these guys are going to get it together.'" Linnell, later singled out in the film's acknowledgements for his unflagging support, gave Metropolis $15,000 to write the first draft of a screenplay.

Lucas spent six months writing, changing the name from *Torture* to *Strictly Business*. Neither he nor Gunnarsson was happy with the result. Despite his best efforts, Lucas could not seem to make the concept work on paper. At the CFDC, the readers' reports were luke-warm, but "kinder than we were," says Gunnarsson. "We couldn't get a handle on it. And we wanted to bail out." They approached Linnell, proposing to put the entire project on the shelf. In its place, they pitched him a new idea—a film about two old people coping with the death of loved ones. Linnell liked the new proposal, but he liked the Latin story even more: he wanted another draft of *Strictly Business*. To sweeten the incentive, Linnell dangled a two-picture development deal, a remarkable offer to two rookie producers, and threw more money (another $27,000) into the pot. "The thing would never die," says Lucas, "even when we tried to kill it."

The second draft was no more popular than the first. "And by rights," says Lucas, "at the end of a disappointing second draft, you're dead. I mean, that's how it should be—two shots and goodnight, Irene." Moreover, under CFDC bylaws, the agency was not allowed to underwrite 100 percent of the development costs of any project. If *Strictly Business* were going to have another life, it would need a new patron. Metropolis found one in Jim Burt, the CBC executive in charge of movies and mini-series. By then, Gunnarsson had become a known and trusted commodity at the CBC, directing network dramas and documentaries. Lucas, too, was rarely without other work. Indeed, during the decade required to make *Immunity*, Gunnarsson and Lucas between them would work on 40 other films.

Glowing reviews for their other work made *Diplomatic Immunity* look more credible. Says Gunnarsson: "People kept looking at everything else and thinking, 'These kids know what they're doing. And they'd hear our passion for the material and go, 'if they could ever get at that, it would be a great movie.' Then they'd read the script and go . . .'hmmm, this is awful!' " The basic problem was that the film had been constructed as an allegory, a kind of morality play in which the characters all represented a particular moral viewpoint. As such, action was largely predetermined and static; it did not flow naturally from the characters themselves. "That was our problem right up to the end," Gunnarsson says, "figuring out how to make them flesh and blood."

With some new development money from the CBC, Lucas gave the film another new title—*Vested Interests*—and produced a third draft. That, Gunnarsson says ruefully, was "the worst of them all. We had completely lost touch with the passion, with why were doing it." Lucas concurs. He had trouble writing a film with a woman as the lead character and driving force. He had trouble writing credibly about Latin America. He had trouble understanding how the foreign service actually worked. ("Even to the people who work in it, it's a mystery," he says.) And he had a lot of trouble not making the entire story wholly predictable. By June of 1986, more than five years and $75,000 after the project began, Lucas was convinced that "I have screwed up. I am nowhere. I am in the middle of a quagmire."

The CBC responded unequivocally to *Vested Interests*: it withdrew. Two developments, however, conspired to sustain the film. One was the creation of the Ontario Film Development Corp., a source of new funding. The second was political—Canada's re-establishment of foreign aid dollars to El Salvador. While Lucas arranged a second fact-finding mission, Gunnarsson pitched the OFDC. Louise Clark, the agency's head of production and development and an old friend of Lucas, had seen the first script drafts at the National Film Board. She still thought enough of its potential to risk more money in the venture. Gunnarsson was also able to wrest some new funds from the CFDC—soon to be transformed into Telefilm Canada.

For Lucas, the second El Salvador trip was a dose of much-needed adrenalin and perspective. "After two weeks there, I finally get it," he told one writer. "I go from being cynical and detached to meeting these people, seeing the dynamics." He heard stories of torture and exile. He met soldiers and guerrillas, mothers of 'the disappeared' and rebel priests on the run, nuns, teachers, Americans, businessmen. "Suddenly we were talking about something real, not never-never land." For the first time, Lucas felt he had a handle on the movie and on the script. The hook was foreign aid. Canadian dollars, he discovered, were spent to subsidize a Salvadoran housing complex that had been turned into a brothel. Re-energized, Lucas returned to Canada to write what was now called *Diplomatic Immunity*.

The problem then, in the spring of 1987, was not too little reality, but too much. To help shape the new draft, Lucas and Gunnarsson decided to hire a story editor—and turned to veteran screenwriter and director Paul Shapiro. That fall, the three men spent two arduous months trying to assemble the fourth draft. "We had a very hard time," concedes Gunnarsson. "Paul's got a very strong sense of how to tell a story. His attitude was basically, I don't care how it works in real life. We're making a movie!" Despite the tensions, Gunnarsson thought Shapiro was the right man at the right time. Indeed, it was the fourth draft that won the first expressions of cautious optimism at the agencies—and inspired the first hope that the film might actually be made. There were criticisms, but no suggestion that Lucas should reinvent the wheel. This was the movie they were making; the question now was: how could they make it better?

By this time, another round of musical bureaucrats had been played. Bill House had moved from the OFDC to run Telefilm in Ontario. Louise Clark had succeeded House. In the changing of the celluloid guard, Telefilm's point man on *Immunity* became Bill Niven. Even before the script was approved, Niven and the OFDC's Clark had told Metropolis that an executive producer would eventually be needed. It was virtually inconceivable that the agencies would otherwise grant production financing. Despite their obvious talent and tenacity, Gunnarsson and Lucas were still first-timers in the world of feature films, with a ballpark production budget of $2.5 million. Both agencies needed a higher comfort level, the presence of a savvy executive producer who could manage the film's finances.

Thus began a marathon search. There was no shortage of potential candidates, but most of them wanted a guarantee of creative control. Metropolis balked. "We couldn't quite wrap our heads around that," Gunnarsson says. "We did all this so that we can give it to you? You're going to be our boss?" One prospective producer told them: "You guys wanna make a quality picture, and the problem with a quality picture is that it's gotta be good." Another well-known producer was on the brink of signing when both Lucas and Gunnarsson had nightmares about him; they abruptly terminated discussions.

Their philosophy from the start was that in order to control the film, creative people had to control the finances. It was different in other countries. Hollywood respected talent; if you delivered box office, you could negotiate a wide degree of independence. The British system was driven by writers and creators. But in Canada the people who clambered to the top of decision-making pyramids tended not to be creative producers. Instead, they were people who had learned to work as extensions of government. "And our take on that," Gunnarsson says, "was that virtually everybody out there would compromise until the cows came home to make the deal." The rationale for compromise is obvious. Because there is virtually zero expectation of back-end profits, the only money producers are ever likely to see are up-front fees. Whatever facilitates the fee payments, whatever it takes to close the deal, is therefore acceptable, including major script changes.

Immunity was particularly vulnerable, because by the time production financing closed, in March 1990, the parties at the table included Telefilm, the OFDC, the NFB, the CBC, Britain's Channel 4 and Astral, the film's distributor. "Every single one of them," Gunnarsson points out, "was a creative department. Every one was a bureaucracy. Every one had its own agenda. And every one thought they were filmmakers. And if you actually do what all these people tell you to do, there's nothing left! Your film has lost its voice, which is what happens to so much of our stuff." Indeed, that is the line that Canadian filmmakers must inevitably walk—accommodating the demands, however graciously tabled, of the financial sponsors, without emasculating the vision. For Gunnarsson "the name of the game right from the word go was control of production. And we got to the point where we would rather not do it than lose control."

One day in the summer of 1988, Bill Niven invited a morose Gunnarsson to meet a friend of his at lunch. The friend was Haligonian Michael Donovan, who had produced four feature films and served as executive producer of CODCO, the award-winning national TV comedy series. Gunnarsson gave Donovan the *Immunity* script to read. Donovan liked it. More importantly, he liked Gunnarsson. "I had seen his film on Bob White [*Final Offer*] and was very impressed," says Donovan. "I liked the politics of the script. But particularly, I liked Sturla and Steve. It was chemistry." The next day, he met Lucas and Gunnarsson for breakfast and shook hands on the deal; for a fee of $125,000, most of which he ultimately deferred, he agreed to become executive producer. Donovan's role was precisely defined—to help raise money and oversee the financial side of the production. "I made it clear that I thought it desirable that Steve and Sturla should take the creative lead, and they made it very clear that they thought that was desirable too."

FINANCING The arrival of Michael Donovan was to represent a major turning point in the life of *Immunity*. Tall and well-scrubbed, Donovan had studied law at Dalhousie, graduating in 1977. He still speaks in crisp, understated, carefully constructed declarative sentences, as if he were swearing an affidavit. Gunnarsson and Lucas came to regard him as a kind of zen master, riding above the fray, talking in parables. Uncertain about pursuing a legal career, Donovan had travelled in Europe for a year and decided, after articling in Halifax, that "I would do something other than law. I am not a filmmaker," he insists. "I am just someone who doesn't want to have to practice law."

With his younger brother, Paul, Donovan had used the tax-shelter film financing regime in place at the time and made a series of movies—*South Pacific, 1942, Siege,* and *Def Con 4.* The latter ran into cash-flow problems that forced the brothers to sell off U.S. distribution rights for a song. When the film started making money, the Donovans tried to recover a share; the attempt failed. Once a producer started dealing in the North American theatrical market, Donovan concluded, he invariably lost control. "[Distributors] make money, and then they just don't give it to you. You have to go to lawyers you can't afford to go to. And they know that. You have to simply accept that fact and work on your career. If there's enough financial incentive, they will make the film successful. If the film is successful, it will help your career."

By 1986, Donovan's career was flourishing; he simply had no money. For seven years, his average annual income had been about $9,000. By then, of course, the tax-shelter system was in tatters, and Telefilm had emerged from the molted skin of the CFDC. The Donovans quickly switched focus and began producing films and television shows aimed, in the first instance, at Canadian audiences. Thus, by the time he agreed to oversee *Immunity,* Michael Donovan already was known as a producer on whom the agencies could rely.

Even before Donovan's arrival, Gunnarsson had gone to England to test the financing or co-production waters. His entree was facilitated by Bob Linnell, who had become Telefilm's man in London and was still an avid supporter of the project. Several companies evinced interest, but Gunnarsson was most impressed by Lyn Goleby, an independent producer at Working Title, the company that had made *My Beautiful Laundrette* and *A World Apart.* The personal chemistry was critical. The rule of thumb for Metropolis, at first accidentally and then consciously, was not to do business with people it did not like. "It makes sense," Gunnarsson says, "but when you're young, you don't know any better. You think most people are assholes, so maybe you have to do business with assholes." Goleby, too, later told people she was investing as much in Gunnarsson as in the film itself.

In London, Gunnarson also managed to see Karen Bamborough, the influential commissioning editor for Britain's Channel 4. (His advice to producers seeking meetings with filmdom's powerhouses: call. "Anybody will see you if you're from out of town. Canada's the only place where people won't see you.") Bamborough liked the script, with reservations, and she liked the apparent interest of Telefilm, as expressed by Linnell. In fact, having Linnell arrange Gunnarsson's meetings at Channel 4 subtly implied that Telefilm was ready to invest. During his meetings, Gunnarsson told everyone that all *Immunity* needed to take flight was the final piece of the financing puzzle—between $500,000–600,000. Everything else, he said, was virtually in place. Strictly speaking, this was a serious distortion of the truth, since not a single penny had yet been committed by any Canadian agency. And the number itself was sheer voodoo. Gunnarsson had no idea what people actually paid for this material; the figure he quoted was simply the difference between what he hoped to raise from Canadian sources and what he thought he needed to make the film. "But what are you gonna do," he says. "Say we don't really know if we're gonna get this together, but would you like to take part anyway?"

Gunnarsson returned with three potential co-producers—Central Television, London Films and Lyn Goleby. It was Donovan's view from the start that although Telefilm Canada would ultimately represent the largest single slice of production financing, 49 percent, the strategic trigger for the deal was the involvement of Britain's Channel 4. Its name was known and respected in Canada. Its creative track record was unimpeachable. And its agreement to participate would give the film exactly the imprimatur it needed. Sign Channel 4, Donovan argued, and the rest was paperwork. All of that was true, to a point. What Channel 4 could not alter was the emerging mindset of the new regime at Telefilm's Ontario offices. Gone were Linnell (to London) and Niven (to Paris). The new mandarins, headed by Bill House, had a different perspective about the agency's mandate. They wanted low-budget, auteur films with a detached, ironic attitude—ones, it was said, that reflected their own sensibilities.

At the OFDC, *Immunity* was on firmer ground. The key player, Louise Clark, was favourably disposed to investing, although she, too, wanted additional script changes. For Clark, it was a question of relative merits. There was good reason to say no to almost everything. "It's not easy to say no to somebody," she insists, "but it's easier to make a no decision than it is to make the leap of faith." With Metropolis, "it reached the point where it was in the lighter grey zone, rather than the darker grey zone. Sometimes that's enough to get you going, to give it some energy." The agency saw itself as making an investment not only in one project, but in two filmmakers, "and what they learned at every stage" would eventually pay huge dividends. The one caveat, she remained convinced, was that Gunnarsson and Lucas needed to acknowledge the problems that continued to lie on the printed page. Otherwise, they would recognize them when solutions were more difficult—in the cutting room.

Telefilm's won't-say-yes, won't-say-no attitude sent Metropolis back to the Ontario Centre of the National Film Board, then headed by John Taylor. Even with Telefilm, the producers knew they would need additional financing. A public offering was out of the question—at once too difficult and too costly. And they could count their contacts wealthy enough to bankroll a private offering on the fingers of one hand. At one point,

Gunnarsson and his wife, Judy Koonar, had dinner in New York with Spectrafilm's head of acquisitions, Karen Jaehne; she voiced readiness to commit half the film's proposed budget in return for another script rewrite and production control. But that, the producers concluded, would have forced them into subordinate roles, and made it into another movie. "It really became clear to us," Gunnarsson says, "that we were right on that cusp where we'd just pushed the envelope as far as possible budget-wise for a film that was essentially a personal kind of thing."

The NFB, on the other hand, had just been endowed with a new $5 million Department of Communications fund, expressly designed to mount co-productions with independent producers in the regions. The Toronto region's share of that pie was $500,000 a year. Gunnarsson thought it was a perfect match. Many of the awards on the NFB's Toronto office walls had been won either by Lucas or himself. And the entire *Immunity* project had originated at the NFB. The Film Board would eventually commit $271,000 to the film's production financing, but not without a serious case of hiccups along the way. The reservations were partly creative and partly procedural. In a debate that would affect several independent productions in the late 1980s, the Film Board wanted—in return for its money—to be treated like, and accorded the status of, a co-producer; that was a complete non-starter as far as the OFDC and other financing agencies were concerned, which saw it as their mandate to support wholly independent producers. To complicate the situation, Metropolis made the mistake at one point of submitting yet another draft of Lucas' script to all the other investors without consulting John Taylor. According to Lucas, an irate Taylor abruptly reversed his position, condemned the script (which was not appreciably different from the previous draft), and walked away from the project. In effect, the producers believed, the Film Board was using legitimate creative concerns— the script's weaknesses—to disguise the real issue, whether it would be acknowledged as a co-producer, and rank ahead of the other funding agencies.

Taylor insists that both objections were genuine. The script was "not as good as it should have been. The central character [Kim] was too passive." And the NFB, given its early role in *Immunity*, was not an investor like the others. Besides, he had only $500,000 to spend on co-productions. In effect, he was being asked to allocate half his entire budget to a production he did not feel was ready. In a bold move, Gunnarsson then appealed that decision to Taylor's Film Board superiors, Joan Pennefather and Barbara Emo. Emo read the script, shared Taylor's concerns, but found unspent co-production money in the Maritime region to add to the Toronto centre's pool (begging the question of why a quarter of a million dollars earmarked for feature productions in Atlantic Canada had not been used). At that point, conditional on another re-write, Taylor again reversed his decision. As for the credit issue, the typical Canadian settlement obtained—a compromise, says

Donovan, "where everyone kept their principles until a workable solution was found." The film's final credits, however, gave no special mention of the NFB's role.

Lucas' new draft received a mixed reception—basically positive, but with recommendations for one more try. He went back to the word processor—producing his sixth complete script (and perhaps his eighteenth counting the versions in between). He did not enjoy the endless requests for script changes, but he was eventually reconciled. "The audience is always right," he would say afterward, quoting Woody Allen. In retrospect, it was clear to him that he was simply at the threshold of his ability as a writer. What he produced was the best he could produce at that time. Even after the sixth or seventh draft, when virtually all the investors were committed and the screenplay had been blessed by the appropriate clergy, Lucas sat in on a cast read-through of the script and "couldn't understand what the heck was going on—and I had written it."

In July 1988, Gunnarsson and Donovan flew to London; their goal was either to close a deal with a co-producer or find extra production money. As it happens, they did both. They hired Lyn Goleby as co-executive producer with a mandate to sell a U.K. broadcast license for the film, preferably to Channel 4. Alternatively, they could have bypassed Goleby (and her fee) and dealt directly with Channel 4 themselves, but decided against it. With Goleby involved, they concluded, Channel 4's bidding price for the license would be a multiple of whatever they would have received acting alone. Moreover, Donovan was convinced that Goleby's presence would give British bureaucrats a generally higher comfort level.

"It was my experience that walking in the door with your script never worked—ever," he says. "You would be well-received. The committee would take it seriously. And they would always, always, always say no." Goleby, therefore, was essential. Although the British film industry is today less clubby than it was five years ago, Donovan felt strongly that without her, Channel 4 would never have participated. Goleby later sold the license for £100,000—about $200,000 Canadian, and probably twice as much as a Canadian producer had ever received from Channel 4. The broadcaster also agreed to buy $100,000 worth of equity in the film.

By the end of 1988, production financing was more or less on track. The OFDC was in for $350,000 (later to rise to $450,000), subject to script changes. For the Ontario agency, the real issue was not so much the script as it was the proposed $2.7 million budget—a fair piece of change for two untried producers, planning to shoot on location in a foreign country. "I don't think there was any question that people were interested in giving this team a shot at a feature film," Clark says. But was this the right one? In the end, the OFDC decided to invest. "You had two people who had committed to the project for 10 years. That's got to count for something, that staying power. Either they're idiots, or they've got something there."

By this time, too, Gunnarsson had negotiated the sale of first broadcast rights to the CBC. The agreement came during a 15-minute meeting with Ivan Fecan, the corporation's vice-president of programming. Fecan, who had already read a later draft of *Immunity*, had a reason to support the project—Gunnarson had been called in to rescue a pilot for a new CBC-TV series called 9B. The show he directed had been well-received. Fecan thanked him for his work and said, "I like you. I like the script. What can I do for you?"

"Oh," said Gunnarsson," who projects a boyish, unworldly innocence that is utterly deceiving. "Well, how about you buy it for $450,000?"

"I can't do that," Fecan said. "I can buy it for $300,000."

"How about $350,000," Gunnarsson suggested. They shook hands on that amount—an agreement that gave another boost of momentum to the financing.

In fact, the CBC sale also helped cement a distribution deal with Montreal-based Astral Films, a company Donovan had recommended. Astral had handled some of Donovan's own features. He respected the organization, which was run by the Greenberg family. And Astral was known to be financially solvent—an important consideration in an economy that was increasingly inhospitable to the industry. After extensive discussions, Metropolis sold Canadian distribution rights to Astral for $450,000. Donovan did approach other distributors, including Cineplex–Odeon, but they were never seriously considered.

The Astral deal was less generous than it seemed. First, in addition to Canada, the Greenbergs acquired distribution rights to potentially lucrative French-speaking territories in Europe as well—a wrinkle that would later complicate the film's attempt to find a foreign distributor and annoy the agencies, which did not learn of it until several months after the agreement was struck. Metropolis, says Clark, claimed that it simply forgot to advise the OFDC of the French rights clauses. "They probably *had* forgot," she says. "But when you've had a tough job selling a product, the last thing you need is to go down to business and legal affairs and say, 'Oh, by the way, you know that nice clear revenue stream we had? Well, it's gone.'"

Donovan says Lucas and Gunnarsson agreed reluctantly to the French rights provision. However, Astral's Danny Lyon, director of business affairs in Toronto, has a different recollection. He maintains there was no pressure from Astral to include French rights. The pressure, he says, worked from the other side. "They needed another $50,000 and this was the way we could come up with it." Astral suggested France because it knew it would have to make a dubbed French-language version of the film for release in Quebec in any event, and it already had sales representation in Paris.

But Astral's $450,000 advance was really only $100,000, because Metropolis pledged to later turn over its broadcast license fee from the CBC ($350,000) to the company. In effect, Astral was providing an advance, an interest-free loan of $350,000 for use in the film's production, a loan that would be paid back when the CBC contract kicked in. Even then, of course, Telefilm's Distribution Fund would effectively reimburse Astral for 75 percent of its acquisition cost. So, not including what it would later spend to market and promote the film (some of which was covered by Telefilm's Launch Fund), Astral's net cost to acquire rights for Canada and France was about $25,000. Its revenues from video cassette sales alone (about $43,000) would push it into the black. Whatever Astral's level of risk, Gunnarson praises the company for its generous payment schedules, saying "they could have paid us out much later than they did."

Even with the distribution guarantee, a glitch in the financing remained: Telefilm Canada. It never issued a flat no, a verdict that would have killed the project instantly. It simply said, 'we are not prepared to invest at this time. We suggest you do another draft of the script and re-apply.' The agency's caution was based in part on a damning reader's report of the latest script. "The report," says Gunnarsson, "read like a review by [the late *Globe and Mail* film critic] Jay Scott when he's in a bitchy mood." It said the film's central character, Kim, was not fully developed. And it questioned whether *Immunity* ought more properly to be a made-for-television movie. Gunnarsson was stunned. Rejecting the movie on those grounds was preposterous. "I mean, all you make here is television movies." he says. "What else are you going to do for three-quarters of a million dollars? That's the cost of an average TV movie. What are you talking about?"

The real problem, Gunnarsson concluded, was not the script, but the kind of movie he wanted to make—a social realism document, "a movie movie, a movie for an audience. It wasn't esoteric, personal, quirky, weird, minimalist." *Immunity* was open to criticism precisely because it was not ambiguous and elliptical. It had a point of view; it declared itself. "How do you criticize these arty films," Gunnarsson asks. "Those who know, know; and those that don't, don't." In terms of the artistic vision that dominated Telefilm in the late 1980s, Gunnarsson "woke up one morning and realized I was a dinosaur."

House acknowledges that he harboured reservations about the script, always believing that it was too earnest and not dramatic enough. He still believes the final film "just wasn't theatrical. There was no drama from what had been shot in Mexico, none whatsoever." *Immunity*, says House, was "one of those films made because of its longevity in the system or in the consciousness of all of us. It became viable because it's as viable as anything else, and perhaps more viable in a system that is dedicated to spending its money. But that film would not be made today." What would have made *Immunity* more theatrical? "A harder edge," says House. He cites Oliver Stone's *Salvador* as an instructive comparison. "In the way it was written, shot, performed, it was all much more 'out there.' Out there in a particularly American way, true. But a much more exciting movie."

Telefilm's request for yet another draft pushed the film back into an asymmetrical development zone. Telefilm and the OFDC again invested in script development (the two agencies together paid a total of $105,000 in development), while the National Film Board contributed a small amount for the rewrite and a larger amount for pre-production. The new money allowed Gunnarsson, early in 1989, to fly to Mexico to scout locations. His mood on departure was sour. Negotiating with the agencies was at once frustrating and enervating. He found himself rejecting other lucrative offers because of *Immunity*, without any confidence that it would actually be made. "I never knew whether we were in business, or out of business," he recalls. "It took months and months to arrange meetings, turn around a script, and then you'd get not even 'maybe,' but 'don't ask us [for a verdict] because you might not like what we say.' " Gunnarsson thought the movie would probably be made, but he could not remember why. "I just wanted out," he says. "It's a stupid way to live."

It was the second leg of his visit, to El Salvador, that turned him around—much as Lucas' 1987 trip had done. His 10 days there, Gunnarsson says, were the most intense time he had ever experienced. Salvadorans were living in terror, caught between extremists of the right and left, yet strangely hopeful. Many people Gunnarsson met were arrested before he left the country. The university was bombed. When the students demonstrated in protest, the army opened fire. Gunnarsson watched it happen. His goal had been to walk through the Lucas script and compare it to the reality—"get more details, the flesh and blood of this thing. It's always that dialectic you're working with." And in the process, he was stirred again by an idealism and hope he had not felt since his own university days. Weary and cynical, angry and frustrated, worn down by the extended nightmare of development and financing, and sorely tempted by big-buck offers from Hollywood, Gunnarsson found El Salvador a form of catharsis. "Going there sort of simplified things," he says. "It made me remember why I wanted to make the film."

For Donovan, who accompanied Gunnarsson, the trip was eventful in other ways. In Mexico City, he was stricken with a virulent strain of food poisoning and "spent the whole day slowly dying in my hotel room, constantly vomiting." A chambermaid recognized his distress and finally summoned a doctor. Then, staying in the beach hut outside of Acapulco, he awoke at 3 A.M. to find three armed thieves in his room. He immediately leaped out of bed, naked and screaming, threw the bedsheet at his intruders and, in the confusion, managed to lock them outside. Mexico, he had been dramatically persuaded, would be no ordinary place to make a film.

In the fall of 1989, Lucas produced another draft and with it submitted a new application for production financing to Telefilm. Metropolis' request: $900,000. Telefilm's response: We will give you an even $1 million—but we want another draft. As Bill House told Michael Donovan: "I want to hold a gun to Steve's [Lucas'] head." Gunnarsson by now had stepped back from dealing with Telefilm directly; there had been too many angry words with House, and the inventory of resentment had built to dangerous levels. The new draft, written over Christmas of 1989, finally earned a green light at Telefilm and an important endorsement from a new quarter, Ian Birnie, the agency's head of development. But while the script was now deemed acceptable, a new problem arose: Metropolis' proposed $2.7 million budget. "I mean, there was an earthquake in one of those scripts," House says. "I kept saying, 'How can there be an earthquake here? What are you guys doing? There was a scene with the army. What can you afford? Three guys and some rifles?' "

But House was not the only doubter—and Metropolis knew it. "It wasn't like the whole world was clamouring for this and Bill House stood at the dike saying no," says Steve Lucas. In fact, as the largest single investor, House had a perfect right to demand a script and a budget that met his approval. "There's always somebody who's in first," Lucas adds, "and there's always somebody who's in last, and the trick is to keep them all sitting at the table until everyone's in. It's a neat trick."

The final production financing picture was:

Telefilm:	$1,000,000
OFDC:	$450,000
NFB:	$271,350
CBC:	$350,000
Astral:	$100,000
Channel 4: ($200,000 license fee and $100,000 equity)	$300,000
Deferrals: (Donovan:$81,000; Gunnarsson:$84,604; Lucas: $44,744)	$210,704

CASTING According to the critics, the acting performances in *Immunity* were generally of a high standard. The Mexican actress, Ofelia Medina, was singled out for praise. But the work of Canadian actress Wendell Meldrum, in the coveted lead role of Kim Dades, drew some particularly harsh reviews. Even the film's distributor, Astral, would later complain that Meldrum had failed the two critical tests for lead characters—the audience had no sympathy for her and no understanding of her motivation. Meldrum, who had appeared previously in *Beautiful Dreamers*, was chosen in December 1989, after a long search. Martha Burns was briefly considered, as was Kate Nelligan. Altogether, more than 50 actresses were auditioned. Of these, says Gunnarsson, Meldrum seemed to be the best, although there was never a firm consensus. "I was the last one on that bus," says Gunnarsson.

Meldrum won the part five months before production began. In those five months, there were two new rewrites of the script and two complete cast read-throughs. Gunnarsson says he had misgivings about Meldrum even then, "intuitions that I didn't articulate." He began to articulate them privately during pre-production in Mexico, and semi-publicly during the second week of shooting, when the first rushes were available for screening. (The exposed film was shipped to Canada, developed, transferred to video, and shipped back.) Stories of the director–actor fireworks were making the rounds of Toronto's film community long before the shoot was wrapped. The role as written, says Lucas, "called for a world-weary sophisticate who is dragged into an inferno and called upon to get it up, if you like, one more time. She didn't do the part that was written." Instead, according to Bill House, Meldrum delivered a "reserved character who basically walks through the film expressionless. It suited the movie somehow. There was no drama." Adds Louise Clark: "[Wendell's] not a bad actor. It was just a bad match."

Donovan, who was then in the middle of an interim financing crisis on the film, was alarmed by the signals from Mexico. "There was a pattern of continuing calls of increasing disappointment." By the time he arrived in Mexico City, "it was clear that things between the director and his leading lady were less than harmonious." Now, long after the fact, Gunnarsson is philosophical. "There's push and pull in every creative relationship. She had her take and I had mine, and we pushed and pulled and got to where we got to. But at a certain point you have to go with what you got, and make it work as best you can."

Still, Meldrum's take on the character caused enormous problems on the set—both with Gunnarsson, who kept trying to steer her closer to the original concept, and with other actors, who were forced to change readings, levels and therefore motivations to match hers. "A lot of doctoring," concedes Lucas, "was done to deal with the fact that people did not like the lead character. There was an inevitable shift in the film's direction."

PRE-PRODUCTION Even after the obligatory handshakes on financing had been exchanged, Motion Picture Guarantors (MPG)—the people who effectively guaranteed that *Immunity* would be made—insisted that Metropolis hire a top-flight line producer to supervise expenditures during the shoot. MPG, like the other agencies, was concerned about untried producers being handed $2.68 million to shoot in a foreign country. Donovan concurred entirely. The line producer is often the critical pressure point of any large-scale production. In the case of *Immunity*, once the button was pressed, the producers were spending about $60,000 a day. It was the line producer who kept the faucet on—hired crews, negotiated contracts, dealt with unions and the Mexican army, arranged meals, prepared cost reports, kept people in line—and the cash flowing. It was not, says Lucas, "a touchy-feely proposition. It was a military exercise."

Metropolis had trouble finding the requisite level of toughness. Several candidates were rejected. The last person they interviewed was Michael

McDonald, a veteran of more than two dozen major Hollywood films and in Gunnarsson's words, "a heavy duty motherfucker, who butts heads when heads have to be butted," precisely what they needed. Eight weeks before the start of principal photography, in May 1990, Gunnarsson and McDonald flew to Mexico to formally begin pre-production. Among the first priorities was to deal with the actors' and technicians' unions, which had what Gunnarsson calls "the most-iron clad contracts in the universe." Every conceivable eventuality seemed to be spelled out in their favour. For example, each union had different definitions of daytime and nightime hours, which meant that a production was into paying overtime almost from the start. And actors were paid from the first day of their shoot until the last, regardless of off-days in between. McDonald managed to win modest concessions on these points; the negotiations were smoothed as much by the amount of money changing hands as by the fact that Mexicans were prominently featured on both sides of the cameras.

It was only at that point, after negotiating with various unions and casting agents, that Metropolis began to get a handle on the real costs of the film. The results were frightening; production had not begun and the film, on paper, was $166,000 over budget. Morever, in order to qualify as Canadian content, and be eligible for agency funding, a certain percentage of the budget had to be spent in Canada. The Mexican overages therefore threatened the producers at both ends. Gunnarsson immediately called Donovan. "Cut the budget," Donovan told him. "Don't even think about trying to raise more money. It's out of the question. Just find a way to do it." Others kept saying Metropolis would not be able to proceed, but Donovan insisted otherwise. "You might not do it the way you would if you had twice as much money," he said, "but so what? You want to make a movie or you don't." So the six-week shooting schedule they had already cut from eight was tightened again to five. With a week saved, the deficit dropped to $30,000, which was available from the contingency budget. But it put enormous pressure on Gunnarsson, who now had been left with a minimal margin for error. "It got everybody out from behind the eight ball," he says, "but me."

INTERIM FINANCING The nature of financing agreements for most Canadian feature films is that money is delivered to the producers by the investors at various stages of the film's completion. Quite often, however, money is needed before it is scheduled to arrive. The bridging mechanism is known as interim financing, which in the late 1980s was principally handled either by the Royal Bank of Canada or by Rogers Telefund. Donovan chose to deal with Rogers, because it had a lower interest rate and charged no fees. The Telefund people had seen the script, liked it, and indicated a high probability of approval for the film's interim financing needs—$850,000. In May of 1990, just as the production was gearing up in

Mexico, Donovan flew to Banff to see the scenery, meet with Robin Mirsky, Rogers' Telefund manager and close the deal. To his dismay and consternation, Mirsky proposed to lend only $425,000, explaining that Rogers was short of money itself.

That offer, Donovan concluded, was no offer at all, since it meant he would need to arrange another interim agreement for the outstanding amount and incur legal fees for two separate financings. Moreover, interim financiers always demanded security—the contract with Telefilm itself or in this case with Channel 4—and it was self-evident that the same contracts could not be pledged to two different organizations. Donovan was "in a state of shock. I couldn't believe it. I said 'this is absolutely useless. I need either all of the money or none of the money; there's no half way.' " And because he was sure that Rogers must have known he could not accept only half the money, the offer itself was in his judgement a form of refusal. "Paranoid about my regionalism," Maritimer Donovan concluded that if he had been "a major player in Toronto, I would not have gotten such an insulting suggestion." Mirsky insists that the answer she gave to Donovan in Banff was the simple truth; at that moment, owing to other commitments, Rogers could only afford to bridge finance half the film. And far from discriminating against regional interests, she notes that 60 percent of Rogers Telefund's dollars in 1990 went to productions outside Ontario and Quebec.

The more critical question was how to respond. Just when the film's cash needs were becoming most urgent, there was no plan B. In a state of near panic, Donovan immediately called Doug Barrett, the production's lawyer at MacMillan Binch in Toronto, and asked him to arrange an immediate meeting with the Royal Bank. The Royal had a well-earned reputation for fastidiousness, but proved to be even more picayune than anyone expected, insisting that every final contract be in place (final contracts often are not completed until the film is in editing). "They were extremely demanding," Donovan says. "All the paper work had to be perfect, not 99 percent perfect, not 99.9 percent, but 100 percent." That, he concedes, "was a reasonable position for a bank to take, but a major problem for me."

It was at precisely this point that Gunnarsson began to telephone from Mexico indicating problems with Meldrum—the equivalent, says Donovan, "of the gas gauge showing red on an airplane." That kind of feedback, he knew, had an excellent chance of spooking the investors and unravelling the entire production. Donovan wrapped up the Royal Bank negotiations, took the money and caught the next plane to Mexico City.

THE SHOOT All feature film shoots are difficult. All feature film shoots in foreign locations are extremely difficult. The on-location filming of *Diplomatic Immunity* in a suburb north of Mexico City was a harrowing nightmare. In the course of it, the unit manager broke his foot. The production accountant became ill and her hair turned white. Gunnarsson himself was sick for much of the shoot, not only with a gastro-enterital parasite so common in Mexico, but with what would later be diagnosed as hepatitis; he lost 35 pounds. Then, the popular leader of the Mexican crew, gaffer Beto Arellanos, was killed in a strange car accident—driving on a straight, divided highway, with no oncoming traffic. (The film was later dedicated to his memory.)

Even before Beto's death, the film's Mexican production manager Rosalie Salazar was convinced that a personal enemy of hers had cast a malevolent spell on the entire project. But rivalry was one thing; death was another. The only antidote, she insisted, was an anti-hex. At that point, McDonald actually agreed to put a witch on the payroll, the only recorded involvement of a supernatural agent in a non-speaking part in the making of a Canadian film.

The mood in Mexico was reminiscent of Malcolm's Lowry's *Under the Volcano*. Every night, bands of *campesinos* strolled through the streets, drinking mescal, playing music, parading the iconography of their saints, and praying for rain. The rainy season had not begun. Water levels were abnormally low, and the bacteria count was soaring; every day, another member of the crew took ill. Gunnarsson, renting a house that had belonged to director John Huston, felt he was living in a Huston movie. "Mexico," he concluded, "is a different reality. It's like being on acid. You know, Gabriel García Márquez is really just a documentarian." The night Beto died, and still unaware of his death, Gunnarsson had pulled back the covers on his bed to find a scorpion in the sheets. "It's not like you get superstitious or anything," he says. "It just becomes the reality that involves you."

Off the set, there were constant struggles with the Mexicans over unexpected costs. Much of this was simple misunderstandings based on cultural differences. Food would be ordered, the bill would be paid, and then a second bill would arrive—for sodas. In addition, the production had to pay a union shop steward to monitor developments on the set. And an official censor had to be added to the payroll, to ensure that the film did not misrepresent the government or the people of Mexico. There were so many unexpected surprises that at one point, line producer McDonald considered having T-shirts printed with the words, "Oh, didn't I tell you?"

POST-PRODUCTION The first assembly of *Immunity* was put together by Gunnarsson and editor Jeff Warren in eight weeks at Pathé Films in Toronto in the summer of 1990. Gunnarsson, still recovering from his bout with hepatitis, set up a cot outside the editing suite and spent countless hours asleep, too weak to work. Lucas, seeing the film for the first time, was pleasantly surprised; after all the trauma, he actually thought he saw the outline of a real movie. The next stage, the first rough cut, constituted an enormous setback, a fiasco. Seeing it, Lucas says, "was one of the most painful days of my life." The film looked like a series of scenes that did not connect.

The OFDC's Louise Clark remembers the first rough cut "as one of those really long screenings where you just sort of sat there and went, 'what is this woman [Kim] in?' The problems were really evident. It was hard to identify key emotional moments. It was hard to identify the main character's turning point—when she decides to go against her masters in Ottawa. There was a huge question of what could be juggled." Lucas thought the second rough cut, while still a little "clunky," at least made sense. "It had a story that I thought I could follow. If I can't follow it, I assume I'm in good company." To his chagrin, the third cut was even worse. By then, says Lucas, "we had done everything we could with the existing footage, and the picture didn't work."

Questionnaires prepared by the filmmakers and handed out to viewers at the screenings confirmed the thesis. Audiences hated the lead character and could not follow the story. The film's opening dragged. "People said it was great once it started, " says Gunnarsson. "That was about half way through." And the audience, he knew, had to be able to track. "If they stop tracking with you," he says, "you're dead. Even if they only stop for two or three minutes, you can't get them back."

For a long time, Gunnarsson had been convinced of the need for a framing device, which would speed up the start of the film and give a better sense of the Meldrum character. (The device had actually been written into an earlier script and then dropped.) "The audience needed to be told how to look at her," Gunnarsson says, "because she wasn't able to tell you herself. We had to give people a pair of glasses to look at the movie. Let's not be precious. Let's get this thing up and running."

The night of the third rough-cut screening, a distressed Lucas walked home in pouring rain and finally surrendered to the inevitable. There were, he decided, only two possible solutions. Either the Meldrum character would have to narrate the entire film, to explain it and make audiences like her more—a road down which Lucas was not prepared to venture. Or another kind of framing device would have to be erected, to tell viewers that it was okay not to like Kim. "I made the decision then," says Lucas, "that I was going to get in there and kick ass. I was going to set up a framing device using another character [Michael Hogan], who said she wasn't a bleeding heart. She wasn't a liberal. She wasn't the warmest person you'd ever want to meet. She's just a good little soldier come down from Ottawa to do a job. If you don't like her, that's okay, because Hogan didn't either."

At the agencies, Clark maintains, there was no particular concern about the post-production problems—a position difficult to credit—because Gunnarsson and Lucas continued to remain their own worst critics. "The good thing," says Clark, "was that they didn't try to keep making what they had on the page. They saw what they had and they adjusted. They absolutely got the best film they could out of the material they had." A fourth rough cut was screened in late October with voice-overs added. The scene containing the opening framing device was shot at Toronto's Brothers Restaurant, a favourite Lucas hang-out, on November 11. By the end of December, the film was ready to show to its distributors.

Among the first to see the fine cut of the film was Wayne Case, senior vice president of distribution at Astral's Toronto office. Like other distributors, Case had been the victim of several unfortunate Canadian experiences, "where you do everything at the film festivals and everybody is excited and you open right after the festival and it does three hundred dollars box office." Still, when he saw *Immunity* for the first time in January 1991, Case "for a change actually enjoyed a Canadian movie and was fairly, cautiously enthusiastic" about its chances. His enthusiasm did not last long.

MARKETING AND DISTRIBUTION Wayne Case joined Astral Films' Toronto office in 1989, after more than decade working with several major American distributors. But by the time the company secured rights to *Immunity*, his job "had become almost not a job. We didn't distribute anything theatrically and there was no interest in acquiring products. The only thing Astral was interested in acquiring were things they were already assured of not losing any money on." Nor did it help the picture's commercial destiny that Case seemed not to be communicating with his Astral colleagues. He rarely spoke directly to his boss, senior vice president Stephen Greenberg in Montreal, and had almost no time for Stephen's cousin, Aubie Greenberg, who had been appointed to handle marketing. Eventually, Case started sending nasty messages to Stephen Greenberg saying, 'since you won't talk to me, I've decided the following.' Inevitably, this practice did not not endear him to his employers; Case was fired shortly before the film's release, an event that presumably colours his account. Astral, it must be said, regards Case's complaint as utter clap-trap. "He was the boss of that operation," insists Stephen Greenberg. "He had a mandate to bring in outside people to augment any shortcomings he perceived. The fact that he's no longer with us speaks volumes."

For Case, the internal problems were compounded by the attitude of Famous Players, the chain that traditionally exhibited Astral's films. According to Case, Famous knew that theatrical release "was an exercise to get it played so that we go on with the video, TV and all the others." But "their thinking was, 'why should we give you theatres and lose money?' They would remind me on a horrifyingly regular basis how they lost money every time they played one of our films. I had a constant struggle just trying to get the film in a theatre in Toronto, God forbid we would discuss which theatre."

The chorus Case repeatedly heard from Famous was, 'we'll play your films if First Choice'—owned by the Greenberg family—bought films distributed by the exhibitor's Canadian affiliate, CFP, for pay-TV release. "I would try to get Stephen to deal with that and he wouldn't do it." Greenberg says he cannot recall any "ransoming of film slots for First Choice sales," but notes that First Choice did not need pressure from Famous Players to buy Canadian films; it has a mandate to buy them.

Repeatedly, Case lobbied to use the theatres of Cineplex–Odeon, which was willing to carry Astral's product. Cineplex already exhibited films distributed by Avenue Cinema, the rights for which Astral owned, and, as one Cineplex booker told Case, "we'll play the Canadian shit as well." Maybe Stephen had reasons," Case says. "I'll give him the benefit of the doubt. But he would not let me go to Cineplex."

Case was therefore stuck with films his own company had no enthuiasm for releasing theatrically, and saddled with an exhibitor that had no real interest in offering good theatres for exhibition. "Famous would not give me dates. Or they would make me beg and plead to get the posters up and the trailer running. I'd have to wait until the last minute. And the directors would be hysterical." Such an attitude not only seemed counter-productive; it made the gloomy forecasts of box-office performance self-fulfilling prophecies. At one point, Case tried to get Famous Players to refuse to date *Immunity*—that would have given him license to go back to Cineplex–Odeon. But as soon as he made the suggestion, Famous' interest was rekindled. "I tried every trick in the book. They didn't want to play it, and they didn't want anyone else to—get the picture?"

Aubie Greenberg, who first saw the film after it was mixed, knew immediately it would be a tough sell theatrically. After 10 years in the political spotlight, El Salvador was not exactly on everyone's lips. American films like *Romero*, *Under Fire* and *Salvador* had already explored political turmoil in Central America. Besides, says Greenberg, "there were no stars to draw anyone into the film. It has its faults. And the audience is a middle-class, educated audience, who frankly don't go to movies that often anymore, or tend to go only to bigger, well-known films."

While Astral pondered a marketing strategy, Gunnarsson and Lucas submitted *Immunity* to the Cannes Film Festival pre-selection committee. The goal was to garner favourable foreign publicity, and ride that crest to box-office success in North America. At first, the tactic seemed to be working. The film was one of three Canadian films (the others were *The Pianist* and *The Adjuster*) chosen for entry in the official competition in 1990. In retrospect, Gunnarsson says, that was "a big mistake," because it put the film in the toughest competition, up against major Hollywood releases like *Goodfellas*. When the Cannes final selection panel eliminated *Immunity*, it was too late to seek entry into the Directors' Fortnight or some lesser category. They had gambled everything on Cannes's main event, and lost. After that, says Gunnarsson, "the extent of their strategy" was to open the film theatrically on the heels of its appearance at film festivals in Montreal, Toronto and Vancouver. They received a boost when Serge Losique selected the film for entry in the Montreal festival's official competition—one of only two Canadian films chosen. Gunnarsson regarded the Montreal honour as a major platform for the film. Of course, being picked as a showcase film in Montreal in August automatically meant that it would not receive the same attention at Toronto's Festival of Festivals in September.

Metropolis knew that Astral's experience in designing marketing campaigns was limited. It was accustomed to distributing U.S. product, which came with pre-packaged materials. According to Gunnarsson, Astral commissioned both the trailer and the poster without consultation, "and we had to get sort of noisy about it." Case recalls that "Sturla freaked out when he saw the trailer," but insists that the final, collaborative effort was virtually identical to the first one, and made "not one bit of difference" as to who went to see the film. The real problem, he maintains, was ensuring that the trailer was actually played in the theatres.

What was missing, from Gunnarsson's vantage point, was any sense of an overall marketing strategy for the film. Everything seemed *ad hoc*. A poster was needed, so a graphic artist was retained to design a poster. A trailer was needed, so an editor was hired to assemble a trailer. But there was no centralized marketing concept that tied the various pieces together. Gunnarsson got involved simply "to make the most of what had already been set in motion." In the end, he thought both the trailer and the poster were better than they otherwise would have been. An electronic press kit was also prepared, based in part on interviews conducted on-location. And Gunnarsson and Lucas drafted their own written press kit, which recounted the film's amazing odyssey from concept to execution. "We decided," says Gunnarsson, "to defy the conventional wisdom and embrace the fact that it was a content film, which may have been a mistake."

In trying to seed a potential audience, Metropolis worked closely with grass-roots agencies like Oxfam Canada and church organizations active in the refugee movement. The film was screened several times before focus groups made up of target-market viewers. Gunnarsson and Lucas scripted questionnaires to be filled out, focussing not so much on marketing issues, but on whether the film's story was coherent. Promotional mailings were also sent to Oxfam, National Film Board and various church donor lists. "We thought there was a natural constituency that had to be reached," Gunnarsson says, "and that this constituency would keep the film alive while we were trying to build a cross-over audience."

Initially, Metropolis lobbied Astral to open the film nationally in major cities. By doing that, they hoped to gain simultaneous media coverage— reviews and feature stories. Opening nationally, Gunnarsson adds, would have raised the stakes, "increasing the resources, and increasing everyone's desire to succeed." Astral resisted the pressure, arguing that it would be too exposed financially. Instead, it recommended that *Immunity* open in Montreal, capitalizing on its exposure at the Film Festival. Astral pointed out that

Romero, a not dissimilar film, had done very well in Montreal, and that the city was more receptive historically to artistic, politically-driven movies.

THE MONTREAL FILM FESTIVAL With the help of a hired publicist, Gunnarsson conducted a promotional blizzard for *Immunity*. The film's stars, Ofelia Medina, Wendell Meldrum and Michael Hogan, were brought in for the occasion and extensively interviewed, generating feature articles in the major daily newspapers. Gunnarsson himself spent a week in Montreal and was involved in scores of interviews with radio, TV and the written press. (Actual reviews were held back, pending the film's release.) T-shirts and a CD of the film's musical score were dropped in press mail boxes. The festival organized three official screenings of the film—including a gala evening showing to a packed house of 2,000 at the Place des Arts. Afterward, Astral hosted a $20,000 party, complete with a Latin American band. According to Astral's Danny Lyon, the company resisted the party, convinced that it would not result in additional "ticket sales, video sales or anything else that would help the bottom line." Only a "fairly intense bit of pleading and negotiating on Sturla's part" succeeded in changing Astral's mind.

THE OPENING *Diplomatic Immunity* opened simultaneously on four screens (one English, three French) on October 4, 1991, nearly two months after the Montreal festival. The timing of its release raised again a critical question for producers and distributors: do festival screenings create momentum for a film? Or do they, by exhausting a primary constituency of filmgoers, actually weaken a film's box-office potential?

The release dilemma is especially acute for "films that have a limited appeal to begin with," maintains Wayne Case. "If you take it out to festivals, and show it two or three times, you really are cutting into your audience. On the other hand, when you don't have any money to promote the film, you have to get all the free publicity you can," which festivals generate. As much as he liked the film, Case had concluded even before its opening that *Immunity* would likely fall flat at the box office. "The people who were seeing it at the festivals were mostly the people who would have bought tickets," Case says, "We were in effect giving it away."

The two-month delay was occasioned by several factors, including the search for a U.S. distributor. No Canadian company, says Case, would dare open in Canada if there were a chance of a U.S. deal, because it could then take advantage of the American materials and promotional campaign. But the delay was also caused by the inaccessibility of Famous Players screens in Montreal. Gunnarsson had wanted the theatres booked before the festival—not only in Montreal, but across the country; Famous Players declined, saying it wanted to use the festival to gauge public response. As a result, the film opened in Montreal with no commitments to screens anywhere else.

And, as Case had predicted, it opened to miserable box office. The opening weekend gross receipts for the four screens in Montreal amounted to $4,794. The first week total was $7,486. The critics were generally favourable. The *Gazette's* John Griffin gave it a money review, calling the film "a power-house" and telling readers "don't miss it."

But the revenues were so soft, says Lyon, that "it was in danger of not being held over after the first week." Inevitably, the filmmakers lobbied for a continuance, arguing that the film needed time to develop word-of-mouth. Inevitably, Famous wanted a new product that might fill more seats. After one week, the film closed at theatres in two French-speaking suburbs (Longueuil and Laval). It continued for a second week at the downtown Eaton Centre and the Parisien cinema.

The second week grosses, not unexpectedly, were worse— $611 at the Eaton Centre; $1,874 dollars at the Parisien. Except for a disappointing week-long run at the Capital theatre in Drummondville (gross: $497), and later appearances on the repertory circuit, the film Metropolis and Astral had hoped would excite Quebec audiences disappeared. In Toronto, the film opened at the mid-town Cumberland #1 theatre on November 8, 1991, grossing only $2,241 its opening weekend, and $3,257 for the week. The second week grosses dropped to $2,208—after which the exhibitor again pulled the plug. Reviewing the film in the *Globe and Mail*, critic Rick Groen said, "Whatever passion was initially brought to the project . . . seems to have gotten waylaid en route. Fairminded, it definitely is. Dramatic, it isn't." The Toronto *Star's* Cathy Dunphy was more sympathetic, calling it a "believable, moving story, lovingly photographed, which pulls no punches.

In Vancouver, the film opened in Cineplex's downtown Royal Centre, a multiplex of 10 cinemas, on December 6. It ran six weeks, and grossed $9,813. The film hung on longer in Vancouver, Lyon believes, because it was running during a slow holiday period. Gunnarsson, however, had always thought the film should have opened in Vancouver—both his and Lucas' home town, and a city more tolerant of left-wing political ideologies. The better box office he credited to better promotion, including a mock confrontation staged in the Granville Mall between the Salvadoran army and a group of Salvadoran street musicians, which three local TV stations covered. Famous Players, he says, pulled *Immunity* even though its grosses at that point were higher than some Hollywood films, including *Thelma & Louise*.

It is difficult, of course, for directors and producers to criticize the performance of a distributor. The Canadian industry is small, and there is a good chance that they may need the services—and the advances—of the same distributor in the future. Still, Gunnarsson believes that Astral's failure to promote his film in TV ads in the weeks preceeding its launch was a critical factor in its subsequent box-office results. "People don't get up and say, 'Wow, *Diplomatic Immunity* opened this weekend. Let's go see it . . . . It has to become a cultural phenomenon before they'll see it." Even Donovan, who led Metropolis to Astral, and considers the firm honest (an adjective rarely affixed to distributors), believes the film "would have done much better in other hands. Marketing is 90 percent of a film." Apart from the Montreal Film Festival, where Astral's effort was said to be exemplary, "there was an unwillingness to commit resources to making it work."

Astral's counter-argument is that no amount of P&A money could have turned *Immunity* into a box-office success. "We acted in a professional, responsible manner," says Stephen Greenberg. "We're part of the North American marketplace. We're fighting for a shrinking disposable dollar. The film played in good theatres. It got the dates Wayne Case wanted. The fact is, we made the party and nobody came."

Despite its lack of theatrical success, *Immunity* did score well in film festivals and on television—perhaps its more natural home. In its November 1992 prime-time airing on the CBC, it was doubtless seen by tens of thousands more viewers than ever would have seen it in the theatres. And by March 1993, it had been invited to appear at 15 separate film festivals outside of Canada, winning Havana's Premio Coral, Houston's Gold for feature drama, San Remo's best actress (for Ofelia Medina), and the Cannes Winter Festival's Grand Prix awards.

U.S. RIGHTS In the summer of 1991, Alliance's Robert Lantos and Victor Loewy were invited to a screening of *Immunity*. After the lights came up, Lantos gave Gunnarsson the most back-handed compliment he had ever received. "Compared to the shit that's been produced in this country in the last couple of years," Lantos said, "this is almost a masterpiece." But Lantos genuinely liked the film, and pursued acquisition of foreign rights aggressively. Uncertain whether to use a foreign sales agent, Gunnarsson took the film to Los Angeles to screen it for other potential distributors. One British firm was interested, as (briefly) was Miramax. Jan Rofekamp's Films Transit in Montreal also tabled an offer, but he was unwilling to mount a theatrical release for the film in the U.S. Lantos, says Gunnarsson, "made us feel wanted." Alliance was Canadian, and there would have been potential political problems with Telefilm had Metropolis tried selling rights to a foreign firm. Alliance won, offering a minimum guarantee of $50,000 and another $60,000 for prints and ads. By July 1993, however, the film had not opened theatrically in the U.S.

Why did *Immunity* not succeed at the box office? There are at least half a dozen theories, all of which have some validity:

1) The natural audience for the film had already seen it at the film festivals.
2) The topic was stale-dated. At least three other Hollywood films had already been made on similar subjects, and El Salvador

itself had virtually disappeared from the evening news and from public consciousness.

3) With the recession starting to bite hard, fewer Canadians were going to the movies.

4) There was not a single recognizable name in the cast, and the lead actress' performance was at best incomprehensible.

5) It was a made-for-TV movie trying to disguise itself as a feature film, and failing.

6) All the money for promotion was basically spent at film festivals.

7) There was no TV advertising for the film—perhaps the only form of paid advertising that has a significant impact on box office returns.

There are lessons here—for producers, to push for creation of an integrated campaign; for distributors, says Stephen Greenberg, to "pay attention to the content. It starts and stops with the written material." And, he adds, to get involved much earlier, long before the film is finished.

FINAL TAKES Sturla Gunnarsson: "Making a feature film in Canada with the expectation that it's going to do well at the box office is like going to Las Vegas with the expectation that you're going to win. If you think the trip's a failure if you don't win at the roulette table, it's not going to be a very good trip."

Steve Lucas: "If it's not working, change it. That's the biggest lesson. You can always change it. That's my motto from here on in."

6
Genius is Pain

Comic Book
Confidential

DIRECTOR:	**DISTRIBUTOR:**
Ron Mann	CINEPLEX–ODEON
PRODUCER:	(Canada); CINECOM
Ron Mann	(USA); FILMS TRANSIT
CO-PRODUCER:	(world)
Martin Harbury	**RELEASE DATE:**
EXECUTIVE PRODUCER:	September 23, 1988
Don Haig	**RUNNING TIME:**
PRODUCTION EXECUTIVE:	85 minutes
Charles Lippincott	**BUDGET:**
CINEMATOGRAPHY:	$700,000 (approx.)
Joan Churchill,	
Robert Fresco	
SOUND:	
David Joliat, Tod A.	
Maitland, Brenda Ray	
EDITORS:	
Robert Kennedy,	
Ron Mann	

"Ron's insane. He's totally committed to and obsessed with his film, a complete and utter perfectionist. Which is bizarre to me, because given the nature of a documentary film, it's limited to people who share the same interest in the subject matter. But there is no point in trying to explain something for which there is no logical explanation. Why anybody in their right mind would want to distribute a Ron Mann film, unless there was a clause in the contract that denied Ron access to you as an individual, and you don't give him your home phone number, is beyond me. The next subject is Ron Mann? Let me take some valium." — Jeff Sackman, distributor

"All distributors—not most, but all—are liars, crooks and thieves."

— Ron Mann, director

SYNOPSIS A feature-length documentary, *Comic Book Confidential* combines interviews with 22 comic-strip artists, including Gilbert Shelton, Bill Griffith and Art Spiegelman, historical footage, and computer-programmed camera movements that mimic animation in an entertaining and informative, if not particularly insightful, tour of the 50-year history of comic books in North America.

ORIGINS It seems almost impossible to credit now, but in 1985, Ron Mann left Toronto for Hollywood to write films for Ivan Reitman. It seems hard to credit because anyone who knows Ron Mann, or knows the work of Ron Mann, will know that, while he likes to be entertained as much as anyone else, and once watched a daytime soap, The Young and the Restless, for 18 months, every day, he is not at heart a Hollywood sort of

Ron Mann, producer, director and co-editor, **Comic Book Confidential.**

guy. Hollywood sells fantasy; Mann prefers reality—and he preferred it on the cultural fringe, a territory not overly populated by documentary filmmakers. Only 26 years old at the time, he had already made a name for himself as a director of off-beat, award-winning performance films—notably, *Imagine the Sound*, a 1981 work about a group of avant-garde jazz musicians, which featured long segments of atonal saxophone music; and *Poetry in Motion*, a 1982 film the *Los Angeles Times* called 'the Woodstock of poetry," which featured long segments of atonal poets reading their work. Mainstream, the films were not. The following year, partly to prove that he could do something else, the *wunderkind* produced, directed and co-wrote (with Bill Schroeder) his first dramatic feature, *Listen to the City.* The script was written in six days, shot in 12, cost $150,000 to produce, and included a part for which Mann persuaded actor Martin Sheen to donate a day of his time (and later had the nerve to edit him out of the film). Like virtually everything Ron Mann did, it was a complete gamble. But as he says: "You're not a filmmaker if you're not a gambler, if you're not a con man." And since he viewed *Listen* more or less as an experiment, he did not regard it as a personal failure.

Others were less charitable. Both critically and commercially, *Listen to the City* was a complete failure. Indeed, it was never given theatrical release, in part because its erstwhile distributor, Spectrafilm, went out of business. The film was, however, later sold to pay–TV. Experiment or not, the experience understandably left Mann feeling more than a little depressed. He was also in debt—as he was after every film—this time, for $70,000. Says Mann: "The way I make films is. I make films. Go into debt. And have to make another film to get myself out of debt. This joyous cycle. Which is not very joyous."

Ron Mann talks like that, in short sound bites that follow the completely unpredictable neural pathways of his brain. "My mind," he concedes, "jumps around like a stone that skips on water." Most of the sentences he starts in conversation never quite finish; they are simply interrupted and superseded by new thoughts, which may or may not be connected to any previous thought. Or perhaps they are connected, but only Mann knows how. His films are generally more orderly, but Mann himself is at heart a charming subversive, a kind of lovable anarchist. He would make a fascinating case study as the first human demonstration of Chaos Theory. Some years ago, a writer asked Mann and some 40 other filmmakers to identify the film they would take with them if they were ever stranded on a desert island. Mann, of course, said he would not take a film at all—he would take a laser disc, because with it, "you don't have to look at film in a linear way." Were they available on laser disc, Mann would have taken the work of the late Emile de Antonio, an American political documentarian (*Point of Order*, *Rush to Judgment*, and *Milhouse: A White Comedy*), whom Mann regarded as his mentor and principal inspiration and whom he has called "my second father. I owe everything to him," he once said, "my style, my thinking, my reflections, my views. He taught me everything." Appropriately, de Antonio told the same writer he would not take any film to a desert island because "I know of no film I would want to see even five times."

And so in 1985, Ron Mann, with more unpaid and seemingly unpayable bills than he had ever accumulated, and not really knowing "where to go," finally succumbed to an old temptation and decided to call up an old friend, Joe Medjuck. A former professor of film at Toronto's Innis College, where Mann had studied in the early 1980s, Medjuck was now an executive producer in Hollywood and had "just finished making a small film called *Ghostbusters*," Mann recollects. "So I called him up and said, 'Joe, why don't you give me a writing job?' " Give me some ideas, Medjuck said. Mann gave him 30 the next day; he liked three. When the paperwork was done, Ron Mann flew to Hollywood with a million-dollar contract to develop three scripts for Ivan Reitman, then and now one of the American industry's top producers.

After six months in the sun—he lived on the lot of the old Burbank Studios, in a trailer that once belonged to the Three Stooges—Mann had retired his debt, had about $100,000 in the bank, and had finished one screenplay, *Hoods in the Woods*, a comedy about a group of juvenile delinquents on an Outward Bound retreat; it eventually settled into that perpetual limbo state knows as Somewhere In Development at Columbia Pictures, but was never produced. Looking back, Mann regards his Hollywood stay as "an imaginary experience. I had anything I wanted. Anything. I had a job that everybody wants. Essentially. But I didn't know if it was real or not."

Of course, he had never entirely relinquished his true identity as a maker of documentaries, and he continued to scout around for some sort of quirky, *noir* cultural phenomenon that might lend itself to film. Among the ideas he explored was comic books. At the suggestion of a Hollywood friend, Charles Lippincott (later to be awarded the largely honorary credit of Production

The film's four-colour poster used icons in the interviewed artists' familiar styles to enhance audience recognition of their names.

Executive), Mann attended a comic book convention in San Diego. Afterward, he discussed the possibilities of making a film on the subject with de Antonio, and with the late poet bp nichol, who had appeared in *Poetry in Motion* and had become a friend. Nichol, a serious comic-book collector, had an enormous knowlege of the industry. But it was de Antonio, better known as 'Dee,' who "got me excited about comics as a legitimate art form."

At that point, Reitman was just getting started on *Legal Eagles* for Universal Pictures. Mann suggested he make a documentary about the making of the film, which was being shot on location in New York. Instead, Universal hired Mann (for $150,000) to assemble an electronic press kit (EPK) that would later be used in promotion. But once he got to New York, he decided to make use of his evenings by filming interviews with various comic book artists, including Will Eisner, creator of "The Spirit," and Jules Feiffer. "I had a film crew at my disposal in New York," Mann explains. "And free film stock. I mean, what would you do?" When filming for the epk was finished, Ron returned to Toronto to edit it. Not surprisingly, Universal executives thought the result was too arty; it somehow managed to draw more attention to Mann, an off-screen presence, than to the stars—Robert Redford, Darryl Hannah and Debra Winger. At which point, Universal instructed Mann to return the footage and had the epk entirely recut to its liking.

By then, of course, he was keen to follow de Antonio's advice—disconnect from Hollywood and resume life as a documentarian (although he insists that he has a standing offer to return to the Reitman entourage at any time). His first plan was to make a film about political theatre, centred on the work of Italian political playwright, Dario Fo. Its working title was *Enemy of the Obvious*. In fact, Mann had even submitted the idea to the Canada Council and had received a $35,000 grant. When he discovered that a friend of his had already made a film on the San Francisco Mime Troupe, one of the leading exponents of political theatre, he dropped the project, turned instead to comic books, and gave back the $35,000—becoming, he firmly maintains, "the first person in Canadian history to return money to the Canada Council." Of course, he immediately re-applied for money to finance *Comic.*

DEVELOPMENT Like most of Ron Mann's films, *Comic* was never officially in development. "I develop my films in the editing room," he says. "They kind of develop themselves." This, too, is an extension of personality. "Everything I do," he concedes, "is haphazard and scattered. I've never had a focus." The first injection of real financial support for the project—$5,000 (US)—came from Jules Feiffer's Swan Foundation, an organization dedicated to the promotion of sequential art. Later, it contributed another $5,000. Shortly afterward, the Canada Council reinstated its $35,000 grant. These funds allowed Mann to continue filming, but he still had no sense of what his film might become. He simply believed that the subject itself had cultural importance. Once, returning home from Los

Angeles, he was reading a new Batman comic in the airport terminal and noticed his fellow passengers sneering at him. For Mann, the establishment's basic hostility to the art form was incontrovertible evidence of its legitimacy. "I knew at that point I was on the right track," he says. "That this was an important medium, and that I could contribute to something culturally significant."

In fact, Mann has always seen himself as an unofficial historian of the counterculture. Notwithstanding his flirtation with The Young and the Restless, he maintains that he is only marginally interested in the mainstream diet of TV and film. When he watches TV, he says, he is "looking for something between the dials," something he rarely finds. His work, he suggests, is an attempt to "put my own form of disinformation out there, a window for understanding ourselves." And his passion flows from a sense of obligation to make a record for future generations of who these people are—largely uncelebrated poets and jazz musicians and comic book artists (and, in his next film, *Sparks*, radio broadcasters.) By design, his films are not about the popular or the well-known—they are always about those whose creativity flourishes on the social margin, in subcultures rejected by the establishment. "That's why I can't stop myself," he says. "I become almost fanatical about it. I have this missionary approach. Essentially, I'm trying to make unpopular culture popular."

At some point early in 1986—although it may have been 1985, "my memory is really bad," he confesses—Ron Mann appeared in Don Haig's basement screening room on Toronto's Church St. with a folder under his arm. Inside it was a proposal for a half-hour documentary on comic books. He intended to pitch it to the CBC, and he wanted Haig to help produce it. Haig, the gentle guru of Canadian cinema, had enormous respect for Mann's work, but he was immediately skeptical. He knew nothing about comic books and regarded them as a childhood, and therefore frivolous, pastime. "The last time I saw comics books," Haig told Mann, "was when I traded them in 1947 in Winnipeg. I mean, who reads comic books?" Mann's retort: "You'd be surprised."

Although the idea itself was interesting, Haig was not entirely sure that it could be translated into film. But Mann had already done a fair amount of research on the concept, had filmed several artists and had figured out—at least in theory—how to make the package work cinematically, by weaving together the talking heads of artists and what appeared to be animation of their art work. Moreover, Haig was absolutely convinced that Mann needed someone to help produce. Indeed, a large part of the problem with *Listen to the City*, Haig thought, stemmed from Mann's insistence on trying to do everything—write, produce, direct, edit, promote, answer telephones. Next time you do a film, Haig had told him some years earlier, do yourself a favour and hire an executive producer to ease the burden. Now, Mann was trying to do just that.

So Haig, who could seldom bring himself to say no to any enterprising young filmmaker, agreed to help Mann launch *Comic*. His thinking at the time was, "this may take three months, but it will be a simple process, a modest TV half-hour, and an interesting film." But the more they explored the subject, the clearer it became that there was simply too much material to contain within a 30-minute film. Haig was overwhelmed by how many comic stores existed, the mail-order business they were doing, what comic books were selling for, the collecting clubs in England and Japan. "I went with him one day to visit one of these stores and I was freaked," Haig recalls. "And I said—I think I was the instigator, or at least I perpetrated the rumour that I was—'this is bigger than a half-hour. This is like a documentary feature almost.' But Ron probably knew all along that that's what he was going to do."

Indeed, Mann had long before concluded that only a feature-length film could encompass the myriad dimensions of the $1-billion comic-book industry. By now, of course, he was already shooting film, doing interviews with selected artists on 16MM, and waiting for grant money to get them processed. Some time earlier, he had sat down in Los Angeles with his friend Charles Lippincott, vice president of Creative Movie Marketing, and drafted a Christmas tree-shaped flow chart, which outlined the history of comic books and all the key creators. By the time they had finished, the tree was decorated with 150 names. Later, back in Toronto, Mann started calling those names, asking if they would consent to be filmed. Most said yes immediately; others agreed after viewing videotapes of Mann's earlier work. The only rejection was from a New York lawyer and former government censor, who unceremoniously evicted Mann and his crew when they showed up on his office doorstep. But having filmed some of the heavy-weight comic book artistic heroes—Robert Crumb, Will Eisner, *Mad Magazine*'s owner, the late William Gaines, and its founder Harvey Kurtzman—made it easier to persuade others. "Having these people in place," says Mann, "was what made me think I could make this movie." In fact, they were the film's critical mass; without them, he knew that he would not be able to proceed.

It was while he was interviewing Gilbert Shelton, creator of the Freak Brothers, that Mann hit upon a possible scheme to breathe some life into the film. Shelton, like many artists, was painfully shy, and difficult to interview. Finally, Mann suggested that he read from his work, and Shelton was immediately able to forget himself and throw himself into the character in the strip. "When you hear it," says Mann, "you can hear how the artist wants that character to sound. The text is really the extension of the artists." Shelton, Eisner, Feiffer and others had been shot even before Mann knew for certain there would be a film. But that was his style—do what you wanted to do, do what needed to be done, and worry about paying for it later. That, too, came from de Antonio. "What [he] taught me was to go out and do it.

I never went to film school. Just go out and do films on your own." It was not an approach likely to endear him to government cinecrats, with strict rules and procedures about when and how film budgets could be spent.

FINANCING In the late 1980s, feature-length theatrical documentaries—even if they had a distribution commitment guaranteeing their exhibit in theatres across the country—were not eligible for funding from Telefilm Canada's Theatrical Fund. Under the agency's guidelines, only films based on fiction could receive money. This constraint forced documentarians to apply under Telefilm's Broadcast Fund, which in turn required them to find a Canadian broadcaster willing to buy a broadcast license worth 25 percent of the film's budget. "The Theatrical Fund simply was not designed for documentaries," explains Bill House, director of Telefilm's Ontario region. In drafting the rules, "we wanted to make that distinction absolute. There were a lot of fictional feature films vying for a relatively small amount of investment, and we wanted to allocate every dime of the fund to that purpose." The agency, however, could not simply ignore the demands of documentarians, particularly in a country with such a long tradition of excellence in the art form. As House notes: "We had a lot of sympathy for the feature-length documentary itself. Canadians have made them with some success, aesthetically. Documentary expression deserves support."

It was as a result of this official thinking, says House, that Telefilm "invented this system to rationalize investing in these films under the Broadcast Fund." In a sense, it was a cultural obligation and, during the late 1980s at least, there was generally enough money around to meet it. In fact, the Broadcast Fund helped financed several much-admired feature-length documentaries including Gail Singer's *Wisecracks*, Simcha Jacobovici's *Deadly Currents*, Kevin McMahon's *The Falls*, Janis Lundman's and Adrienne Mitchell's *Talk 16* and Katherine Gilday's *The Famine Within*. But as the easy Eighties gave way to the nervous Nineties, pressure increased on the federal agency to invest in films more likely to deliver better box-office results. Accordingly, Telefilm's enthusiasm for theatrical documentaries began to wane.

"No one's being categorical about anything," House maintains. "But the theatrical documentary is a very, very difficult beast. Difficult to finance, and extremely difficult to exploit commercially, domestically and internationally. People don't want to spend $8 to see a documentary film. The primary market [for them] is television." Good promotion campaigns are not the answer. Alliance mounted a "very inventive campaign" for *Talk 16*, House notes, only to be seriously disappointed by the results. Successful theatrical documentaries—Madonna's *Truth or Dare*, *Roger & Me* and *Paris is Burning*—are rare. In the future, House cautions, "it's going to be difficult to get [these films] financed through Telefilm. We have to consider the efficacy of this form."

In the meantime, Ron Mann set out to find a broadcaster willing to fund

25 percent of his original budget—$360,000—and he found one in Toronto's CITY-TV, a long-time backer of Canadian films in general and of Mann in particular. In March 1986, he sold the broadcast license for *Comic* for national French and English television, including pay-TV, to CITY for $90,000, payable in 48 monthly installments beginning with delivery of the film. The contract called for the film to be ready by September 1987—a naive hope, as it turned out—and gave CITY the right to unlimited runs of the film for a 15-year period. Jay Switzer, then program director, said at the time that the station was excited by the "opportunity to build [*Comic*] into a commercial television hit." CITY's support, Mann acknowledges, has been critical to his career. "If Jay Switzer wasn't there," he says, "I would be out of work permanently. I don't care if they play my films until the sprockets come off. The more people who see the film, the better."

But a theatrical feature, by definition, also needed a theatrical distributor—and Ron Mann had never met a distributor he did not distrust. The distributor for Mann's feature, *Listen to the City*, had gone out of business before the film was released. The distributor for another, earlier film had reneged on a $100,000 commitment. "I have not had good experience with distributors, period," Mann says. The core of the problem, he believes, is that "distributors don't have the same investment in a film as you do, or aren't as passionate as you are. It's just in their catalogue or it's the film they're releasing this week." Other filmmakers, he knows, are willing to devote time to taking the film around the continent, watching their film a hundred times. Mann has taken his documentaries on the college lecture circuit, but it is not a tour he relishes. "I don't want to do that. I see my film once, that's it. I never see it again. My role ends with the first screening."

In the end, Mann went to Cineplex-Odeon, principally because he had liked its work on *P4W, Prison for Women*, a documentary by Holly Dale and Janice Cole. He talked first with Murray Gough, a vice president of Film House, a Cineplex subsidiary, and another loyal supporter of Mann's films. Gough, in turn, directed him to Cyril Drabinsky, brother of the company's then high-flying chairman, Garth. It was Cyril who made Cineplex's original distribution commitment to *Comic*—then handed the project off to Cineplex vice president Jeff Sackman. "So I inherited Ron as if a stork had dropped him on my front porch," Sackman recalls. "Here's this cute baby with Phyllis Diller hair. How can I leave him out on the porch? I have to take him in."

Mann, however, was not exactly a helpless infant. Or, as Sackman says, "he wasn't shy about asking for things." According to Sackman, Mann would figuratively say, 'okay, I'm going to run my finger nails on this chalk board unless you give me what I want.' Afterward, of course, he was "always gracious, always appreciative." For the Canadian theatrical and video rights to *Comic*, Cineplex offered a minimum guarantee of $200,000, and an advance of $40,000, which Mann would use as part of his production financing. Cineplex also became the agent for any U.S. sale, for which it would be entitled to a commission.

With his distribution agreement in place, and his broadcast guarantee secured, Mann then turned to sources whose *modus operandi*—their obsession with form, method, paperwork, reporting—he detested, but whose cooperation he needed: Telefilm Canada and the Ontario Film Development Corp. At the OFDC, officials who reviewed the dossier initially planned to contribute $25,000 on an equity basis, and interim finance the CITY broadcast license ($90,000), for a total of $115,000. But it soon became clear, recalls Judy Watt, the agency's business affairs officer, that the CITY license was payable over too long a time-frame for interim financing to work. As a result, the OFDC simply decided to invest a straight $115,000, freeing up CITY's deferred $90,000 as revenue. It was ultimately split between Telefilm and the Ontario agency.

At Telefilm, the essential problem had nothing to with the film proposal and everything to do with the filmmaker himself. Mann, by this time, was a known quantity—known, that is, for not feeling bound by the normal constraints of an approved budget. From a bureaucratic standpoint, Ron Mann's films were virtually synonymous with overages and delay. True, he had Don Haig looking over his shoulder. And true, Haig had agreed to be the film's completion guarantor—some insurance, at least, that *Comic* would one day be finished. But in the agency's skeptical eyes, Haig was too busy with other projects to keep a firm financial leash on Mann. Haig's counsel would be invaluable on the creative side, Telefilm officials thought. But what Mann really needed, they insisted, was somebody with control of the chequebook.

The OFDC's Watt was actually working at Telefilm when the *Comic* application for production financing was filed. "It was one of the first projects I worked on there," she recalls. "The budgets would never add up. You could never get one column to match another. That's why we asked for another executive producer to be involved. I mean, I refuse to add up another Ron Mann budget."

Various officials, Watt included, are careful to avoid accusing Mann of outright duplicity. "It's not questioning Ron's integrity," Watt insists. "He has a strange and wonderful way, a creative way, of putting down figures, that once you get on to his wavelength, which I'm trying to, you're okay. But if you look from the outside, you're totally baffled." The overages resulted from what Mann's many backers would call perfectionism; he simply would not allow anything with his name on it to leave the editing suite until it resembled something of which he could be proud. Others said the delays had more do with simple confusion and lack of focus. Steve Weslak, the first of several editors who worked on *Comic*, says the first question he always asks the director is, "Who are you making this movie for? Ron Mann couldn't answer it. He kept saying 'I'm making it for my friends,' he said. 'They would enjoy this film.' " Weslak considered that an inadequate response. Ten months into the edit, he walked away from the project (or was fired, depending on whose version is believed).

Focussed or not, the extended costs of editing inevitably yielded cost overruns. In the case of *Comic*, these were aggravated by Mann's desire to use expensive technology to create the illusion of animation, and to re-shoot sequences until he judged them satisfactory. He was not easy to satisfy. By one account, he either fired or lost half a dozen animators during post-production. Telefilm, says Judy Watt, never could get a proper handle on the animation costs.

Once again, Haig offers the counter-argument. A film budget, he says, is not much more than a pre-nuptial agreement. Everyone declares their assets with the best of intentions; but between the promise and the fulfillment lies a series of perilous and unmappable minefields. There are simply too many aspects of a film that cannot be costed out in advance with exactitude. "I'm not saying Telefilm should just say, 'Go ahead and just send us the bill,' " Haig insists. "But you're dealing with an artist. There has to be a reasonable [response]." Mann himself, frustrated by the agency's endless and, in his view, frivolous and time-wasting demands, would often get so exasperated as to declare that he would pay for it—a threat he was more than willing to carry out. "I know they want to know what they're investing in," he says. "They want a piece of paper. But I didn't know how the hell the thing was going to look. I was finding the form as I went along, and that's kind of risky."

Finally, Telefilm insisted that Mann hire an executive producer—in addition to Haig—to watch the money. Find someone of your choosing, they told him, but find someone. And the agency agreed to pay the cost of his fee. It was at that point that Mann turned to his old friend, Martin Harbury. A native of England, Harbury had by then been in the business more than a dozen years. In 1986, when Mann approached him, he was working at Insight Productions on *The Truth about Alex*, a made-for-television movie. Harbury had known Mann for years, had always wanted to work with him, and so "without really thinking about it much, because it all seemed so straightforward," he said yes. "That, of course, was my first big mistake." The agreement was signed within days, Harbury accepting a modest flat fee and what he calls "minor equity in the film—not that it means anything." Harbury's consent was the last shoe. With it, Telefilm finally agreed to participate in *Comic*. The production financing as struck in 1986, then, was:

Cineplex–Odeon advance:	$40,000
Canada Council/Swan Foundation:	$40,000
Telefilm Canada:	$141,000
OFDC:	$115,000
Deferrals:	$25,000

The initial budget for *Comic Book Confidential* was $361,000. It later jumped to $500,000, with agency permission, but Mann ultimately spent $700,000—putting him $200,000 in debt, even before the film had been released.

Initially, says Martin Harbury, he had no great expectations for how Comic might perform. On the other hand, he, too, was impressed by the burgeoning subculture of comic books. He thought the film might have potential as a cult video, and that "everybody would start buying it in the comic book stores. Maybe it will sell ten million dollars worth of videos. I mean, everyone who makes a living in this business is, by definition, an optimist. You wouldn't last a year if you weren't." Harbury's arrival was also welcomed by Don Haig. "I had about 10 things going," Don Haig concedes. "So I said to Martin, 'I'll look after the creative side, to make sure that Ron does something that's commercial and not too arty. And you handle the money.' "

In his role as de facto co-producer, Harbury's first assignment was to sign "lots of documents," swearing that he believed Mann's budget was credible, that the schedule was doable, and that he "would stay involved until the bitter end, whenever we managed to make that happen." Harbury, feeling charitable, is sure now that Mann must have explained to him exactly what had been done so far, and what he planned to do. But because he was preoccupied with his own film, "I didn't take it all in." It was only some months later, therefore, that Harbury realized that Mann had already shot "vast amounts of interview footage, on his own hook, without any money raised," that he already had an editor, Weslak, working on the material, and that he had "laid enormous plans to interview dozens more people in the United States." In fact, by the time Harbury was able to devote his full attention to the project, Mann had already interviewed 50 or 60 people on film. "I thought, 'this is going to be a really fast-paced film.' "(Only 22 artists made it into the final edit.) At one point, Mann decided that he needed to interview the musician Frank Zappa, on the subject of censorship. He tracked him down, flew off to Los Angeles to do the interview—and never used the footage.

It is not fair, Harbury nonetheless maintains, to suggest that Ron Mann behaves without consideration for budgetary factors. However, in his view, the budget was always Mann's secondary concern. "With Ron, it's always, 'this has to be done. Therefore, we'll do it, and worry about what it means later.' " To some extent, such an attitude is both exemplary and necessary. "Everyone in the industry who has done anything worthwhile always puts the project first," Harbury observes. "My job was to keep him closer to the bounds of reality." Harbury tried to pin Mann down on exactly where he was going, and what he was going to do, and how much he could shoot. By and large, Mann was good to his word, but "there were always exceptions." Harbury would say, "Ron, how are you going to pay for this?" And Mann would say, "Don't worry about it."

Thinking he had bought into a part-time job, Harbury soon discovered otherwise. "I was running around like a lunatic, trying to track down what Ron had done, calling the lab to see what was being developed, just getting the information." Periodically, says Haig, "Martin would call me up and say, 'Jesus, that Ron. We're in deep fucking trouble. He won't listen.' And I'd say, 'I'll have a talk with him. See what the problem is.'" And Harbury would say, "I know what the problem is. The problem is he's shot another 75,000 feet of film in New York and no one at the agencies knows about it. You've got to tell him to stop. No more film!" To appease Harbury, Haig agreed to talk to Mann, but it was a pointless exercise. "I knew that Ron would find a way around it."

Still, Haig considered the pain of Ron Mann always worth the gain. The bottom line, he firmly believes, is that the funding agencies were created to support talent. Mann—it was undeniable—was the sort of filmmaker who might, at almost any point, announce that he could not finish his film in time for the festival that he had already committed to attend, and then add, "oh, and by the way I need another $80,000 just to make sure I can finish it at all." On at least one occasion, Haig remembers, Mann changed the entire subject of his film only days before an Ontario Arts Council jury was scheduled to rule on his funding application. Other referees were dumbfounded. "What is this?" they asked. "We spend two months reviewing the proposal for a film about X and now he wants to make a film about Y? What the hell does he think he's doing?" Haig was less concerned. "You've got to just swallow it and say, 'listen, you'll get your film, a sellable film. Give him the money. He'll work it out.' And in the end, he does. It might take three years, but he delivers."

Former OFDC production executive Louise Clark agrees with Haig. Clark remembers the *Comic* dossier as being entirely typical of any Ron Mann venture: "It just goes on and on and on and on. That's the way Ron is always going to be. He's his own little institution, and he's always going to drive everybody crazy. And he's always amazed that people think he's caused trouble. There's absolutely no way to get through to him." Having said that, Clark adds: "He's going to keep coming up with popular films. Play a Ron Mann film in Berlin and the mobs come out." Clark, in fact, accompanied Mann to Germany for the 1989 screening of *Comic* at the Berlin Film Festival. One night, she wanted to see a new film about the French revolution that was completely sold out. "So Ron said, 'Let's go.' And I said, 'But you can't possibly get in.' But with Ron, you can get in." That sort of brazen, can-do irreverence has been part of Mann's character since he was a youth. At 15, he began making regular knapsack pilgrimages to Cannes, sleeping on the beach and scalping film tickets, cadged from a sympathetic distributor, for food. At 20, needing an executive producer for a film, he introduced himself to and quickly befriended de Antonio. At Berlin, says Clark, "we followed the official French delegation into the theatre. They were dressed to the nines, and we were in blue jeans and running shoes, and we walked behind them, and everybody nodded and went 'bonjour,' and we went up to the main balcony and sat down and watched the movie."

POST-PRODUCTION *Comic* almost became the first film ever named as the result of a Name That Movie contest. The contest was advertised, appropriately enough, in the back pages of a Marvel comic book. There were dozens of responses. But the actual title was suggested by artist Art Spiegelman (*Maus*), who suggested *"Comics Confidential,"* an allusion to the garish, police-action magazines of the 1950s. Mann liked the idea, because the film is "like an expose of comics. And what I'm doing is making comic books, which have always been something sleazy and confidential, unconfidential."

Steve Weslak first met Ron Mann in 1984, when the latter was recutting his failed feature, *Listen to the City*. Weslak did some sound editing on the film and, Weslak says, "we got along quite well." In 1986, just after Weslak had finished work on David Cronenberg's *The Fly*, Mann approached him about editing *Comic*. In June of 1986, he started screening the footage. At that point, he says, Mann had shot about 75 percent of the film. In retrospect, Weslak regards the editing experience as "very, very, negative." In his eyes, the root of the problem was that although Mann had an idea for a film, he had no sense of how to organize the material. "He'd interview an artist for 90 minutes, getting his life story on film, when the contribution that artist had actually made to comic books was maybe worth two minutes. We ate up an enormous amount of time compressing these interviews."

Early on, says Weslak, they agreed to give *Comic* a chronological structure, based on the history of the art form. By definition, therefore, certain artists had to be slotted into those segments of the film where they were most relevant. So Weslak would edit them into sequences during the day only to find that Mann, working most of the night, had undone his work by the morning. "Ron can't pre-visualize things," Weslak says. "So that meant you'd have to do the work, and then he'd look at it and decide he didn't like it. He burned out a lot of people that way."

But the film's fatal flaw, according to Weslak, was the technical format Mann tried to impose. In the conventional movie house, the screen is almost twice as wide as it is high—the ratio is 1:1.85. But Mann wanted the film to look more vertical, like an actual 7 x 10-inch comic book. That attempt caused some of the "animation" sequences to look jerky. Technically, of course, it was not animation at all. Mann never wanted the characters in the comic strips to physically move; that would have violated the integrity of the art. What moved was the camera, zooming in or out, or across the panels, in computer- programmed sequences that gave the illusion of animation. These movements were often accompanied by the artists' readings of their own work.

Even before Mann and Weslak started editing, Martin Harbury and Don

Haig knew that, given the footage shot—an estimated 70 hours—they were in for a strenuous post-production experience. The first rough cut, completed in October 1986, was four hours long; during the screening, Don Haig actually fell asleep. "There were, like, five people in the room," Mann says, "and one of them was snoring. Not a good sign." Harbury agrees. "I thought, 'we're in trouble here,' I didn't know how we'd ever get it into shape. There were too many talking heads, too many people to follow. You kept thinking, 'Who are these people? How do they connect?' There were just so many possibilities at that point that finding the through line became incredibly difficult. Of course, Ron—optimist that he is—wasn't seeing what I was seeing."

It was here, Harbury insists, that Don Haig intervened "in a fairly major way," telling Mann that far too many voices were represented and that he would risk losing his audience unless he started making some hard choices. The loss of those voices, however, was partially offset by the gain of animation—an attempt to make the film more accessible and entertaining. Harbury applauded the cutting, but was less enthusiastic about the animation, if only because "I knew how tight the budget was. I knew how little animation we could actually afford."

Mann, Weslak and assistant editor Robert Kennedy spent another two months re-cutting the film, adding some material, eliminating more and revising the animation. To Weslak, the second rough cut—about three hours long—seemed to have promise, but Mann still was unhappy. "So we started again," Weslak recalls, "pulling it completely apart." Aiming to finish it by April, "we put a major push on, working every night and every weekend. It was crazy." At one point in the film, artist Lynda Barry says, "genius is pain." Weslak became convinced that Mann had appropriated this motto as the definitive summation of his life. "He seemed to believe that the more hours you worked, and the less you saw of your wife and kids, the better the project would be." Weslak remembers spending one entire weekend—"my wife was really pissed"—editing a single 45-second sequence. By Sunday night at 9 P.M., both he and Mann had something they were content with. But when Weslak returned on Monday morning, Mann was still there and not a single frame of the finished sequence still existed; "Ron had stayed through the night and pulled it all apart."

Later, Mann was featured in a short CBC profile, and interviewed by Peter Gzowksi. The CBC crew spent three or four days in the editing rooms. The televised film shows Weslak badgering Mann to finish *Comic* and joking about his disregard for deadlines. " 'C'mon Ron,' Weslak said. 'If we don't finish soon, we'll still be here editing a year from now.' " Ironically, Mann was still cutting his film a year later.

The third rough-cut was almost there, Weslak maintains. "It was a very solid effort. Another six weeks, and it would have been finished. But again, Ron didn't like it. He went back to his old routine. He wanted to start over, recut, do more animation, more shooting." After the screening, Haig, Harbury and Mann went for drinks—several drinks—and, according to Mann, made the decision to fire Weslak. "He's a brilliant, incredible technician," Mann says, "but he just wasn't able to contribute any more to the project. I mean, he'll tell you this, honestly, that he went insane." Weslak says he did not go insane; high anxiety is closer to the truth. He had simply hit the absolute limit of his tolerance for Ron Mann. "I quit," he insists, but adds: "whether I was fired or walked out is irrelevant. It's like, who ends a bad marriage? It took me a long time to recover from that experience. I spent the whole summer not doing much of anything." (The Canadian film industry being what it is, this schism was not permanent. A few years later, Mann asked Weslak to edit a fine cut of his 1992 documentary, *Twist*; Weslak declined. "Ron's a likable guy. I just didn't want to be locked up in the same room with him for 10–12 hours a day.")

After seeing later rough cuts of *Comic*, Telefilm's Bill House urged Mann to "get some analysis going here. Let's get the story straight. I mean, there was a point where we [Telefilm] felt that Ron didn't really know how to make it into a feature-length presentation." The central problem, he says—"and it affected its commercial success"—was the absence of a through-line through the film: some thematic take on what the comic book form means to its audience. "There is no clarity around that issue. It's a difficult film on a difficult subject, with a lot of different elements." Telefilm, says House elliptically, wanted Mann "to make the film he wanted to make, if he could determine himself what that film was. We wanted him to solve his own problem."

Weslak, of course, was not the only member of the post-production team to run afoul of Mann. At about the same time that Weslak departed, so did the woman who supervised his animation sequences, Ellen Besen. "My problem in making a film," Mann explains, "is that most of the time you order a grilled cheese sandwich and you get garlic on toast. That applies from the lab to the editor to . . . . It's very hard for people to give you what you want. I would re-shoot animation 20 times because it was crooked or not smooth. People would say, 'No one will notice.' Fuck, no one will notice. *I'm* noticing it; that's enough. That's why it took years to finish this film. Because people just couldn't get it right."

Besen, predictably, has quite another take. Originally, *Comic* was to include only 20 minutes of what is known in the trade as animatics. By the time she was hired in the late summer of 1986, those 20 minutes, she says, had been carefully thought out. The real problem was the rest of the film. Mann, she says, had shot hours of footage, but all of it was talking heads. There was no action movement, no film of the artists doing anything but facing the camera and talking. "You couldn't have a 90-minute film like that—20 minutes of animation and 70 minutes of just heads." That, says Besen, is why the production decided to double the time devoted to animation—except that for the second 20 minutes Mann did not seem to know what he wanted.

Like Weslak, Besen became frustrated by Mann's inability to read a story board—the outline of what the animators planned to do. Inevitably, she says, he loved the ideas in rough form, but hated the finished product. "He was getting precisely what he had requested, but he'd be terribly upset. People were stars, then they were shit. He burned through a major portion of the animation community. He'd look at the footage over and over and over again, and tell you an edge was crooked. I'd tell him the edge wouldn't show on the screen, but there was a breakdown of trust."

By March 1987, it seemed to Besen that "the whole production was spinning out of control." Both Don Haig and Martin Harbury were by now preoccupied with other projects. By April, Besen was having trouble reaching Mann. She had already notified him of her forthcoming wedding, and the week-long holiday that followed, but that had been some time earlier. Unable to contact him, she took the week off as planned—and returned to find that she had been dismissed. Working with Mann, she says, was like being sucked into a vortex. "You see the warning signals, but you get caught up in the excitement. He has an extraordinary ability to talk to people. But I've been to the Ron Mann school of hard knocks. I'll work *with* people now, but I'll never work *for* someone again."

After Besen's exit, Mann turned for help with the animation sequences to art directors Gerlinde Scharinger and Steven Lewis, but did, he claims, a significant portion of the work himself. And he had no compunction about abandoning everything and starting over. "Whatever the cost—$20,000, $30,000—I just didn't care. I mean, this is not the way to make movies, but if it didn't work for me, I would throw it out." Later, Mann and Harbury had a meeting with the film's bookkeeper, and realized that *Comic* was facing an imminent fiscal crisis. "We knew then how much money we had, and how much it would take to finish the film, and it looked grim," Mann says. That night, the two of them sat on the curb outside the bookkeeper's office, "with our heads in our hands, just like that scene from *The Bicycle Thief.*" The only recourse was to ask the agencies for more money. But both Telefilm and OFDC wanted evidence that Mann was not already over budget, and given "Ron's particular style of doing things," says Harbury, "that was not an easy thing to prove." The agencies did, however, inject more money, raising the overall financing to $500,000; according to Don Haig, "there wasn't much choice. If they didn't agree to it, they wouldn't have had much of a film." But Mann continued to spend, incurring another $200,000 in expenses. The debt forced him to turn to another old friend, Marvin Pludwinski, an entrepreneur/accountant. Pludwinksi personally loaned him $25,000 and purchased the director's equity in *Comic*, which was worth another $25,000.

With Robert Kennedy, Mann continued to edit for almost an entire year after the departures of Weslak and Besen. Often, he stayed in the editing suite until 4 A.M., "trying to figure out how to put it together. The rats would be eating the crusts in the pizza boxes in the corner." And early one morning, leaving for home, he recalls: "It was snowing outside. There was nobody there. It looked like a kind of post-nuclear holocaust. And I'll never forget feeling very cold and very alone and saying 'why the hell am I doing this?' My wife is at home sleeping, you know. And then I realized—because what you're doing is important. If I didn't feel that, I wouldn't feel the need to make movies."

By the following fall, *Comic* was ready for its premiere—at the Toronto Festival of Festivals. Afterward, the artist Will Eisner approached Mann and said, "You really did a great job." That, says Mann, "meant everything in the world to me. I couldn't care less about what the critics said. Here's someone who was there at the beginning of the medium. For him to say that was incredibly moving. Because a film is never really finished. You either run out of money or you run out of energy. And I had run out of both."

MARKETING & DISTRIBUTION Like Don Haig, Martin Harbury and Ron Mann before him, Cineplex–Odeon vice president Jeff Sackman was initially optimistic about the box-office potential of *Comic Book Confidential*. Shortly after he became involved in the project, he accompanied Mann on a Saturday morning visit to the Silver Snail, a Queen St. store specializing in comic books. "I just stood there thinking, 'geez, all these people coming to buy comic books. That's our easy audience,' " Sackman recalls. "And then you can expand beyond that. There's nostalgia. There's interest in this creator or that creator. There's all kinds of reasons why people would go see this film."

At the time, there were some two dozen comic book stores in the city of Toronto alone. The film had received a few forests of free publicity. It had been a smash hit at the Festival of Festivals, both among critics and regular movie-goers. In *Maclean's*, Brian D. Johnson called *Comic* "dazzling . . . Mann brings static images to life with vivid editing and camera movement." *Variety* was more restrained, calling the film "not the definitive comic book retrospective, but a primer . . . a lively enthusiastic look at a maligned art form." *Comic* had a brilliant one-sheet, composed of 22 four-colour squares showing the work of the artists; the poster had been plastered all over the downtown core of the city. Promotional brochures, postcards, T-shirts, buttons and flyers had been distributed to all the obvious channels and quite a few less obvious ones. The press kit included sea horses (of the kind once sold by mail order from coupons in the back pages of comic books), as well as an entire comic book, which told the story of the film, complete with quotes from the artists and samples of their style; 10,000 were printed and distributed. The founder of *Mad Magazine*, Bill Gaines—and four other artists featured in the documentary—came to Toronto for the premiere and plugged *Comic* at in-store book signings. The movie had tie-ins with Pizza Pizza and Licks, a hamburger chain. Mann claims to have spent about $60,000 on promotional materials—all out of his own pocket; not independently wealthy, he somehow managed to find credit that would only be repaid with the fees from his next project. "Cineplex wasn't going to do it, and I knew it had to be done in a certain way, or [*Comic*] wouldn't have gone anywhere." He also paid for ads in the Toronto weekly tabloid, *Now*. Some 39 separate articles about Mann or the film were booked for magazines and newspapers. Writing to CITY–TV's Jay Switzer two months before *Comic*'s opening, Mann said, "what makes me most confident about the film is that audiences like it, and that in the end is what really counts."

Attempting to piggyback on its appearance at the Festival of Festivals, *Comic* opened simultaneously at Cineplex–Odeon's downtown Carlton and midtown Canada Square cinemas on September 23, 1988. The film was scheduled to open at the Eaton Centre as well, but Cineplex ultimately decided against a third screen; it was a wise decision. In five weeks at the Carlton, the movie grossed a mere $13,768. It grossed another $3,300 during its one-week run at Canada Square. According to Jeff Sackman, more people saw *Comic* in its two screenings at the Festival of Festivals than during its entire run in Toronto. "That may be a slight exaggeration," he concedes, "but not much." In October, the film opened at Vancouver's downtown Royal Centre, grossing $3,665 in two weeks. Thereafter, its appearance was limited to two- or three-day runs at repertory houses in Toronto, Kitchener, Hamilton, Ottawa, Windsor and Halifax, always grossing less than $1,000. It also had a short run in Montreal, at the downtown Egyptian theatre.

Mann was both disappointed and surprised. The pattern was the same everywhere—decent to rave reviews, lots of free media attention, "but nobody showed up." Mann cannot explain why. "If I knew, I'd be very rich. It opened my eyes. I really did think we'd at least make our money back. [Distributor] Ben Barenholtz once said something to me that's very true: 'Making documentary films is five times as hard and five times the heartbreak.'"

Sackman's own analysis of *Comic*'s theatrical performance is that very few documentary subjects actually have crossover potential. However popular a trend or hobby or cult might be, the likelihood of its capturing a large film audience is remote. Many thousands of people, Sackman observes, are now caught up in the sports-card craze. "I'll bet any amount of money in the world that if someone does a film on hockey cards and baseball cards, it will go right down the toilet. Because the film transcends the actual media. People don't want to see films when they feel more comfortable in a different environment."

Comic, Sackman concludes, worked about as well as it should have worked theatrically. The problem with the film's promotional campaign was that it was wholly disproportionate to the expected pay-off. Says Sackman: "We just shouldn't have put in that kind of effort. I got caught up in the excitement . . . Youthful naivete." Would he do it again? "I would not be so committed to a film of the same stature," he concedes. "I'm more cynical now. I've had more experience releasing films. It's not a matter of commitment. It's a matter of being realistic and knowing how to allocate the limited amount of time in a day."

By December 1991, Cineplex had reported net theatrical revenues in Canada of $13,029, and foreign revenues of $24,236, for a total of $37,334. Against that, however, it had claimed some $226,620 in recoupable costs, as well as its $40,000 advance. On paper, at least, *Comic* was still showing a loss of $155,656.

U.S. RELEASE In September 1988, immediately after its appearance at the Festival of Festivals, Ron Mann took *Comic Book Confidential* to the Independent Feature Project (IFP) in New York City. Several distributors saw the film and voiced interest in acquiring theatrical rights, including New York based Cinecom Pictures, Miramax Films and New Line Cinema. Several others were ready to discuss acquiring TV rights, including Home Box Office, which wanted to play the movie to its cable TV subscribers and was prepared to pay a handsome price. Mann, of course, was eager to secure a full theatrical release, regardless of the dollars involved. Cineplex's Jeff Sackman—eager to recoup his company's investment in the film—was looking to maximize the U.S. distribution guarantee. Indeed, when New Line representative Nancy Moss, who had seen the film at the IFP, approached Sackman, he told her he was seeking a $350,000 (US) advance; New Line quickly dropped out. So did Miramax's Harvey Weinstein and New York-based distributor Ben Barenholtz, who said *Comic* had more potential in video than it did in theatrical.

Mann's choices were narrowing quickly. Mann preferred Cinecom because its catalogue of films included filmmakers he respected, including John Sayles and Jonathan Demme. He also liked Cinecom's Ira Deutchman, who first saw *Comic* at a staff screening in New York and later outlined a platform plan (quite ambitious for a documentary) for small openings in 10 American cities, or more "if the film performs well." According to Don Haig, who accompanied Mann to New York, Cinecom was "young and aggressive," was handling specialized film quite well, and was already feeding films to Cineplex in Canada, so it was a natural tie-in." When Cinecom asked Mann how much he wanted for U.S. rights, he suggested $200,000, representing $150,000 for video and television, and $50,000 for theatrical. Cinecom later agreed to $80,000.

Mann claims HBO was prepared to offer $500,000 (US) to gain the first window; that sounds like an inflated figure to Sackman, although he does concede the HBO offer was substantially more than Cinecom's. Naturally, Sackman preferred the HBO deal. "I wanted to sell it for the most money, but Ron wanted a full theatrical release." What may have changed Cineplex's mind, Mann suggests, was his offer to pay for the sound mix bill of *Comic*. Whatever the inducement, Sackman says Cineplex was "not terribly exposed financially. There was a commitment from Cinecom. And there was no good reason to deny a theatrical release."

Mann's usual misgivings about distributors were magnified when his friend Ira Deutchman announced—one week before the contracts were signed— that he was leaving Cinecom for a new job. Deutchman was no doubt anticipating the company's imminent fiscal crisis; not long afterward, Cinecom filed for protection from its creditors under U.S. bankruptcy laws. Mann immediately asked whether, in his absence, Cinecom could still handle the project. Deutchman felt sure it could, and agreed to monitor it from a distance. Again, a media promotion blitz was organized. A New York public relations firm, Seifert & White, was hired to handle media, and generated everything from mentions of the film to feature articles to reviews in *Elle*, *GQ*, *American Film*, the *Village Voice*, the *New York Times*, and several other publications. It was even promoted on David Letterman's late-night talk show, courtesy of artist Lynda Barry. The Canadian consulate in New York contributed $2,500 towards the film's promotional expenses.

Comic Book Confidential opened at New York's prestigious Film Forum on June 14, 1989. The post-premiere party was at the trendy Mars. The movie was generally well-received, although the *Village Voice* was snarky, calling it "pedestrian, if evocative." Eventually, *Comic* played in about 40 U.S. cities, mostly in repertory and art film houses, and Mann—uncharacteristically— was pleased with Cinecom's distribution effort.

Haig thinks *Comic* probably performed "better in the U.S. than Ron will ever know." By 1990, Cinecom was in receivership, but every few months they would receive word that it had run on HBO or some other network. "Somewhere along the line," he remains convinced, "the film did well." Haig does not subscribe to Mann's unqualified condemnation of distributors, but he does acknowledge that many companies cross-collateralize, selling packages of films and distributing the revenues in such a way that some producer is always a loser.

WORLD SALES In 1987, Mann retained Jan Rofekamp's Films Transit to represent *Comic* in foreign markets. By 1993, Rofekamp had reported gross sales of about $100,000, selling the film to TV networks in several countries.

FINAL TAKES Martin Harbury: "To be in this industry, you have to be an optimist. To be Ron Mann, you have to be doubly so. He's a very bright, very talented binge filmmaker. Binge: he can outlast just about anybody. But expecting to get your money's worth out of a production, from distribution, is somewhat akin to relying on the fact that you're going to be born again in another life. What did I learn? To ask more questions before I get involved in that role again. What *is* the role? What are the *other* roles? And more specifically, what is intended? There's an old military maxim: time spent in reconnaissance is seldom wasted."

Ron Mann: "I really liked working on *Comic*, even though it was hell to do. Making these films, you sort of feel like you're in this kind of war zone. But I really thought it would make me, not a lot of money, but some money, and man, I was in real shock. I am now convinced that you can't survive in this country making documentary films."

7
No Sure Things

![line]

Perfectly Normal

DIRECTOR:	**DISTRIBUTOR:**
Yves Simoneau	ALLIANCE
PRODUCER:	ENTERTAINMENT
Michael Burns	RELEASING (Canada),
EXECUTIVE PRODUCER:	THE SALES
Rafe Engel	CONSORTIUM (UK);
WRITERS:	FOUR SEASONS
Paul Quarrington,	ENTERTAINMENT (USA)
Eugene Lipinski	**RELEASE DATE:**
DIRECTOR OF PHOTOGRAPHY:	February 1, 1991
Alain Dostie	**RUNNING TIME:**
SOUND:	105 minutes
Douglas Ganton	**BUDGET:**
EDITOR:	$3.775 million
Ronald Sanders	
ACTORS:	
Robbie Coltrane,	
Michael Riley	

"Movies are the oddest things. You start with a story, it could be worth nothing, or it could be worth a hundred million dollars. You develop it into a screenplay, taking sometimes years, and it's finally finished and you like it; it could be worth nothing, it could be worth a hundred million dollars. Then you raise the money, and shoot the film, and at the end of principal photography, it could be worth nothing or it could be worth a hundred million dollars. Then you cut it, do all the stuff, all the marketing, and on the day of release you could be worth zero or you could be worth a hundred million dollars. And then literally, nine days later, at the end of the second weekend, you know and they know exactly what you're worth. — Michael Burns, producer

SYNOPSIS A black screwball comedy, *Perfectly Normal* is the story of Renzo, a wimpish, introverted young man who works in a beer factory and plays goalie for the brewery's hockey team. After the death of his mother, Renzo's life and apartment are invaded and taken over by a complete stranger, Turner. A large and boisterous American, Turner eventually uses Renzo's inheritance money to open a restaurant whose waiters sing opera in drag.

ORIGINS It would have come as no surprise to Robert Lantos or to his associate Victor Loewy to learn that, as a student, Michael Burns had been a discipline problem. It was Lantos' Alliance Entertainment that, in the spring of 1989, bought the Canadian distribution rights for Burns' *Perfectly Normal*, paying $350,000. But the relationship between Burns and Alliance—beginning with a feud over the issue of foreign distribution rights

Yves Simoneau, director, **Perfectly Normal.**

and descending into bitter acrimony over Alliance's performance as a distributor—would become something of a legend in the annals of contemporary Canadian cinema.

Normal is noteworthy on other counts as well. In director Yves Simoneau, it had one of Canada's most talented and most cinematic directors; in Michael Burns, one of the country's most aggressive producers. It had a recognizable star (Robbie Coltrane) in a lead role. It had a solid script. And it had, by Canadian standards at least, a generous budget ($3.775 million). If ever a Canadian film seemed likely to work at every level, this was it. And yet—a phrase that might constitute the unofficial anthem for Canadian cinema—outside of Toronto, the film had almost no theatrical resonance, prompting the culture czars in the funding agencies to ask, with Bill House of Telefilm, "if no one is going to see *Perfectly Normal,* what *will* they go and see?"

Ironically, the genesis of *Normal* ultimately owes something to Burns' troubles in public school. As a result of his erratic behaviour, his step-father, Lloyd Burns, a founder of Screen Gems, arranged to enrol him in Upper Canada College, a Toronto private school and the elder Burns' own alma mater. About two weeks after the start of grade 9, the UCC housemaster summoned Burns' parents from New York for a little chat. " 'This school has been here for 100 years,' he told them. 'Your son is not going to change it.' " Burns—wiry and intense, but suffused with comic energy—was eventually thrown out of UCC in grade 12, but not before forming a friendship with Harry Ditson, who later moved to England and became an actor. And it was Ditson who, during a visit to Toronto in 1987, told Michael Burns about the screenplay that his neighbour, Eugene Lipinski, another expatriate Canadian actor in London, had written.

Lipinski says he was "fascinated with the idea that someone could be a victim of his own circumstance; someone who never knocks on the door but, by twists of fate, has it opened for him." The script's central character, Renzo, was autobiographical. Like Renzo, Lipinski had worked in a brewery and, by temperament and ethnicity, felt like an outsider. "I ran away to England," Lipinski says. "I wanted this film to explore what happens if you can't run away." He wrote the first draft, long-hand, during a two-week holiday to Portugal in 1987. Pretending to be a friend of Steven Spielberg, he then managed to show the script to various potential backers in Toronto, all of whom, he claims, were interested in its development. But he eventually chose Burns, who seemed the most enthusiastic about the project.

Burns, 40 years old at the time, was then developing a package of film properties in association with a wealthy New Yorker named Abe Rosenberg. Earlier in his career, Burns had worked as an assistant to Hollywood producer Burt Schneider and director/writer Bob Rafelson on a series of successful films, including *Five Easy Pieces*, *The Last Picture Show*, and *Drive, She Said*. On his own, Burns later produced *Threshold*, a $5.5 million feature film about heart transplants, starring Donald Sutherland. When Eugene Lipinski knocked on his door, Burns was looking for new projects.

DEVELOPMENT Eugene Lipinski did have an idea for a film, an idea, as Burns puts it, "that really did sing." But the script itself, while oddly appealing, was "basically gibberish. It wasn't by any means a movie." Burns reorganized and rewrote the material and sent it back to Lipinski, who loved it. In fact, according to Burns, "he thought it was the great American novel and—not in a political way, but in an emotional way—he basically said, 'this cannot be changed.' He didn't want to change a punctuation mark." But it had to be changed. "The writing was impossible," says Burns, "and Renzo was a metaphor for what every young, latent homosexual probably goes through, which is that he meets someone who opens him up to the world."

Still, Burns was convinced that a genuine film lay buried within the Lipinski script. In search of development money, he had shown the draft to officials at Telefilm and the Ontario Film Development Corp. On the strength of a noncommittal letter of distribution interest from Cineplex-Odeon, Telefilm had invested modestly in the script's development. Later, in July 1988, and despite harshly critical readers' reports, the OFDC's Bill House reluctantly committed $10,000 to *Normal*'s development. A year later, the OFDC would contribute another $25,000 in late-stage development.

But no one at the agencies thought the Burns-revised Lipinski draft could or ever would be produced. According to the reader's report done for the OFDC, there would be no audience for the film Lipinski had written. The script was "confusing and unsatisfying. It attempts to appeal to everyone and therefore satisfies no one." Lipinski contends that pressure from Telefilm Canada forced Burns to seek script changes. The agency, he believes, would not accept key elements of his original story, including scenes set in a Calgary drag club. According to the writer, Telefilm viewed the drag club sequences as politically incorrect, risking accusations of "fag-bashing." Burns, however, needed no prodding. In London, he tried to persuade Lipinski "to re-envision parts of the movie," and to turn the drag club into a restaurant whose waiters dressed as characters from classical opera. Lipinski declined. "I can't do that," he said. "It compromises the story. We have a chance here to go out on the limb and make a statement." Lipinski was completely immovable. "He was in love with his own work," says Burns. "He began to pray to it."

Informally, the agencies suggested that Burns find a new writer. It was at that point that he asked novelist Paul Quarrington, a Governor-General's Award winner (*Whale Music*), to essay a second draft. Burns invited Quarrington up to his cottage in the Kawartha Lakes for a few days to discuss new approaches. While Quarrington fished, Burns talked, "planting little ideas in my mind," says Quarrington, "that quite cleverly made me think I was having an epiphany. He worked me until I said, 'We need this great, huge fellow, sort of larger than life to play Turner,' and Michael said, 'I know just the fellow who could do it.' "

Burns had in mind Robbie Coltrane, a British comedian who would later gain international acclaim in *Nuns on the Run*, but who was largely unknown at the time, at least outside the U.K. In fact, shortly after Quarrington's draft was complete, Burns sent it to his old school friend Harry Ditson in London and asked him to show it personally to Coltrane. Ditson did, and Coltrane immediately agreed to act in the film—subject, of course, to scheduling and fees. He would later sign for a seven-week shoot for $180,000. In the meantime, Quarrington was still wrestling with Lipinski's original draft. The most glaring problem was still the Turner character's covert homosexuality. "See, nothing overtly homosexual actually happens in this movie," says Burns. "And so Lipinski was already prepared to say it's not gay. But it was, understand?" Quarrington shared Burns' uneasiness about the script's homosexual undertones. "It's not that we were homophobic," Quarrington says. "I just didn't think it justified all of the activity in the story."

In the fall of 1988, Lipinski came to Toronto to record voice-overs for *Love and Hate*, the CBC drama about Colin Thatcher in which he had acted. Burns introduced him to Quarrington—a potentially awkward encounter. Lipinski remained convinced that the original draft, as reshaped by Burns, was a work of genius. Now he was meeting the man who was about to eviscerate his *magnum opus*. Over drinks, Quarrington started by alluding to the smaller changes he wanted to make, trying to get Lipinski's blessing for, as Burns says, "the kind of things a professional editor might add, a little polish." Lipinski's reaction to the suggested revisions, Quarrington insists, was "fine." But the script that emerged, while it retained many of Lipinski's original images and its unconventional hockey-meets-opera structure, was a new movie entirely. In fact, of the original dialogue, concedes Quarrington, "I don't think anything, really, survived." And, as Burns would later discover, Eugene Lipinski was anything but amused. "I thought

Michael Riley plays a brewery worker, Renzo, whose life is turned upside down by the sudden appearance of a forceful stranger, Turner (Robbie Coltrane) in **Perfectly Normal.**

it became character neutral," Lipinski says of Quarrington's script. "I thought it lost some gutsiness. I thought it would be a boring film."

Hoping to capitalize on Coltrane's interest by selling either a U.K. broadcast license or equity, Burns had early on sent the Quarrington script to British Satellite Broadcasting (now defunct), and The Sales Consortium, the foreign sales agent for British Screen. When he arrived in London to pitch BSB on buying the TV rights, Burns' contact, Cici Dempsey, could not understand why he wanted to produce it. "While working at a different company, Cici had actually read Lipinski's unedited original and of course hated it," Burns explains. So when the Quarrington script arrived with the same title, she had simply thrown it out.

To underline the fact that an entirely new screenplay had been crafted, Burns asked Lipinski's agent in London, Elizabeth Dench, to courier another copy of the Quarrington rewrite to Dempsey. Not having her own copy, Dench had Lipinski's original photocopied and sent it over. Apparently, Dench did not look too closely at the script. The copy she forwarded to BSB came complete with Lipinski's unexpurgated marginalia. "Now when I walk into Cici's office," Burns recalls, "she says, 'We really like the script and one of the things we found especially entertaining were these remarks in the margins.' Because Eugene had written things like 'shit' and 'fuck' all over it. In crayon. It was like the most humiliating experience a producer can possibly have." Still, it was agent Dench who ultimately helped "tame Lipinski, the savage beast," Burns says, thanks largely to Coltrane's interest in the project.

It was this first Quarrington script, delivered in January 1989, that finally convinced Burns that he had a real movie. "There were a lot of hurdles still to jump over," he says. "I didn't know how much money I could raise. But that script was the critical moment. Because good screenplays just don't come along. Scripts come to my office every day, and in a sense I might pick one and do it. But I'm telling you . . . dream on, buddy."

FINDING THE DIRECTOR With his film starting to take shape, Burns' next task was to hire a director compatible with the script. The search was to prove exhausting. In fact, Burns went across the country interviewing prospective candidates, 15 or 20 in all, the very experienced and the very untried. He made his final decision only two weeks before pre-production was scheduled to begin. High on his original list was Phillip Borsos, director of *The Grey Fox* and, at the time of Burns' search, just back from shooting My Nightmare in Beijing, or, as it was officially known, *Bethune, The Making of a Hero*—perhaps the single greatest cinematic fiasco in Canadian industry. In preparation for the meeting, Burns spent two entire days writing the essence of each scene onto little blue index cards, a common scriptwriter's device. "Burns thought it was a stupid idea," Quarrington says, "but he said Phil liked this sort of thing." Later, Burns methodically tacked up each of the cards on a wall in Borsos' office. But during several ensuing hours of script discussion, Borsos never referred to the cards—not once. Says Quarrington: "I could see Burns sitting in the corner, getting madder and madder. I kept on trying to refer to the cards. I'd say, 'You know that scene where Renzo meets Denise . . . There . . . It's right up there!' Borsos didn't care. And I think there was a schism established there. That was when Burns started to think about someone else."

After several conversations, it also became clear that Borsos was not accustomed to working with a producer as "hands-on" as Burns fully intended to be. Burns therefore rejected Borsos not on grounds of talent, but to avoid what showed signs of turning into a battle for control. Afterward, he concentrated on directors known to be visually stylish. Several candidates had directed TV commercials. "Some part of being a movie director," Burns believes, "is not intelligence. Is not learnable. It's literally muscles you are born with. I'm serious. It's like Olympic diving. Greg Luganis is not just somebody who worked hard. He brought something to the table *before* he started to work hard. "Movie directing is like this. No matter how smart you are, there is something else . . . a cinematic idea . . . of knowing exactly where the edge of the frame is. And to some extent, being suspended in the air like that, the way a diver is, is a lot of what making a movie is, especially a low-budget movie. It's a very daunting experience.

A writer can rewrite his book. A director doesn't have too many shots at it. Once you move on to the next scene, that's it. It's tightrope walking, and you need someone who is really self-assured."

In the end, Burns was torn between two directors—Winnipegger John Paizs (*Crime Wave*) and Quebec's Yves Simoneau (*Pouvoir Intime* and *Belly of the Dragon*). What he liked about Paizs' work was his sense of comedy—an essential ingredient in *Normal*. What he feared was Paizs' relative inexperience. As for Simoneau, Burns considered him "a born movie director. I was knocked out by his technical fluidity and his sense of cinema." But Simoneau had never directed an English-language film, and his command of English was, from Burns' standpoint at least, suspect.

"This language thing is crucial," Burns says, "because you're listening to actors do scenes, and you have to know whether they got them, and it's not just 'did they say the lines right?' or 'was their facial expression correct?' There's a sort of *patois* that is really challenging. And our script was literary. I mean, it's hoser language, but it's damn good hoser language."

Simoneau himself, according to Burns, "originally did a bit of a dance" in their negotiations. Simoneau wanted to do some re-writing; Burns objected, "As of now," he told Simoneau, "I have something I like. I don't want to turn it into something I don't like." For a time, Simoneau walked away from the project. A few weeks later, he returned, suggesting only changes to the film's ending. Burns told him to call Quarrington. "Yves was very . . . I don't like to say sneaky, but he's a writer himself," Quarrington explains. "He has a lot of strong opinions. He was bringing a darker, more Gallic sensibility to the film, and I was not at all resistant to that."

Simoneau says he was drawn to the project because of Quarrington's script, by his ability to write dialogue and to mix the metaphors of sport and art. But despite the quirky story and a bizarre accumulation of themes, Simoneau felt "there was no focus. I don't think it was a film until I came in. So I sat with Paul and I made it my story, in a way." The offer also came at the right time. Simoneau was increasingly discouraged by the film climate in Quebec, where the rules seemed to change every month. And he felt ready to look elsewhere. He knew *Normal* would never be *Crocodile Dundee*, but it was "so crazy, so unusual, so off-the-wall" that it appealed to him.

The major unresolved issue was always the ending. Simoneau did not like the ending as written, but he would not know how to change it until he had done the film. Burns kept asking him how he thought it should end. "You understand, Yves. I can't sign the contract with you if I don't know how you're going to end it." "If I do the film," Simoneau replied, "then I'll tell you. I have to get into the project, go around it, swallow it, then spit it out."

Such creative tensions Simoneau regarded as, well, perfectly normal. He had by that time directed four feature films; Burns was producing his second. In terms of experience, in terms of vision, Simoneau felt himself the senior executive. Still, he understood that Burns had been working on the project for two years and was reluctant to suddenly yield control of the material to someone else. "I was coming in and saying, 'This is mine now.' I knew that was going to be tough for Michael to accept."

So in the end—despite a clear sense of risk on the language question—Burns opted for Simoneau. The director's fee was $125,000. Even then, Burns spent the first three weeks of the shoot listening to the actors on headphones, making sure it all sounded right. "I had a Scottish guy [Coltrane], playing an American, directed by a Francophone," Burns says. "It wasn't easy." Simoneau's own confidence was never threatened. "To be convincing," he says, "you have to be completely convinced. When you have that clarity, there is no limit, no budget, language, schedule, weather, that will interfere with you. You're the strongest person on the set, the spirit, the captain."

The clear loser was John Paizs who, with Simoneau's contract always in doubt, had hung on to the end, believing he was about to direct his first major film. "You end up having to string people along," Burns concedes, apologetically. "John did not find out about Simoneau until pretty much the last minute." In fact, according to Paizs, he didn't find out at all. "The last thing I heard from Michael Burns was that he would be flying me to Toronto to meet with him. I never heard from him again. I thought I was the front-runner. I was left hanging. I guess that's how it is in the movie business."

The selection of Simoneau had another critical consequence: it cemented the interest of Robert Lantos and his Alliance Entertainment. Lantos says he had "quite liked the script," even before Burns had found a director. But in the absence of a talent like Simoneau, whom he regarded as a stylistic master, "the material could risk becoming pedestrian." Indeed, "the best stylist I knew who could be engaged for material he didn't himself write and was looking to work in English was Yves Simoneau." It was Lantos who therefore facilitated the Burns–Simoneau union and, once consummated, "felt more of a proprietary interest" in the project and "wanted to be involved in creation and marketing." The trajectory of that desire would eventually put him on a collision course with Michael Burns.

FINANCING Michael Burns' proposed budget for the film was $4 million, a miniscule sum by Hollywood standards, but a very big gulp for Canada. Indeed, at its final $3.775 million budget, *Normal* was the most expensive Canadian film financed in 1990. "Here's how budgeting works," Burns explains. "You have your script and you go around and you raise every fucking nickel that you can, okay? And magically, as if by a stroke of genius, that same number appears at the bottom of your budget." To access the feature film funds at Telefilm and the OFDC, Canadian film producers must first persuade a distributor to support the project with a minimum guarantee—an advance against the future earnings of the film. To that end, Burns approached Cineplex–Odeon and Robert Lantos' Alliance Releasing. Cineplex was interested, and had early on drafted a pro forma letter to that effect, but the corporation was starting to sink into the miasma of debt that would eventually lead to the palace coup staged against its controversial chairman, Garth Drabinsky.

Alliance, on the other hand, liked the script so much that Lantos wanted to executive produce the film—an idea that had some prima facie appeal. Alliance was an emerging powerhouse in the film industry; its involvement would virtually guarantee that the film would win the necessary agency permissions and investment; and in a stroke, it could solve any potential cash-flow problems.

According to Burns, Lantos was willing to pay $350,000 for Canadian rights and an additional $250,000 for the world. But the latter amount was contingent, says Burns, on his agreeing to make comedian Howie Mandel the co-star. At that time, Lantos did not believe Robbie Coltrane's name alone had sufficient drawing power to ensure box office success; in fact, like most Canadians, he had never heard of Coltrane. And Mandel, Lantos assured Burns, was available. Burns rejected the offer. "I knew the movie. And the Renzo part   later played by Michael Riley "wasn't a Howie Mandel part. At that point," Burns says, "I realized this was not a cooperative venture." Lantos, for his part, says the notion of becoming executive producer was "a passing thought four years ago. The film occupied perhaps an hour or two of my time." He has no specific recollection of any discussion involving Howie Mandel.

But it was only after draft contracts were circulated that Burns decided to abandon any notion of co-producing with Alliance. He was appalled not so much by the Mandel issue, as by what he considered the "gigantic up-front fees" being claimed by Alliance's lawyers in Montreal (Heenan, Blaikie) and by Alliance itself. In the cash-rich climate of the late 1980s, the fees were probably within the norm. Still Burns thought them excessive. "These kind of people [like Alliance] are omnivorous," Burns concluded. "They want their name on everything. They want to seem like they're the progenitor of the whole world." Burns advised Alliance that Canadian distribution rights were available, but Lantos would not be executive producing.

Snubbed, Lantos then sent what Burns calls "an extremely unpleasant memo, to everybody in the world but me," announcing that Alliance was withdrawing its support and had been forced out of the project by Burns. Lantos, he concluded, may not have actually wanted to sabotage the entire deal, but he would not have been upset to see it collapse, because a collapse would have implied that only Alliance had the necessary muscle and moxie to make it go.

Good film projects being rare species, Lantos was still prepared to buy the Canadian rights. In a subsequent discussion, Alliance offered $350,000 as a minimum guarantee for Canada—less than it had bid the same year for

Patricia Rozema's *White Room* ($400,000). Burns was offended by the judgement that his film was worth less than Rozema's, but he considered the Lantos bid "a very substantial offer" nonetheless and later accepted it.

Burns had asked Lantos to pay $400,000 for Canada. But at that price, Alliance also wanted the right to represent the film abroad. Because advances for Canadian films were more subsidized by Telefilm's Distribution Fund, Burns explains, "many distributors at that time would pay a legitimate fee for Canadian rights and try to persuade producers to throw in world rights for next to nothing." Alliance's head of distribution, Victor Loewy, seemed to adopt precisely this strategy with Burns. "Every contract or deal memo that I got from them contained one formula or another for last right of refusal, first right of negotiation, for the U.S., for Europe, for the world," Burns says. "I continuously told them that what they were buying was Canada; the world wasn't for sale."

It was not for sale because Burns had already managed to secure a high level of interest in the European theatrical rights from the London-based Sales Consortium, one of the largest foreign sales organizations in the world and, in Burns' mind, the best agency for a film of this kind. In addition to its expertise, The Sales Company, as it was generally known, charged a much lower than standard commission on sales (12.5 percent) and had a reputation—rare in the industry—both for low expenses and for integrity in reporting. On the downside, under the terms of its own corporate constitution, The Sales Company—then, jointly owned by British Screen, Zenith Films and Palace Films—could not put up minimum guarantees.

As for U.S. theatrical rights, Burns had from the start expected to retain and to sell these himself, once the film was complete. And at least initially, he was not prepared to yield to Alliance on this point. "There's only five or six companies that can distribute the film in the U.S., and you can call them up and get them to do it," he says. "I did. There is no advantage to having an agent, unless that agent has a reputation for marketing. So unless you get a lot of money, you're being scammed if you sell U.S. rights" to a Canadian distributor.

As the film's Canadian distributor, however, Alliance was legally entitled to a first right of negotiation for world rights. In bidding for those rights, Lantos initially offered Burns an extraordinary deal—five percent of gross sales, worldwide, off the top. In return, Alliance would be free to take whatever commission on sales it could persuade the agencies to let it take, probably between 25 and 30 percent. That, for example, would have meant that if Alliance had sold *Normal* to Germany for $100,000, Burns' personal share would have been $5,000. Alliance would have taken its commission, plus expenses incurred in selling the film. The rest of the proceeds would have been returned on a pro-rata basis to the film's investors.

Burns considered the proposal highly questionable. In effect, he was being offered a five percent incentive to give Alliance the world rights. Says Burns:

"For a producer to be making money before the film is recouped out of gross sales, while Telefilm, the OFDC and all these other investors were in deficit, were standing in line to recoup, and I'm taking dollars off the top, struck me as unbelievable. It's wrong, in my opinion, to earn money over your fees, while your partners aren't recouped." Burns reported the offer to the agencies, but without result. Their basic attitude was, 'what Alliance does with its fees is its business.' Lantos says such a procedure is "not particularly common at Alliance, but it certainly happens in the film business—that producers get a percentage of the gross in lieu of a percentage of the net. Alliance, he adds, "will make whatever deal we feel makes sense on each occasion. And we will be creative about deal-making as long as it's in line with the market value of the product or the individual behind it."

THE TWIN In his continued search for production financing, Burns felt reasonably assured of a favourable hearing at Telefilm, to which his friend Bill House had recently moved from the OFDC. But at the OFDC, Burns' dossier still bore the stigma of damning reader reports of both the first Lipinski screenplay and the first Quarrington script. Both scripts, as it happened, had been perused by the same reader. The first report called Lipinski's script incompetent; the second waxed nostalgic for it after reading Quarrington's. In pure, bureaucratic theory, of course, producers, directors and writers never see readers' reports, favourable or otherwise; actual practice is rather different. But Burns also had an important contact at the OFDC—chief executive officer Wayne Clarkson. In fact, Clarkson was probably the single most important ally the film had, responsible not only for securing a major chunk of production financing ($725,000), but for setting in motion the events that would lead to "the twin"—the co-financing marriage of *Normal* to *The Reflecting Skin*, a British film written and directed by Phillip Ridley (screenwriter on *The Krays*).

Clarkson first read the Quarrington screenplay on the beach at the Cannes Film Festival in May 1989 and, according to Burns, "loved it so much, he'd come running into the hotel to read jokes from the script." On his way back from Cannes, Clarkson arranged to meet Burns in London. The script had already made its way to Simon Relph, head of British Screen Financing Ltd. Relph liked the script. And he especially liked Robbie Coltrane's name attached to it. But what he liked most of all was the tantalizing prospect of saving *The Reflecting Skin*, a $3-million film, of which BSF was lead investor. Approaching the start date for shooting in Alberta, *Skin* was a project on the brink of collapse. One of its key investors, Charles Denton's Zenith Productions, had developed a terminal case of nerves and wanted out. Relph's imminent shortfall: $1 million.

The twinning idea was essentially an exchange of equity. The Canadian funding agencies would take a modest position in *Skin*—thus salvaging Relph's production. In turn, BSF and *Skin*'s other investors would purchase either equity or U.K. licensing rights for *Normal*. Those injections would boost Burns' own production budget (in fact, he had finally sold pay–TV rights to British Satellite Broadcasting for $343,000—at the time the largest pre-sale to a single medium in Canadian history).

So despite the byzantine complexities of negotiating the agreement—at one point, the Brits had arranged 19 separate tiers for recoupment, with the OFDC near the bottom—the twin was a win–win arrangement, an exchange of paper that made both projects viable. Simon Relph managed to secure an additional $750,000 ($375,000 from Telefilm, $125,000 from the OFDC and a $250,000 advance from Alliance), enough to complete production of *Skin*. The same total was invested by the British participants in *Normal*'s production financing. Burns agreed to complete post-production in England; Relph would do post-production in Canada. To legitimize its investment in a British film shot in Alberta, the OFDC had to scrape the barrel for Ontario justifications, and ended up with the art director and the gaffer.

Moreover, under terms of a co-production treaty with Great Britain, the CRTC was prepared to recognize both *Perfectly Normal* and *The Reflecting Skin* as Canadian content, while Great Britain was prepared to recognize the two films as British. As such, the potential value of the films to sub-distributors, free TV networks, pay–TV, video and other ancillary sources of revenue increased. Indeed, that was the tacit agenda of the entire scheme—to inflate values at both front and back ends, making both films potentially more profitable.

What complicated the twinning negotiations was not only the novelty of the arrangement for feature films (most previous twins had been conceived in the womb of television), but the hard bargaining. Every decision, says Clark, seemed to have 20 ramifications. The serpentine discussions dragged on for months, in large part because of disputes about recoupment schedules. *Skin*'s negotiators claimed that since it was public money, the Canadian agencies could afford to take a back seat to British private investors. Telefilm and the OFDC resisted, convinced that the British were simply seeking financial advantage. On the Canadian side, Burns and executive producer Rafe Engel—as the final piece of their financing jigsaw—planned a fallback position: to raise $425,000 from a consortium of private investors. And they had persuaded Telefilm and the OFDC that these investors should rank first on the recoupment schedules. The British resisted that tier placement, perhaps dimly assessing *Normal*'s probable box-office performance and its revenues from world sales. And *Skin* could afford to drag out the negotia-tions; by the late fall of 1989, it was already into post-production and its need for the Canadian investment was therefore less urgent.

As a result, negotiations did not conclude until Burns was well into post-production. The delays forced him to prepare two separate legal closings of *Normal*, one that assumed final agreement on the twin, and one that did not. Since the twinning deal included $750,000 worth of British investment, the non-twinning closing faced a $750,000 shortfall. Through various fee deferrals and feats of financial *legerdemain*, Burns finally managed to persuade the agencies that he was missing only $70,000—money he then borrowed from the bank against his mother's guarantee.

Even with the twinning issues resolved, Burns was still between $250,000 and $425,000 short of what he felt he needed to make the film, and feeling quite desperate. As a consequence, he asked Eugene Lipinski to defer the $100,000 writer's fee owed to him on the first day of principal photography. Lipinski declined the invitation, promptly hired a lawyer, and later agreed to a series of staggered payments. But the incident added further strain to their relationship.

To breach the financing gap, Burns had lined up private investors, but he would have preferred not to have needed recourse to their funds, because it constituted equity and their presence was complicating the negotiations on the twin. Far better, if he could, to arrange a big-dollar deal for foreign distribution rights; that money would represent an advance against the film's future earnings, but once recouped would leave a larger revenue pie to be split with the agencies and the other equity partners. The pecuniary consideration was not unimportant. Other Canadian filmmakers make culturally driven films. Michael Burns, by his own admission, "is not in the first instance culturally motivated. I'm always pointed toward making money and as a rule, I think private investment, from lawyers, dentists, etc., is scary. It's not a way to construct a Canadian film industry." So it was at that point that he went again to Robert Lantos at Alliance and virtually begged him to make a bid for international rights.

Meeting for more than two hours at Alliance's Yonge St. offices in Toronto, Lantos and Victor Loewy tried to convince Burns that Alliance could effectively represent his film abroad; in fact, it was setting up a new sales organization to do just that. That, says Burns, was the Alliance agenda: "to show me how serious they were about foreign sales." Despite his need for cash, Burns felt his bargaining position was strong. *Normal* had a script Alliance liked, a lead actor who was becoming a major star and, in Yves Simoneau, it had a director Alliance respected and had made money on in Quebec. So his agenda, says Burns, "was make me an offer. Make my head swim." Lantos asked what sort of number he had in mind for world rights. Two million dollars, Burns suggested, boldly.

Lantos says that Burns attempted to justify this demand by calling *Normal* "the best film that would be made anywhere in the universe" that year. "It's great to be enthusiastic about your own film," Lantos said to Burns. "But how do you know it's the best film in the universe? To know that, you'd have to know about all the other films that are being made." Burns' answer to that, according to Lantos, was, "no one has ever made a film of this quality. So I know it's the best film in the universe because nothing of this quality has ever been done before by any filmmaker, anywhere, in any country."

Burns then asked how many new staff people Alliance would be hiring to handle foreign sales. None, said Lantos; Victor Loewy would handle everything. "Victor knows Cannes," they said. "He knows how to get things done at Cannes." Burns did not dispute the claim. Victor Loewy is widely respected as one of the most astute buyers of cinema.

Then Burns asked what films would be included in the new sales catalogue. There were, at that point, only two—Sandy Wilson's *American Boyfriends* and Steve de Marco's *Thick as Thieves*. Burns was unimpressed. These were, in his view, unsalable products. Other films Alliance had produced were not in the catalogue; their foreign rights had been sold off to sub-distributors. "They were trying to make a big deal out of my not giving them foreign rights, and they weren't even taking their own. They wanted me to do something that they don't do themselves!" Burns had another reservation that he did not voice—the expensive lifestyle of Alliance executives. Of course, there was prudent motive to renting yachts at the Cannes Film Festival. It was an aspect of Alliance's overall marketing strategy—an accepted part of the Cannes subculture—and it worked. But if there were 20 films in the foreign sales catalogue, the costs of that lifestyle could be easily absorbed. If there were only two or three films, the expenses incurred in selling those films would be, from Burns' perspective, punitive.

Still, under the terms of his contracts with Telefilm, Burns was required to give a Canadian export agent, of his choosing, first and last matching rights. In other words, a Canadian company had to be given a chance to match or beat whatever deal Burns struck with Carol Myer, head of The Sales Company. The requirement was less rigorous than it seemed, because any producer who struck a good foreign rights agreement could easily find a Canadian exporter to say no. In this case, Burns had already persuaded Telefilm to waive the clause, because Myer's company, using estimates of foreign sales, had essentially guaranteed British Screen's investment in *Normal*—that is, her projections allowed British Screen to borrow the money needed for its Canadian investment. Burns did not tell Lantos about the waiver, "because politically, I knew he'd scream and yell." So Lantos, Burns concluded, was falsely assuming he could win foreign rights simply by matching The Sales Company's offer.

"So I'm saying, 'You're the new kids on the block. You have no sales force, you're not hiring anyone, you have two dogs in your catalogue,' and they're sitting back very self-righteous because 'Victor knows Cannes,' alright?" Still, Alliance had money, enough to put *Normal* into a break-even position even before it completed shooting. Even if it had offered only $500,000, Burns would likely have surrendered.

Alliance never offered $500,000. Instead, in a letter to Burns' executive producer Rafe Engel a few days later, the company effectively matched the offer Burns was getting from Carol Myer—no minimum guarantee and a commission of 12.5 percent on sales. The sole sweetener, according to

Burns, was that Alliance proposed to drop its commission to 7.5 percent on the first $750,000 of gross foreign income; after that level, Lantos would be entitled to recoup the five per cent he had cut, and take 12.5 percent on any additional revenues. Since "the most incompetent sales company in the world would have reached $750,000," Burns considered the Alliance offer essentially the same as The Sales Company's. On Burns' behalf, Engel rejected the offer, and shortly thereafter (with Telefilm's blessing) Burns signed with Carol Myer. The problem with Alliance, Burns maintains even now, was simply: "I had it. They wanted it, and they wanted it for nothing. And then they got hurt when they didn't get it for nothing."

"Hurt" may be something of an understatement. When Lantos learned of the agreement with The Sales Company, he threatened to enjoin the movie, blocking its release. Incensed, Burns called Lantos and engaged in a verbal slanging match, both men literally screaming at each other. "If you're going to sue," Burns told him, "don't talk about it. Sue me. Go ahead." Burns would later wish that he had been "a little more presidential, and just let it fade away. I genuinely regretted making the call because I couldn't really believe Robert would be this angry over something that was so completely above aboard. There weren't any grounds to sue."

Lantos disagrees. "We probably had sufficient legal grounds for action that we chose not to take, in deference to the other parties—Simoneau and Telefilm Canada. There were legal engagements made that would have stood up under examination, that gave us priority access or first rights of refusal. But in the process, we would have damaged the film itself and the other parties." His response to the situation, Lantos says, was not anger, but frustration, born of "watching someone simultaneously wrong the best interests of his own film and the best interests of Alliance." Launching low-budget Canadian films without stars "in the face of the weekly onslaught from the multinationals that produce Hollywood movies is an extraordinary challenge," he says. "It cannot be done simply by launching a film in Toronto or Montreal or Vancouver." The only chance of attracting sufficient attention to such movies is by "carefully strategizing a worldwide marketing approach," so that it stands out without having $20 million in advertising, like many Hollywood movies. "And you can't do proper positioning and launching if you can't control substantive and essentially worldwide rights." By control, Lantos means making the decisions about which festivals and marketplaces a film appears at, where it premieres, which journalists see it first, and of course the campaign of ads, posters and trailers that accompany it. "If you can't control that process," he says, "then you can't possibly control the destiny of the film."

That is the generic truth of Canadian films, which with rare exceptions are low-budget—a truth "the producer didn't understand and probably still doesn't," Lantos says. With the single event of failing to acquire international rights, Alliance lost control "of the proper professional launching" of *Normal*.

Economically, the Canadian market alone "made no sense to the film and no sense to Alliance. We believed we were buying the international rights and when that turned out to be not the case, we felt we had been double-crossed."

The OFDC's Louise Clark believes the right decision was to go with Carol Myer. "It's a great company with a great track record and they made a better offer." The choice, she acknowledges, ran against the strict grain of Telefilm policy, giving Canadians first right of refusal on foreign rights. But "policy and practicality don't always correspond." That, she says, is the problem with cultural subsidies.

Lantos demurs on that point. If Burns had been able to find a company willing to pay $2 million for world rights to the 'best film in the universe,' Alliance, for one, would not have stood in the way. But Burns was not getting a $2 million advance from The Sales Company. He was getting nothing. "It makes absolutely no sense," Lantos says. Why should millions of Canadian taxpayer dollars be invested in a film so that a British company can then have all the international rights without paying an advance? "All things being equal," he says, "the government has no business funding films where the benefits go to a foreign company." It was after this episode, Lantos says, that Alliance held discussions with Telefilm Canada to tighten the policy on international rights. Where federally funded Canadian features were concerned, Lantos argued, the economic benefits of that film should accrue to a Canadian distributor. Telefilm agreed. Henceforth, international rights would only be available to foreign firms if no Canadian company were interested, or if the foreign firm were offering an amount of money that no Canadian distributor could match.

Without Alliance's money, Burns was now forced to invoke the financial aid of his private consortium (including himself), which invested $425,000. These investors ranked first in the tier schedule for recoupment. Burns also agreed to defer $25,000 of his producer's fee. Indeed, in theory at least, the private investors stood to benefit handsomely. Because of Normal's pre-sales, the Ontario Film Investment Program agreed to reimburse more than half ($220,000) the total private investment after final cost reports were submitted. Their actual risk, therefore, was only $205,000. And because they were also entitled to the first $400,000 of the film's earnings, the private investors had a reasonable shot at making almost 50 percent on their money.

The final production financing picture was:

Telefilm:	$1.5 million
British equity:	$750,000
OFDC:	$725,000
Private investors:	$425,000
Alliance:	$350,000
Deferrals:	$25,000

BURNS VS. SIMONEAU In choosing Yves Simoneau, "a tough, self-assured, somewhat aggressive personality," the strong-willed Burns knew that he would have to struggle to keep control of his film. Burns compares the relationship between director and producer to the one that exists between a racing driver and his car. "If the driver wins the race, essentially he drove a brilliant race. But if he doesn't win, the car fucked up. And I'm the vehicle, okay?" Despite the tension that occasionally prevailed, Burns was grateful for Simoneau's presence. "You don't want to fight with somebody who's a lesser," he explains. "You worry then that if you have a bad idea, it'll end up on the screen. So Yves' toughness is his single best quality. It just took him a long, long time to realize that I was smarter and less egomaniacal than the person he expected."

As for Simoneau, he found Burns tenacious and hard-headed. To change his mind on any point, you "have to go through the armour cement block. Michael was very protective of his project. Anyone approaching was considered a potential enemy, unless he was declared as a friend. You know, 'you have a white flag; okay, now you can come into the fort and talk.' " That toughness also had its advantages, Simoneau concedes. For example, Burns originally negotiated the right to use 12 minutes of music by Prokofiev in the score; in the editing, Simoneau used 19 minutes. Burns went back to the rights holders and persuaded them to give him the extra time at no additional cost.

In the editing suite, Burns and Simoneau remained at loggerheads. Burns felt the opening of the film was "too slow, too dark, too downbeat. You don't find out you're in a comedy until four minutes into the film. That's not good. I mean, Yves did articulate a vision before I hired him. But it didn't involve a four-minute death sequence." Burns wanted to speed it up; Simoneau resisted. However difficult their relationship, Burns insists that it did not defeat either of them. And the final product, he believes, is "Yves Simoneau's movie as much as it could be, given that he didn't write it."

Only two full weeks into editing, Michael Burns put a very rough cut print of *Normal* in his trunk and drove at high speed to Montreal. The next day, January 23, 1990, was the last day on which the Cannes pre-selection committee would screen Canadian films for possible entry into the world's most prestigious film festival. The rough cut was two hours five minutes in length. Friends later told him it was the highest rated Canadian film of the year. The next day, it was shown in Toronto to officials of Telefilm, the OFDC, other agencies, Alliance executives, investors and various press people. Burns still remembers being embraced by Louise Clark after the screening—a silent confirmation that the film had been well received.

The only negative for Burns was the unwelcome presence of Helga Stephenson and Piers Handling, executive director and deputy director respectively of the Toronto Festival of Festivals. "This was a screening for people who had invested money in the film," Burns explains. "Helga and

Piers were consumers, and you just don't show consumers a half-done product." Burns therefore felt compelled to remove them. In the case of Handling, who was recuperating from a broken leg at the time, Burns actually "had to take his crutch and say, 'you're out.' " (Apparently, no lasting damage was done; Stephenson later made *Normal* the Opening Night Gala at the F of F.) After the rough-cut screenings, Burns returned to the editing room to work with Ronald Sanders, his editor. The film was largely finished by the end of February, but when the film was rejected for final selection in the Cannes competition, the final mix dragged on until May.

DANCING WITH THE AMERICANS To secure his U.S. distribution deal, Burns arranged back-to-back screenings in July 1990 for potential bidders in New York City and Los Angeles. His goal was to generate some heat for the film—if not genuine heat, at least the illusion of heat—that would push his U.S. advance to half a million dollars or more. That was the arbitrary floor Burns had set for the American rights. Anything less, in theory, would simply not be considered. Anything more would be a bonus. The day after the New York screening, Miramax president Harvey Weinstein summoned Burns to a 9 A.M. meeting.

"Let me ask you this," said Weinstein, getting straight to the point. "Would you take no advance and $250,000 guaranteed in prints and advertising?"

"No," Burns said. "I've already told you, Harvey, that the minimum price is half a million dollars."

"Alright," said Weinstein. "Would you take a $250,000 advance and no guarantee on prints and advertising?" Again, Burns said no.

"Okay," said Weinstein. "Give us a few minutes to discuss it." Weinstein and a few aides then left the room, and returned a few minutes later. "Michael, we have another offer for you," he said. "And you're going to like it. But we're not going to tell you what it is until tonight at seven o'clock"—Burns' pre-set deadine for concluding a deal. "We don't want you going around trying to improve on it."

There had also been a favourable response from Avenue Cinema, which would later use the number $250,000, but never make a formal bid. During the day, Burns called New Line's vice president of acquisitions, Tony Safford, in Los Angeles, indicating that Miramax and Avenue were seriously interested. Both, in Burns' view, were quality distributors—a fact that would, he believed, further whet New Line's interest in securing the rights to *Normal*.

By four o'clock Los Angeles time, Burns had a verbal offer of a $400,000 advance and $500,000 in prints and ads from Tony Safford. "I wanted $750,000 in P&A," he says. "I would have accepted six [$600,000], but I only managed to get him to five [$500,000]. That's as far as I could get." Burns told Safford he would call him back by the end of the working day in L.A.

He then called Harvey Weinstein, a frank attempt to push the still undisclosed Miramax offer higher. "Okay, Harvey," Burns said. "Here's the deal. I've got four hundred thousand from New Line, but I'd much rather work with you." There was, he says, "no untruth in that" statement, even though Miramax had a reputation for being extremely tough with producers and for cutting films ruthlessly. But by seven o'clock, Weinstein's position on *Normal* had suddenly changed. In the intervening hours, he told Burns, he had had the chance to look at the film's opening sequences again—something Burns says he technically had no right to do—and had decided that the editing changes would be more difficult than he originally thought. "I'm going to pass," Weinstein said. "I can't beat $400,000." Indeed, he was not even going to match it. (Burns later sent him a note saying, "you're the most charming guy that ever low-balled me.") So the bidding war Michael Burns had hoped to ignite had been settled even before it had properly begun. And he was left with New Line, a company he did not really want to do business with, a company that Alliance's Victor Loewy had warned him against.

The talks with New Line had actually been ongoing for several weeks, sometimes via long-distance telephone. New Line, as Loewy had advised, played hardball. They would issue a take-it-or-leave ultimatum, and give Burns five minutes to make up his mind. Eventually, Burns and New Line initialled a deal memo that would have given him $400,000 (US). Burns expected to announce the sale of the film's American distribution rights at the Toronto Festival of Festivals; New Line's president Bob Shea was scheduled to fly in for the occasion. Unfortunately, Burns was about to discover that he was negotiating with "people who were not in a position to make the kind of concessions they made." The central issues were the length of the film, 110 minutes at the Festival, and editing control. New Line wanted to cut it. Burns was agreeable, but insisted on retaining control of exactly what was eliminated. "If they wanted to do their own cut for pay–TV, for video, for whatever, that was okay," he says. "But for the theatrical version of the film, I refused. If they had paid for it, they get to control it. But they didn't pay for it." And while New Line's $400,000 advance was significant, it represented only an eighth of the film's budget, while buying them a territory expected to yield 40 percent of all of *Normal*'s revenues. Not atypically, Burns was prepared to stand his ground. An impasse resulted.

On the Tuesday following the Toronto opening of *Normal*, Burns received a fax from New Line's head office. The fax made two proposals to break the deadlock. The first was that Burns should edit the film according to his own judgement and that New Line would absorb the costs of the edit. If it liked the edit, the distribution deal would proceed as previously agreed. If it did not, the deal was null and void, and the costs of the edit would be a charge against whatever company later bought the rights.

That first proposal gave New Line an obvious escape route; the second virtually guaranteed that it would be taken. It wanted Burns to slice a full 15 minutes, delivering a film that played no longer than 95 minutes, including credits. That, says Burns, "seemed like an impossible thing," because it would have meant cutting into many of Simoneau's long shots, essentially destroying the integrity of the work. "Both conditions," Burns concluded, "were impossible to agree to." Later, Burns would contemplate suing New Line for damages, trying to recover the difference between its offer and the film's revenues in the United States. But he finally decided that legal costs would consume most of any potential gain.

Burns was convinced that New Line's enthusiasm for the film had waned in part as a result of a negative review in *Variety*. Despite pressure from Alliance, Burns had refused to hold press screenings for local critics before or during the festival. He had finally relented only after assurances from Alliance that no reviews would appear until the film's actual release date. The screenings would merely facilitate the writing of feature stories and contribute to the general promotional buzz. But in the middle of his negotiations with New Line, and on the eve of its Toronto Festival opening, Toronto *Star* entertainment writer Sid Adilman wrote a review in *Variety*, which suggested that *Normal* would be difficult and expensive to market successfully. "Adilman cheated," says Burns, still upset about the review three years after the fact.

With the collapse of the New Line bid, "everyone ran for the hills." Burns attempted to revive interest in the film at Avenue, at Orion Classics, at Castle Hill and even at Samuel Goldwyn, whose agent had walked out of the screening 20 minutes before the end. For a time, there was some hope that Orion would pick up the U.S. rights for no advance—an offer a now-desperate Burns would have embraced. Orion, he believed, at least would have guaranteed that the film would be seen and seriously reviewed. But even with no advance, Orion could not be persuaded to bid. Director Simoneau, watching developments from a distance, concluded that Burns was largely responsible for his own failure. "Michael was really acting like he was a big producer, that he had the hottest movie and one of these distributors had to have it. Which is the last thing you do with them. He just kept holding his position, and they just got disinterested. He lost the momentum because of his attitude."

Burns dismisses this critique. New Line, he points out, offered twice as much money as anybody else. He had no choice but to pursue it. And its wallet-waving, in turn, scared off other potential buyers. Admittedly, he might have simply accepted New Line's opening $400,000 offer, but that demanded that he relinquish "all rights, in perpetuity." It would have been like surrendering his first-born. "Due diligence required that we attempt to negotiate a good deal." If anything, he maintains, it was his lawyer, Rafe Engel's, skill in negotiating a contract that defended the film that led to New

Line's backhanded attempt to extricate itself. And when it walked, *Normal* quickly became perceived as damaged goods.

Now, Burns was deep into the autumn of 1990. Despite Alliance's objections, the film's Canadian theatrical release had been held, pending a U.S. sale. The Festival of Festivals and all the attendant hype it had generated was history. Burns felt like he was "really on hands and knees. It went from this hot film to where nobody . . . I mean, I was quite panicked, quite desperate." His choice of last resort in U.S. distribution was Four Seasons Entertainment, a small, "tin-can" operation run by his own uncle, Peter Meyers. Its bid, in December 1990: $110,000 (US) and $603,000 for prints and ads. Despite the family tie, Burns had "no better relationship" with Four Seasons than with anyone else. For Canada, the P&A budget would have been magnificent. For the U.S., it was paltry—about half of what Robert Lantos "calls the minimum, rock-bottom" needed to launch a low-budget film. With that budget, Four Seasons could commit only to a New York/Los Angeles opening platform, followed by a market-by-market roll-out, rather than one national simultaneous opening. "And they really had," says Burns, "no better idea of how to market it than Alliance did."

So for a territory generally worth 10 times Canada's value, Burns ultimately received an advance worth less than one-third of what Alliance had paid. "How logical is that," asks Lantos. "And what does it say about Alliance's commitment to the film, versus that of his uncle?" And if Burns by then had no other choice in the United States, "how did he become desperate? He had the option not to be."

THE CANADIAN CAMPAIGN   As the months of 1990 passed, the ugly wound of the Burns–Alliance relationship deepened. The agencies, reluctant middle men in the war of titanic egos, did what must have seemed like the reasonable thing; they ducked. "It wasn't something you wanted to get involved in," admits Louise Clark, "because it was out of control. The relationship was so bad, nothing good could come of it."

Alliance insisted it had done everything it possibly could have for *Normal*. It had spent $250,000 on prints and ads, had aired expensive television commercials, had rolled it out nationally across the country, opening simultaneously in 25 theatres. And still the film had died—instantly and everywhere except in Toronto's Carlton Theatre, where it played an astonishing 40 weeks and earned more than $255,000 in gross box office revenues. It owed its success there, they argued, to two factors: a largely homosexual audience, drawn by the film's gay subtext, and default—moviegoers often chose to see *Normal* after other films in the 10-theatre multiplex were sold out.

What went wrong? There was plenty of blame on both sides.

Alliance complained that Burns had thrown up roadblocks in the way of unit photography; the result: a poor selection of stills from which to create the film's one-sheet, the single image that often decides whether filmgoers will or won't see a particular movie. Burns had run a closed set; the result: lost publicity opportunities and coverage by local and foreign press. On one occasion, Alliance claims, Burns had gone apoplectic when Toronto *Star* entertainment reporter Rita Zekas tried to gain access to the set—on that day, the *Star*'s own parking lot. Burns had not made Robbie Coltrane available to the press for the film's opening; the result: there was no genuine star power attached to the features run in newspapers or on television. Burns had produced a film substantially different from the film as it appeared in script form; the result: a wonderful movie, but total confusion about how and to whom to market the film.

Burns, of course, is positively eager to answer these charges. He denies categorically that unit photographers were denied access to the set or that the materials produced were insufficient to create a compelling poster. Both the British and the Americans distributors used the same materials, he says, and both produced a superior poster. Of the Rita Zekas affair, he says, "it is entirely indicative of how lame Alliance is that they think not being in her column at least 10 months before the film is released is an impediment to the box office that they generated. Even if it happened right on the release date, it wouldn't matter. But it sure didn't matter a year earlier."

Given his tight, 30-day shooting schedule, Burns felt he had no choice but to close the set to journalists. Had he opened it for Rita Zekas, he would have been besieged by other reporters demanding equal access. He did not have the luxury of that time. "I'm not going to waste my time, and the patience of my director, my actors and my crew for idiocy. It was the Toronto *Star*, okay? I did $250,000 box office in Toronto, alright? The argument is idiotic, alright? The idea behind it is that you can make a shitty movie, but if you play the press correctly, you're going to be alright, okay? Trust me: that is not the case."

It is true, Burns acknowledges, that Robbie Coltrane was only contractually available for promotional purposes for two days. But it was Alliance that "chose to use those days during the Festival of Festivals." To the charge that the final cut was not the film that lay between the pages of the original screenplay, Burns agrees: something was lost in translation from script to celluloid. "In the way of fall-down comedy. I hoped it would come out a lot funnier." But he thinks Simoneau more than compensated visually, "and the film is, if anything, *better* delivered from script to movie." For Burns, "distribution is marketing, alright? If one company is better than another, it's because they figure out some line on a movie—how to make people interested, how to spread the word beyond the limited confines of a little audience that might be aware of the film."

Case in point: the first one-sheet that Alliance produced. The poster was an artist's rendering, not a photograph, of the two lead characters sitting on chairs, with newspapers in front of their faces, drinking coffee, in a framework house made of string; there is no such corresponding scene in the actual film. The sell line was: "The meeting of the ordinary and the extraordinary." Alliance went to artwork, says Mary-Pat Gleeson, the company's director of marketing, because still photographs from the shoot were generally inadequate, because those that might have been adequate were vetoed by Burns as too suggestive of a homosexual theme, and because in Quebec, such renderings had proven drawing power at the box office. Burns had seen five mock-ups of artwork posters in the fall, had hated the concept from the start, and had communicated his frank sentiments to Victor Loewy, saying, "This won't do at all," or words to that effect. All-artwork posters, he felt, represented the lowest common denominator kind of film, and he had never seen an upscale urban film promoted in that fashion.

Burns' venom is strictly professional. Alliance people, he insists, are "nice people. I like them personally. Tony Cianciotta [Alliance's vice president and general manager], is an extremely nice guy. But there's no savvy." On January 16, 1991, the night the Persian Gulf war started, Alliance scheduled a screening of *Normal* at Montreal's Place des Arts. It was there that Burns saw the finished rendering for the first time. More incensed than ever, he conveyed his displeasure to Pierre Des Roches, the man who sits astride the Telefilm colossus. A short time later, Alliance agreed to create a new poster for English Canada, based on the still photographs; the string house poster was used in Quebec, where the film bombed. But the poster used in English Canada, Burns says, was literally finished two days before the film's release and was up in bus shelters "maybe on the day it was released. Now, Alliance saw the rough cut more than a year before they actually released it. Did they discuss their marketing reservations with me? No. These are the people who used a one- word pull quote in the first newspaper ad. One word—'wacky.' *Wacky.*"

Burns' frustration mounted as the months passed. From House and Clarkson, he kept hearing that Lantos and Loewy, loved the film. But Burns was not concerned about their opinion. What he wanted to see was marketing strategy, "an all-out blitz of effort." He became increasingly obsessed. At Alliance, there was concern about the film's ambiguous ending. Various executives urged Burns to change it. Gleeson suggested it end at one point. Lantos suggested it end at another (with the characters singing music from the opera *Norma* in drag; Simoneau threatened to quit if that ending were imposed). Burns found the suggestions interesting, but "none of their business. We make the film; they distribute it. However it ends, you still have the problem of who to sell it to and how." For the producer, Alliance's complaints were "static around the edges of this giant, fantastic hole. Which is what did they do? Where were they marketing? What audience did they aim at? What message were they communicating?"

Indeed, his frustration was all the more acute because he regarded Lantos,

Loewy & Co. as the best in Canada at what they do. "These guys," Burns maintains, "live in an unreal world. [Telefilm's] Distribution Fund allows them to have a success like *Black Robe*. But *Black Robe* is an anomaly. It's not efficacious for the industry to work like that. At the moment, the government pays for the film, pays for the marketing. Maybe what it should do is buy some theatres and pay the audience to go."

To this complaint, Robert Lantos is not eager to respond. "I'm not interested in engaging in any public debate about anything that Michael Burns has to say on any subject whatsoever. Alliance," he points out, "has devoted its life to Canadian films and to finding an audience for them. Films stay in theatres because we fight for them."

A reluctant referee, Peter Katadotis, Telefilm's head of production and development, observes that good marketing "is not about money. It's knowing your target audiences and then buying judiciously in the appropriate market for that." Many Canadian films, he says, are better than American films that have done more box office in Canada. But Katadotis thinks many Canadian films are seriously flawed. Even *Normal*, which he "adored," had "some very serious script problems. So I'm not prepared to say that was a great film that got fucked. It was a film that was as good as a lot of American films in its class and should have done better." It would not have done even as well as it did, he concedes, without Burns' relentless hounding. "And more power to him." Katadotis views the rift between Alliance and Burns as almost natural. "Producers feel the distributors are not doing enough for their baby, and distributors figure they've got this crippled little ass thing, and what does he think I should do with this invalid? That's normal. But there's no question the films could be better marketed, much more clearly targetted," using, he adds pointedly, some of the skills perfected by Americans.

THE CANADIAN RELEASE Alliance believed that, with Simoneau's track record in Quebec, its decision to open the film in Montreal two weeks ahead of its opening in Toronto was the right one. The film would score some big grosses in a multi-screen release in Montreal, and everyone would take notice. Instead, the film dropped quickly out of sight in Quebec, generating only $27,000 at the box office ($18,000 in French-language cinemas, $9,000 in anglophone houses). In Toronto, it threatened to do the same, but was rescued by a stroke of serendipity—the introduction of the *Globe and Mail*'s starred mini-reviews. These began to appear about four weeks into *Normal*'s run—the *Globe* gave the film four stars—and the effect on the box office at the Carlton was almost instantly measurable. Slowly, the grosses began to build, propelled by what few Canadian films ever stay long enough in theatres to generate—favourable word-of-mouth. Burns also spent $7,500 of his own money, taking small ads ($211 apiece) in the weekend editions of the *Globe*. He remains convinced that what he helped achieved in Toronto might have been achieved elsewhere. But it was not. Across the country, *Normal* never parked long enough to develop word-of-mouth. In Saint John, the box office gross was $1,563; in Vancouver, it was $5,619; in Winnipeg, $3,045; in Calgary, $6,622. Its Canadian total: $291,000. These numbers, Alliance's Lantos agrees, were disappointing but not entirely suprising. "Anyone who thinks box-office receipts from Canadian films in Canada is a viable business," he says, "needs very immediate medical attention."

THE U.S. RELEASE T.C. Rice, the Four Seasons marketing vice president who conceived the film's U.S. campaign, still regards *Perfectly Normal* as one of the undiscovered classics of the cinema. Celluloid to Yves Simoneau, Rice says, is what paint was to Picasso. And in his hands, *Normal* became "a *noir* screwball comedy, an entirely new genre." Four Seasons tried to project that light-hearted, off-centre notion with its poster, which featured one image of the Renzo/Turner characters at the top and another image of them at the bottom—this time upside down. The sell line was: "Have you ever had a friend who could make you do anything? . . . Absolutely anything?"

Rice thought the film would "either go right through the roof in terms of box office" or fall on its face. He perceived the core audience for the film as being dedicated (rather than occasional) filmgoers, who would respond to an 'it's different, but you'll like it' campaign. Six separate trailers were made, and rotated through theatres in major markets. For Four Seasons as for Alliance, the limited availability of stars Coltrane and Riley hampered publicity, but a promotion company was hired to spread word-of-mouth about the film. No TV air time was purchased because, says Rice, for a film playing in a single theatre on an exclusive basis, TV advertising is wasted money. Such advertising may work for blockbuster films opening simultaneously in 800 cinemas. It will not work for small, specialty films.

Still, given enough time, he believes the campaign could have worked. What killed it were two harsh movie reviews, one by the *New York Times'* Vincent Canby, the other by the *Los Angeles Times'* Sheila Benson. These, says Rice, constituted "critical assassinations, a stake through our heart." Describing the film as "precious and slightly out of joint," Canby called it "ghastly." ("You can't get much worse than that," says Rice.) Benson said *Normal* was "crammed with so many engaging characters that it's like licking a soft-eyed cocker spaniel to mention that those dreams are a device that simply makes no sense." The *Village Voice* said Simoneau's "arty angled camera work succeeds only in making everyone look like they're standing on the decks of the *Edmund Fitzgerald*. The plot is as pedestrian as a crosswalk."

New York and Los Angeles being the foci of the film universe, these reviews made the task of finding exhibitors in other cities difficult. "It put us at the bottom of everyone's list," says Rice. "We got played because we knew who to bug and who to badger." Ultimately, the film played in some 50 U.S. markets, and performed well in Washington and Seattle. In New York, *Normal* lasted only two weeks, opening at the 68th St. Playhouse and moving to the Angelika film centre. "If you can't perform there," says Rice, "you can't perform anywhere in Manhattan." Those who saw the film loved it, Rice says. The problem, once again, was that *Normal* was never allowed to stay long enough to develop the momentum of word-of-mouth. In 1991, Four Season Entertainment became another casualty of the North American recession, and returned the film's pay– and free–TV U.S. rights to Michael Burns.

THE FOREIGN RELEASE In May 1990, Michael Burns bought a new summer suit, in anticipation of taking his film to the Cannes Film Festival. He never had the chance to wear it—at least not there. The Cannes selection committee rejected the film. The rejection was all the more stinging because the committee only saw the first very rough cut of the film, patched together in two weeks to meet the deadline. A further insult was that *The Reflecting Skin*, Phillip Ridley's first movie and *Normal*'s twin, was selected to open critics' week at Cannes—an inferior film in the judgement of most observers. As a result, The Sales Company generated far greater revenues for *Skin* than it did for *Normal*. And *Skin*'s Canadian investors recouped a greater percentage of their investment from it than they did from *Normal*.

At the time, Burns was disappointed, but not discouraged—owing principally to the early enthusiasm of U.S. distributors. Their reaction persuaded him that *Normal* was not exclusively an art film and had a commercial motor. In retrospect, he concedes that being at Cannes would have given the film an enormous boost. It needed some sizzle as well as the steak—to generate what was needed to sustain it at the box office. Myer and Burns did go to Milan for MIFED, Milan's annual film market; almost immediately Myer sold it to the Germans for $190,000 (US), bidding up from the original asking price of $150,000. Burns was thrilled, but Myer was cautious. "I don't want you to think this is an indication that we'll exceed our high estimates in every territory," she warned him. "I always do well with the Germans." The warning proved prophetic; thereafter, she barely made any more sales. Says Burns: "It was shocking how little interest there was in the movie."

In England, *Normal* had a two-week run in London's Prince Charles cinema, a theatre, according to Eugene Lipinski, that normally plays pornographic films, before moving into pay–TV and video. Less than two years after it was released, The Sales Company resigned the rights, which were then transferred to Majestic Films, international agents for *Dances with*

Wolves and *Driving Miss Daisy*. In his first year with Majestic, Burns grossed an additional $350,000 in free- and pay-TV sales.

It is *Normal*'s dismal international performances—in the U.S. and elsewhere—that Robert Lantos uses to refute Burns' critique of Alliance. "The film did better in Canada than in any other country of the world," he notes. Indeed, compared to the rest of the world, the film [in Canada] "actually had a spectacularly successful theatrical career. It actually did some box office, versus no box office. In the rest of the world, this film disappeared in a deep black hole. So here is a situation where a film failed colossally in every single market—except one," a market handled by Alliance. "So how could it be that the marketing department of Alliance is reponsible for the failure of the film, since it had nothing to do with its distribution in 99 percent of the world? I find it absurd."

FINAL TAKES Bill House: "*Normal* was a very hard film to market, because nobody figured out who would want to see this film or why. But you can't ask for any more care and fight, energy and passion, from a producer than we got from Burns. And I am personally prepared to put up with whatever down side there is to that. This was a real movie, in English, for everybody—not a $350,000 film. Very few of us had had a real movie to deal with. It was a seminal piece in all of our little lives here in these jobs.

Yves Simoneau: "*Perfectly Normal* is a very strange beast. It's quirky, peculiar, baroque. It's not obvious, and it's full of mistakes. But to be able to show something so abnormal so normally—that's the message for me. It doesn't matter who you are or what you think. You're as normal as the other person if you see yourself as normal."

Michael Burns: "The sad thing about independent films is that they never create any wake. You know what I mean? So you never get people to take any risks. It's a very odd business. And as a result you have very crazy people. Because it's ethereal. As much as they will tell you—studios, independents—that they know what they're doing, they don't. There are no sure things."

8
Adventures in Cultland

Tales From the Gimli Hospital

DIRECTOR:	Angela Heck
Guy Maddin	**DISTRIBUTOR:**
PRODUCER:	CINEPHILE (Canada);
Guy Maddin	CIRCLE FILMS (USA)
EXECUTIVE PRODUCER:	**RELEASE DATE:**
Greg Klymkiw	September 30, 1988
WRITER:	**RUNNING TIME:**
Guy Maddin	68 minutes
STORY CONSULTANT:	**BUDGET:**
George Toles	$22,000 (approx.)
DIRECTOR OF PHOTOGRAPHY:	
Guy Maddin	
SOUND:	
Guy Maddin	
EDITOR:	
Guy Maddin	
ACTORS:	
Kyle McCulloch,	
Michael Gottli,	

"A cult film, any cult film, is unlike any other. It's more than just an alternative film. It's more than just an art film. It is totally unlike anything else." — Greg Klymkiw, producer

"I do think that Guy's love for the transitional movies, the late silent films, is real. He always thinks that it's worth going back and doing each of those things that have somehow fallen into oblivion in film history. You can't pretend to cultivate taste in your styling that does not live within you. Both of us are past-haunted people, and film is this strange freezing and holding of things in some kind of time-space limbo. Guarded, in some sense, against destruction, but mutable, too. And so if you get these two things happening at once, even in a brand new film, you're getting very close to the ghost of the essence of what the medium is." — George Toles, story editor

SYNOPSIS Almost silent and essentially plotless, *Tales from the Gimli Hospital* is a bizarre, surreal fairy-tale about two strangers, Gunnar and Einar, who meet while quarantined during a smallpox epidemic in a small Manitoba fishing village. They befriend each other, but the relationship sours when the clinic's nurses begin to favour Gunnar over the hero, Einar. Later, they disclose to each other the darkest secrets of their past, leading to the film's absurd climax, in which the two men engage in a kind of buttock gouging.

ORIGINS In 1988, when producer Greg Klymkiw sent the script for Guy Maddin's second feature film, *Archangel*, to Telefilm Canada for evaluation and financing, the agency immediately called back with a complaint.

"This script is only 40 pages long," the official said, aghast. "We can't have this. Industry standards dictate that a script must be about one minute per page."

"Well fuck industry standards," said Klymkiw, a plain spoken individual, "do I have to remind you that Guy's screenplay for his first feature, *Tales from the Gimli Hospital*, was maybe eight pages long? And that it was just nominated for a Genie award for best original script? So don't give me this industry standards bullshit." As it happened, *Archangel* was subsequently funded by Telefilm.

As for *Gimli*, it originated in Guy Maddin's very lively and utterly unduplicatable imagination as a film loosely based on the history of the Icelandic settlement in the town of Gimli, on the shores of Lake Winnipeg, about an hour north of the provincial capital. In conception, the film was only a short feature, about 40-50 minutes. The working title was *Gimli Saga*. Maddin had no specific audience in mind. "I just wanted to sort of aggravate my relatives," he says. "I wanted to make a flash like Bunuel did. Basically, it was made for a few friends."

Then in his late twenties, Maddin had been working as an occasional house painter in Winnipeg and "sort of being a slacker," attending film classes at the University of Manitoba, "just killing time, napping a lot. Actually," he says, "I think I slept through most of my twenties." He had already made one short film, *The Dead Father*, and eventually hoped to make another.

Father was a 30-minute, semi-autobiographical account of a young man coming to terms with his father's death. George Toles, Maddin's film professor at the University of Manitoba, and later his sounding board, editor and partner in screenwriting, still regards *Father* as one of his strongest works, a "totally finished, astonishingly mature short film." Indeed, Toles was so impressed by it that he "determined to be of any use that I could in Guy's development." Among other things, Toles brought an intellectual grounding to Maddin's work and ranked among his biggest fans. Toles recalls that even before *Father*, Maddin had written a mock-heroic biography of former Boston Red Sox outfielder Carl Yaztrzemski. Maddin admired Yaztrzemski, but wanted, says Toles, "to do a film that took the clichés of baseball and bent them a bit."

All of these early scripts, he adds, were alike in not being structured in any linear way. "They were just bits and pieces of scenes that could be described in a wonderfully evocative sense. They didn't aspire to narrative wholeness." In fact, from Toles' perspective, Maddin's floating, unconnected suggestive set pieces seemed to imply "a terror of finishing, or rounding things off." He would later note this habit even in *Gimli*. Just when events seem to be reaching a dramatic climax, with the two men (Gunnar and Einar) grappling with each other, Maddin declares a de facto dream amnesty. The two characters shake hands. "And the movie," says Toles, "just strolls away from the consequences of its own nightmare." For Toles, who collaborated on the script for Maddin's 1992 film, *Careful*, *Gimli* fails to come to terms with

Guy Maddin, director, writer and editor, **Tales from the Gimli Hospital.**

the import of its various themes—jealousy, disease, necrophilia. "The ideas are all present," he says, "and they saturate the narrative. But they don't quite find each other and engage in a formally satisfying way."

Part of the problem, Maddin believes, is that his interest in the conventional, whether it be cinematic style or theme, is virtually non-existent. As a filmmaker, he is consciously and constantly flirting with the boundaries of tastelessness. "But whenever things threaten to become too explicit, I always try to figure out a tasteful euphemism, like Nabokov writing about pedophilia in *Lolita* without ever being obscene." In *Gimli*, however (and later in *Archangel*) the euphemism seems to reign. Toles—to whom Maddin read the script aloud before shooting—did try to eliminate some of the confusion, suggesting scenes that, according to the director, "were sharper, that people could latch onto, and understand. This isn't a euphemism. This is actually happening."

Maddin actually began work on the film in 1987 after hearing that the Winnipeg Film Group was awarding $20,000 to the best new film proposal; the deadline for applications was the next day. He quickly "scraped together some odd ideas into about three or four very sketchy pages" and submitted it. "It seems that my entire film career so far has been made up of eleventh-hour scramblings," says Maddin, who has raised the art of self-deprecation to a new level. Most of the ideas in the script were simply made up, drawn from his own Icelandic background (his maternal grandmother was one of Gimli's original settlers). Others were based on a book of Icelandic stories from the ninteenth century.

What impressed Maddin most about the Gimli settlers was the never-ending tragedy of their lives—it was so absurdly tragic that it became comic. Forced to leave Iceland because of famine and volcanic eruptions, they were victimized by typhus on the journey to North America; thousands died. A long trek from Kingston to Minneapolis to Grand Forks followed, the migrants arriving in the middle of a locust plague. Coming north by boat to Gimil, they landed just as winter was setting in, bringing ocean nets useless in the waters of Lake Winnipeg. The men immediately set off on a hunt for food, returning six weeks later completely empty-handed. The tiny community was living in buffalo tents, and had started raising families, when a smallpox epidemic struck. "It was actually beyond dreams," Maddin says, "sad and funny, the perfect combination of doom and gloom and stupidity." The poems and sagas were crudely written, but still effective as stories—a nice match, he says, for his own "filmmaking abilities at the time, which were crude at best."

He submitted his proposal to the WFG contest—and lost. He then sent it to the Manitoba Arts Council, asking for $9,000 in production funding. It granted him $20,000 instead, saying the review committee had examined his budget and decided that he would need more money. In fact, after the film was complete, Maddin approached the Winnipeg Film Group for another $2,000; it gave him the money, along with a little lecture about the merit of applying for funds *before* a film was made. So the final production financing for *Gimli* was officially $22,000—a preposterous figure that even Maddin is not sure is accurate. "It might have been a bit more," he concedes. "But it might have been a bit less. I'm terrible at business. I guess it could have been as high as $30,000, or as low as $14,000, because some of it was mixed up in my own food and rent. I'm not really sure."

PRODUCTION Given its budget and Maddin's lack of experience, it is not entirely surprising that the making of *Gimli* had a strange, improvisational feel to it. The film was shot over a one-year period in 1987 and early 1988. A few outdoor scenes were done in Gimli, and a few others on the perimeter highway en route, but most of the interior action was shot in a former beauty salon—the main floor of a house that belonged to Maddin's aunt Lil and above which, as a child, he had lived. The director asked his aunt's permission to convert the salon into a mini-studio, and built the set himself in one day, using lumber from a demolished garage down the street. "I'm thoroughly convinced you can shoot almost any movie just in your apartment or your backyard," Maddin explains. "I wasn't paying anyone, and I didn't like inconveniencing anyone, so I did as much of it as possible by myself."

The cast included a few professional actors, including Kyle McCullough, but several were rank amateurs, who were not being paid, who had no expectation that their work would ever be seen, much less become part of a cult classic, and who grew increasingly reluctant, as the months passed, to volunteer their time. Creatively, their work as actors also left something to be desired. Making a virtue of necessity, Maddin decided to simply cut most of the dialogue from the script. "There's nothing worse," says Toles, "than having actors who aren't up to the demands of the project."

Indeed, Guy Maddin's fascination with the silent film, and the transitional period between silent and talkie, "was in part expedient," says Toles. "He said, 'We'll concentrate on visuals at this point, and voice-over the sound track.' It was like we could control those elements." Maddin concedes the point. "I didn't want to fuss with a synchronized sound track," he says. "It's so much simpler making a movie without sound, creating the sound track later in a studio where it's really clean. You don't have to worry about excluding a take because the sound is bad."

The part-talkie itself was a technological quirk, a catching up period while Hollywood's studios readied film lots for sound stages. Most historians of the cinema have viewed these films and this period as somehow inadequate, but Maddin had always "watched these films with excitement, because it was like giving a painter another option, or a pitcher another pitch. It's the most flexible movie of all because it gives the director more on his palette. It's not for everybody," he concedes, "but I like it." So the decision to use voice only when necessary was not merely based on expedience. In too many movies, Maddin maintains, dialogue is just filler. With Hitchcock, he holds that dialogue should just serve as part of the sound track.

Even when it comes to non-vocal sound, Maddin feels no compunction about shattering dramatic illusion. His motto is, "just include sounds that are important." Hence, if the sound of a door closing were not relevant to a scene, it would not be heard on the sound track. "If someone is hanging herself off-screen, and you're not showing the hanging, then you have to hear the sound," he says. "But if I'm showing the hanging, the sound is overkill."

Although the *Gimli* story revolves around a smallpox epidemic, Maddin was reluctant to satirize its victims. "There's nothing funny about people disfigured with smallpox," he says. To find humour, he needed hopeless exaggeration, so he marked his characters with gruesome-looking cracks and bodily fissures. That, he says, "seemed more metaphorically useful anyway, having people cracking up all over the place." Certain scenes had no roots in reality, nor any specific thematic intent. For example, black-faced minstrels appear in *Gimli*, a dim likelihood in nineteenth-century rural Manitoba. But the minstrels are a good example of his willingness to swim against the prevailing currents of cinematic correctness. More specifically, the minstrels are an answer to the "nauseating liberal comfort about everything in the late 1980s. In the art house scene, everything was getting so formulaic," Maddin says. "Those platitudes were really starting to annoy me. And the black face was very common in the early days on cinema. I don't have an opinion on it. I just wanted to throw it in. Make of it what you will."

Matching the mood of the story, Maddin shot in black and white. He did his own camera work, his own lighting and occasionally stood in for actors. He knew absolutely nothing about operating a camera when he started, and had actually hired a cameraman to handle the entire shoot. "The guy showed up for the first day and then he didn't show up," Maddin recalls. "So I phoned him and he was in bed.

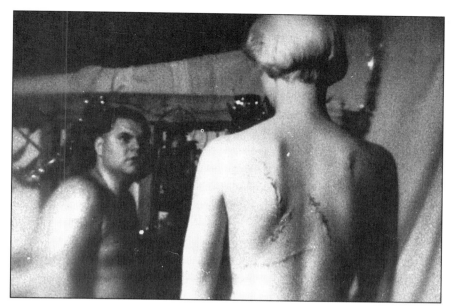

Maddin used haunting lighting and an intermittent sound track to capture the cinematic style of 'part–talkie' films from the early years of this century in his Canadian cult classic, **Tales from the Gimli Hospital.**

"What do you mean you're in bed?," Maddin said. "You're supposed to be here shooting." When the cameraman declined to rouse himself, Maddin went to his house. "C'mon," he said. "You've got to get up. You've got to help me make this movie." No luck; the cameraman refused to stir. Instead, from his bed, he explained the use of a 16MM Bolex. "It only took him about five minutes," Maddin says. "It was really quite simple. Then he just rolled over and went back to sleep. I never really saw him again. Actually, he's dead now."

Thus did Guy Maddin rather reluctantly plunge into the arcane world of cinematography; he will be forever grateful. "I don't think any of my films would have been the same if someone else had been the cameraman," he says. "So many of the things I've filmed I accidentally discovered just by looking through the viewfinder. I'd see the actors or the set framed in a certain way and I'd say, 'freeze,' and do the shot just like that. If someone else had been doing the camera work, I'd have been a little less involved, or had them do something more conventional. I strongly recommend that all beginner filmmakers use the camera themselves."

Lighting, too, was a process of trial-and-error discovery. "I quickly learned that the most visually pleasing pictures were the ones in which I use very high contrasts, with lots of dark shadows and slightly over-exposed faces," Maddin says. But he learned that lesson in part because no one had taught him to read a light meter. Shot in daylight, "the footage kept coming back reading 'night.' So I finally figured out how to make it look like a night, and then kept the script night." It was while he was shooting one of the film's few daytime scenes that Maddin discovered the utility of vaseline. With his camera set up on a freeway bridge, Hydro power lines intruded directly into the frame. "I put vaseline right on the lens, and the power cords just magically disappeared, although if you look carefully, they're just visible."

Having studied the cinematic work of the German expressionists, he knew he wanted *Gimli* to be a film "that felt like that, scored with music from scratchy records in the public domain." The score includes music from Jean Vigo's *Zero for Conduct*, an early Vess Ossman banjo solo and Icelandic folk tunes from his aunt Lil's collection of 78s. And knowing that film sets were always "mind-numbingly and nauseatingly boring," Maddin tried to arrange his shoot so that his unpaid actors could come in, do the scene immediately, and leave. "I tried to storyboard scenes so that I could isolate people one shot at a time, like [Sergei] Eisenstein does. I constructed as much of the movie as possible in close-ups. I'd set the light—in most cases, it's one light—exactly the distance from where I knew the actor would be when he showed up, measuring it with a tape and a meter reading. Then I would turn off the light and wait for the actor to arrive." If he arrived, and was not ready to begin, Maddin and the actor would "watch TV and have a couple of beers for half an hour, then go down and do the shots." Eventually, he finished shooting, edited it into a rough cut, and invited Greg Klymkiw to come see it.

POST-PRODUCTION In his characteristic army fatigues, black boots and black t-shirt, the bear-like form of the chain-smoking, mustachioed Greg Klymkiw is reminiscent of some ex-U.S. marine drill sergeant who has spent too many weekends in Bangkok. But beneath the extra layers of tissue that he carries lurks an astute student of the cinema, a master of the economics of filmmaking and of marketing. His connection with Maddin actually dates back to childhood: Maddin's father was manager of the Winnipeg Maroons, Canada's national hockey team in 1963; Klymkiw's father played goalie for the same team.

The two sons—neither of whom was ever likely to be scouted by the Winnipeg Jets—first met at the University of Manitoba. There, they collaborated on what Klymkiw calls some "rather sophomoric comedy review," roomed briefly together, and studied film in courses taught by George Toles. Maddin, an economics student, earned his degree, and worked briefly in a bank before realizing that he neither knew nor cared to know anything about banking. In fact, he has a near-total aversion to anything financial, including the filling out of grant application forms. His informal understanding with Klymkiw is that the latter handles "all the business end of things, the distribution, the schmoozing and leaves me to make the movies."

It was Klymkiw, Toles insists, who first recognized the film's cult potential and who pushed it aggressively. "Guy has no interest in business and no ability to beat the drum and market his own stuff. It was a very fortuitous collaboration." Every young filmmaker, he adds, would do well to find a Greg Klymkiw-like character with complementary skills. After viewing the rough cut, Klymkiw became the film's executive producer. Technically, there was no producer; *Gimli's* credits (extended to ridiculous proportions to help stretch the film to something approaching feature length) say that it was produced by "Snyder." Snyder, it turns out, was Steven W. Snyder, another professor of film at the University of Manitoba and a friend of the Winnipeg film community and of Maddin. The credit is largely a thank you for Snyder's inspirational role, and for meals and pocket money given to Maddin during his days as a struggling young filmmaker. "He let me audit his film courses without paying tuition," Maddin explains, "and he'd buy me dinners at the Salisbury House. One night I said, 'if you buy me two cheese nips [the restaurant's name for cheeseburgers], I'll make you the producer.' So he did. Two cheese nips and two chocolate donuts." Klymkiw was irritated by Maddin's cavalier allocation of credits, on the grounds that if *Gimli* later won a Genie award, Snyder, the mythical producer, would get to claim it.

Snyder also appeared briefly in the film, as did Maddin's daughter, his uncle and his niece. Klymkiw, too, had originally intended to act in the film, in the role of Gunnar. But in the summer of 1987, when Maddin started shooting, Klymkiw was otherwise engaged, running his own film booking agency. By the time the film was complete, Klymkiw had sold the agency and was working as director of marketing at the Winnipeg Film Group. And one of his mandates, as he saw it, was to take "these films that people had been secretly making for so many years and get them out there."

As a finished product, *Gimli* seems to many viewers completely unfinished, technically and thematically. In the rough-cut stage, it had all of those liabilities and more, among them, no sound track whatsoever. Still, it was at that stage, Klymkiw says, that he concluded "that Guy had something that wasn't the sort of thing you just sit on a shelf. I was convinced that we had something here that no one had seen before, and maybe even never wanted to see before. But by golly, we were going to find a way to ram it down their throats."

At that point, Klymkiw encouraged Maddin to shoot more film, and pump up the movie to feature length. And he set about to find money for marketing, ultimately raising about $40,000 from the Winnipeg Film Group, where Klymkiw was already employed ("that certainly made it a lot easier"), the Canada Council and CIDO, Manitoba's Cultural Industries Development Office. Because the latter had not invested in the actual production, they were sympathetic to Klymkiw's pitch for marketing support.

DISTRIBUTION The world premiere of *Gimli*, appropriately enough, was held at the Winnipeg Film Group Cinematheque in April 1988. In keeping with their fondness for satirizing cinematic convention, Klymkiw spent $5,000 on the event, renting Hollywood-style film lights and a few acres of food and liquor. The tactic paid off. The pre-screening promotional hoopla reached the citizens of Gimli; after the premiere, they were, in Klymkiw's words, "completely and totally and utterly outraged," claiming that the film had distorted the history of the town. Gimli's mayor complained that *Gimli* portrayed the people as "some sort of barbarians." The reaction caught virtually everyone by surprise. Until that time, Maddin had made only *The Dead Father*, and "the only people who had seen it," Klymkiw says, "were Guy's friends and the 10 people who showed up at its Festival of Festivals screening in Toronto in 1985. So I don't think he was ever concerned about offending anyone. And then all of a sudden, there was this controversy with the Gimli-ites being up in arms over the film." The ensuing outcry generated far more publicity than Klymkiw could ever have planned.

The buzz was everywhere, perhaps, but in Winnipeg. Even the non-Icelandic community had trouble understanding a half-silent film, with what seemed to be poor sound quality and bad lighting. Toles compares the Winnipeg premiere to visiting a morgue. People who approached Maddin afterwards made either openly disparaging remarks or very backhanded compliments. Says Toles: "Guy has been stewing about that ever since."

Since even the most determined optimist would never have believed in the possibility of a theatrical life, the initial marketing strategy for *Gimli* was always heavily dependent on film festivals. Klymkiw had early on filed applications to appear in all three major Canadian festivals—Montreal, Toronto and Vancouver. He later added Halifax. He was pushing it as a real—as opposed to an experimental—film, "with a sort of cult flavour to it." The press kit for the film was full of deliberate lies—"wonderful lies. Lies done in the old Hollywood way, so that anyone reading it would know they were lies."

For example, in describing the history of the film, Klymkiw wrote, "Gimli architects furnished the designs. Gimli engineers, Gimli electricians, Gimli carpenters, Gimli interior decorators, Gimli artists and other Gimli specialists, laid out and constructed the vast settings. Gimli costumers designed the gowns. And with the exception of Mr. Guy Maddin, who wrote the story, directed the production, photographed almost everything you see on the big screen, edited everything, and played the supporting role of the Pioneer Doctor, nearly all of the other players in this photo-play were Gimli-born." The press kit also invented an elaborate mythical history for the Klymkiw-Maddin production company, Extra Large Productions, calling it a 78-year-old film company based in Lockport, Manitoba, that once had a "virtual stranglehold on the Canadian film market and was threatening Hollywood's monopoly in the American midwest."

The film festival approach, Klymkiw hoped, would generate enough publicity and word-of-mouth to make a cult film classic, appealing to the kind of audiences that turn up at Midnight Madness screenings in repertory houses across the continent. Before he became involved in distribution, Klymkiw had run a small rep house called Festival Cinema in Winnipeg and, in the late 1970s, had scored a modest success screening David Lynch's cult classic, *Eraserhead*. The first time he screened it, *Eraserhead* had died terribly. But Klymkiw "believed in it, and just kept pumping it and playing it and pushing it." It ended up playing for a full year, every Friday and Saturday midnight, grossing between $300–500 a show, "which for Winnipeg is very, very, very, good. I always thought that *Gimli* might have it in it to go that route."

But creating a cult classic, and the aura that surrounds it, is no small marketing challenge. The traditional hype machine so necessary in promoting conventional films is quite useless when it comes to cult films. As Klymkiw told one interviewer, "It either is [a cult film] or it isn't. You open it quietly, softly, and hopefully, it garners the word-of-mouth that makes it a hit." After its Winnipeg premiere, Klymkiw sent the print to the Montreal festival organizers, who quickly confirmed it for August. But he had more difficulty with Toronto's Festival of Festivals, which declined, for a long period, to return his calls. Seated on the three-person festival selection committee was Geoff Pevere, then program coordinator for the festival's Perspective Canada series. Pevere was an unqualified fan of the film, but he was encountering serious problems persuading the other two members of his committee to recognize its artistic merit.

One day, Klymkiw recollects, he received an embarrassed call from Pevere. "Geoff said, 'I think I know the answer to this question, but I've been asked by other people to ask you about the quality of the film's sound.'" (Pevere does not remember making that call, but concedes that he might have been asked to make it.) At that point, Klymkiw had to explain that what appeared to be amateurish sound had in fact been designed exactly that way. "Every hiss, snap, crackle and pop was there for a reason," Klymkiw notes. "The film was not only attempting to recreate the whole era of the part-talkie. It was attempting to recreate a film that might have been made in that period, as if an old nitrate print had been discovered in some projectionist's barn 45 years later."

Finally, after further delay, Pevere phoned with the bad news: the selection committee had voted against accepting *Gimli*. Pevere now says that the film was victimized by the selection process itself, which requires groups of people to sit together for three weeks and make decisions about "an unholy number of films. That process hurt Guy's film." However, as Pevere points out, Maddin has since used the rejection to enormous advantage, making it part of his burgeoning mythology. The Festival of Festivals did not seem too embarrassed by what some observers would call the myopia of its own selection committee. In promoting Maddin's next feature, *Archangel*, it brazenly referred to *Gimli* as "one of Canada's biggest cult hits ever."

Klymkiw's immediate reaction to Toronto's no was "My God, I've got all this money, and I've budgeted to take this film to this festival and I'm not officially in the festival." Undeterred, he decided to "go anyway," and do what he could to hustle the film without having it actually screened there. First, however, there was Montreal.

Andre Bennett saw *Gimli* for the first time at its official screening at the Montreal Film Festival in August 1988. He walked into the film never having heard of Guy Maddin. "I was just totally mesmerized, especially by the opening. It was amazing. It just haunted me." Almost immediately, Bennett approached Klymkiw and Maddin to acquire Canadian rights for his aptly-named (and now defunct) film distribution company, Cinephile, offering the princely sum of $5,000. The deal also made Bennett a sales agent for the film internationally, entitled to commissions ranging from 25–30 percent. One other Canadian company was interested in the rights, and was offering more money. But Klymkiw was sold on Bennett himself—on his enthusiasm for Maddin's work and on his obvious love for the art of filmmaking. "I just felt that I could trust him," Klymkiw says. "But I actually remember looking into Andre, in the credentials sense. We called Atom Egoyan, director of *Family Viewing* and *The Adjuster*, and told him we were thinking of signing with Andre and asked him for his opinion; Cinephile was also distributing Egoyan's work. And Atom said, 'Well, Andre's a great guy. Why not?' " In fact, Bennett was so enamoured of Maddin's work that he became executive producer of his next two films, *Archangel* and *Careful*.

In Montreal, Klymkiw immediately approached Jacqueline Brody, a press attache for Canadian films. She had already seen *Gimli* and loved it, and laid out a plan to promote it at the festival. One of Brody's ideas was to organize a panel discussion on the topic of cinema versus television, inviting major names to appear. Klymkiw was unimpressed.

"How will such an event promote this film?" he asked her.

"Well, number one, my dear," Brody said, "the moderator is Roger Ebert, the Chicago film critic, and he will guarantee a turnout." Number two was a piece of advice Klymkiw "will never forget and always uses. Whenever you're involved in a panel discussion, always discuss the topic at hand in the context of the film you're promoting, and mention the title as many times as you can." Klymkiw also used "the taxpayer's money" to print t-shirts with the distinctive *Gimli* poster (green and purple on black), stuffed them in media boxes and handed them out at the screening of the film preceding his own. And "at the last minute," he called the Canada Council and asked for money to fly Maddin to Montreal to do press interviews. It agreed; Brody arranged the interviews.

At the time, five English-language repertory cinemas in Montreal had recently closed. A group of exhibitors then decided to open a new, 1,000-seat rep house, the Rialto, which had previously been a Greek-language cinema. Hearing the positive buzz about *Gimli*, the new owners approached Klymkiw, offering to make the film their opening feature. The film opened September 30, 1988 and played for a week.

Moving on to Toronto, where he had been officially spurned, Klymkiw decided to hold underground screenings for the press and other industry types. He stuffed announcements and press kits in the Festival of Festival's press boxes, and used the festival's own screening rooms as well. Klymkiw remembers the distinguished Boston film critic Gerald Peary approaching him one day in the hall at Sutton Place, the official festival hotel, and asking why he could not find *Gimli* listed in the program. Klymkiw explained that the film had been rejected. Peary was outraged. It was, in his view, the best Canadian film he had seen that year. Peary then helped promote attendance by his fellow critics at Klymkiw's informal screenings. Peary also introduced the producer to David Chute, a reviewer for the highly regarded *Film Comment*. Chute would later write that *Gimli*, while weak on plot, was "exactly the kind of audacious filmmaking Canada needs if it is ever to spruce up its dour, stiff, humanistic, NFB image."

Klymkiw then took the film to the Vancouver International Film Festival, whose audiences seemed even more receptive to Maddin's work than did filmgoers in the east. The question then was how to give the film international exposure. Through Telefilm's Festivals Bureau in Montreal, organizers of the Mannheim Festival in Germany had seen the movie and invited it to attend. Klymkiw regarded the invitation as a coup, because many young filmmakers had premiered their work at Mannheim. The only decision was whether to reject Mannheim, in the hope of winning an invitation to the even more prestigious Berlin Film Festival in February 1989. Klymkiw decided to take the bird-in-the-hand option, reckoning that he could always screen *Gimli* at the Market Place in Berlin, a forum for films not officially part of the festival.

Gimli was exhibited at Mannheim in the fall of 1988, and again at Berlin in February. It was there that Ben Barenholtz, head of New York-based distributor, Circle Films, saw the film for the first time. Barenholtz, now a producer, thought it had something of the same cult potential as *Eraserhead*, which he had distributed a decade earlier. In fact, as he told Elliott Stein of the *Village Voice*, not since *Eraserhead* had he "come across anything so original." Barenholtz had experienced the same early problems with the Lynch film in the United States as Klymkiw had in Winnipeg. But he had exactly the same faith in its ability to generate subterranean word-of-mouth. The first time Barenholtz screened *Eraserhead*, there were 25 people in the theatre. The second night there were 26. "Don't worry," he told director Lynch. "It's working." The film eventually took two years to build its audience in New York.

"Cult films," Barenholtz explains, "can't be deliberately made. They're created by the audience. You can only create the environment for something like that to thrive." What drew him to *Gimli* was the "sensibility, the weird sense of humour. This is a filmmaker who's going to be doing some important work," he says, comparing Maddin's films to the Coen Brothers' early work, *Blood Simple*, and to John Sayles' *Return of the Secaucus Seven*. Barenholtz then reached a joint-distribution agreement with André Bennett to share costs and distribute the film in U.S. markets.

Three months after Berlin, Barenholtz and Bennett took the movie to Cannes. Although not officially part of the festival, they rented a theatre for a midnight screening, hired people in sandwich boards to give out free passes, invited a few key people to attend and played to a packed audience. Quite deliberately, no buyers were invited—either at Berlin or at Cannes. The Berlin screening was for media people only. At Cannes, it was a general audience. The only objective was to stimulate word-of-mouth, so that, as Bennett says, "buyers start saying to themselves, 'when am I going to see this film?'"

After Cannes, Barenholtz screened *Gimli* at the San Francisco International Film Festival, its American premiere. Klymkiw remembers an almost full house and an appreciative audience laughing all the way through. It was after that, he says, that both he and Maddin felt that "no matter what kind of money we made or didn't make on the film, it didn't matter. There was no stopping us. After this film, by virtue of what it was, and how it was affecting people, both critically and from audiences, we just felt we could keep going. And we did." It was also in San Francisco that Barenholtz met Maddin for the first time.

"Tell me something, son," Barenholtz said. "You're not all there, are you?"

"I guess not," said Maddin.

After San Francisco, *Gimli* began a round of midnight madness showings in most of the major U.S. cities, including New York, Chicago, Philadelphia, Seattle, Washington and Los Angeles. The New York opening was held on July 7, 1989 at The Quad, an art house in Greenwich Village run, at the time, by the enterprising Barenholtz. He hosted a pre-opening party at the Mars Club—the dress code was "hospital-chic." The film did its best business in New York—steady, if not phenomenal—grossing perhaps $400–500 per show over a period of weeks (one showing each night). Barenholtz actively courted free publicity, arranging long-distance interviews for Maddin (then in Winnipeg shooting *Archangel*) with members of the New York media. He was able to interest the media, Klymkiw explains, because "Ben is Ben. Ben is a God. If Ben said something is good, people pay attention, you know?"

In Canada, Bennett arranged regular first-run screenings in repertory houses across the country, then shifted to the midnight madness format. Box office was always "very, very modest," the film barely covering its exhibition costs. Trying to explain why it failed to generate better box office revenues, Bennett contends that *Gimli* was "ahead of its time in North America." That problem was compounded by the difficulty of finding an exhibitor who would take the film and let it run and "not worry about how many people are going to be in there," an attitude that may have more in common with altruism than with exhibition, and one not widely shared in exhibiting circles. Barenholtz had slightly more success with the same strategy in the U.S., largely, says Bennett, because there were 10 times as many possible venues. Outside of North America, Gimli played to excellent reviews and "okay" box office in Tokyo in 1991, double-billed with Maddin's *Archangel*. It played to less enthusiastic reviews in Germany.

By May 1992, the film had earned revenues in Canada of $116,000. This sum included about $9,700 from theatrical sources, about $2,400 from non-theatrical and $105,000 from free and pay–TV. (A black and white film is almost never shown in prime time in pay–TV; black and white is reserved for midnight to 4 A.M., a time slot, says Klymkiw, that can "justify giving you the lowest possible license fees.") Against that, Cinephile recorded expenses of slightly more than $29,000, most of it for prints, lab work and advertising. *Gimli*'s foreign revenues amounted to $22,380 by mid-1992, all of it in minimum guarantees. Cinephile's share of that sum was $5,300. Expenses incurred in foreign distribution were $22,513; again, prints ($12,900) and advertising materials ($7,000) constituted the lion's share of costs. By that date, says Klymkiw, nothing had been recouped beyond the original investment, but "we aren't worried about it. The film will have a very long shelf life."

FINAL TAKES Greg Klymkiw: "You couldn't do *Gimli* for $22,000 now. It would be $80,000. In many ways we were lucky to be part of that golden period. We made the films because we loved them. It wasn't our livelihood. If the picture was a hit in some way, gee, that would be nice. If it wasn't, no skin off our back. It's harder now. But I think it's easier for an independent filmmaker in Regina or Winnipeg than it is in Toronto or Vancouver. I mean, the unions are so much more powerful. Here, we just tell our actors, do the film [without scale]. If you get fined, we'll pay the fines. It's cheaper than dealing with ACTRA."

Guy Maddin: "If I were doing it over again, I would definitely have come up with a couple of plot twists. I would give the script another draft. It's thin on plot. And there's that pace, you know. It's a slow movie. But I'm proud of many things in it. The thing almost exceeded my wildest dreams. I say almost because every filmmaker, bad or good, dreams of winning an award for their film and then at other times you realize it's a piece of crap. But I think what happened did exceed the farthest the pendulum swings to the successful side."

9

Manoeuvring Through Icebergs

Deadly Currents

DIRECTOR:	**DISTRIBUTOR:**
Simcha Jacobovici	Cineplex–Odeon
PRODUCERS:	(Canada); Alliance
Simcha Jacobovici,	Releasing (USA)
Elliott Halpern,	**RELEASE DATE:**
Ric Esther Bienstock	October 4, 1991
EXECUTIVE PRODUCERS:	**RUNNING TIME:**
David Green, Jeff	114 minutes
Sackman, Robert	**BUDGET:**
Topol	$1,101,636
ASSOCIATE PRODUCER:	
Jane Logan	
CINEMATOGRAPHY:	
Mark Mackay	
SOUND:	
Chaim Gilad	
EDITOR:	
Steve Weslak	

"To me, this wasn't just a film. My guts were up on the screen. And that's exactly the film I wanted to make." — Simcha Jacobovici, director

SYNOPSIS *Deadly Currents* nearly manages the impossible, explaining ancient Israeli and Arab claims as if both were equally persuasive and, rare for a political documentary, doing it without narration. Beautifully photographed, complete with dramatic crane shots seldom used in documentaries, the film consistently surprises, turning stereotypes and prejudices on their ears. Jews tended to find it pro-Arab in its sympathies; Arabs viewed it as pro-Israeli—a tribute to its evenhandedness, and further evidence, if it were needed, of the unbridgeable gulf that separates the two sides in the labyrinth of Middle Eastern politics.

ORIGINS In the summer of 1988, a young Torontonian named David Green approached Simcha Jacobovici about a film he wanted to make. The film was about the *Intifada*, the Palestinian uprising on Israel's West Bank and in the Gaza strip. Green, an orthodox Jew, was concerned that superficial media coverage of the event was distorting reality; photographs of soldiers confronting children, Green believed, or fleeting images of rioting youths throwing Molotov cocktails on the evening news, could provide no serious context for understanding either the forces shaping the rebellion or the reaction of Israeli authorities. Initially, Green only wanted to hire Jacobovici to write a treatment; he had privately raised $5,000 for that purpose.

A native Israeli, Jacobovici had never actually considered making a film about the Middle East. It would, he thought, be like making a film about his own parents' divorce; "it would tear a strip off you." But Green could hardly have made a better choice. Although it had been many years since he had lived in Israel, Jacobovici, then 35, had actually spent the first nine years of his life in Petah Tikvah, a suburb of Tel Aviv. Later, after his parents, Holocaust survivors, emigrated to Canada, he took a bachelor of arts degree at McGill University, returned to Israel to spend a year in the Israeli army, and came back to Canada to take his masters degree in international relations at the University of Toronto. He had studied Israeli politics, written about it, lectured on it. He knew the culture, the language and the incendiary demographics of the state of Israel as well as anyone. For him, Israel was not simply a subject; it was a passion.

The two men held a series of preliminary discussions about the proposal. "I wanted to make sure he didn't have some kind of propaganda agenda," Jacobovici says. "And I wanted him to know that the film I might make might not be the one he'd be happy with." Green insisted that he was not interested in propaganda, but in the truth—believing that one should never fear the truth. Perhaps, Jacobovici agreed; but the truth, honestly told, can hurt. And of course, there are always differing perceptions of truth—based on the prism through which it is observed. In the case of Israel, he noted, there were many prisms—human rights, morality, geopolitics, religion. "A lot of people look at reality through one cylinder or another," he says, "and have no clutch mechanism to shift gears." Pro-Palestinians would always insist on the creation of a Palestinian state, arguing from a human rights point of view. But for Israelis, such a state would have major geopolitical ramifications—an armed and hostile entity against which almost any human-rights abuse seemed justifiable. The documentary's title is drawn from those opposing currents.

His partners in Associated Producers, Elliott Halpern and Ric Bienstock, regarded Jacobovici's early conversations with David Green as the indulgence of an intellectual hobby. Certainly, no one in July 1988, when Jacobovici first sat down to write the treatment, believed the proposal would ever be turned into a feature documentary film. Like most Canadian filmmakers, he had other projects in development; like most, he needed money. He would write the treatment, shake hands with Green, pay off some nagging creditors, and go on to other things. Or so they thought. But the more he delved into the subject, the more persuaded Jacobovici became that the material not only lent itself to a powerful film—he wanted to make it. He wrote the treatment, a 20-page document, in a single day, from the start envisaging a full-blown theatrical release.

"David was doing a film specifically about the *Intifada*," Jacobovici says of his treatment. "I saw the *Intifada* as a passing phenomenon, and wanted to use it to examine the broader Arab-Israeli conflict." As in the finished film,

Simcha Jacobovici, co-producer and director, **Deadly Currents.**

the opening footage would be black and white, and grainy. Different characters—soldier, settler, revolutionary, mother— would be caught in the camera's lens, but the viewer would not know who they were. They would have no clear identity. That's what the film would do; switching to colour, it would "pull the people out and bring them to life." He intended to return to the same faces, the same black and white footage used at the beginning, at the end, to provide a sense of dramatic closure. "I saw it so clearly. Suddenly, there would be recognition that these people fighting each other were people. The issue might still be black and white, but it would have a human dimension."

Even with the treatment, says Elliott Halpern, the project did not seem quite real until it went to Cineplex–Odeon. From his work on his 1984 documentary on Ethiopian Jewry, *Falasha: Exile of the Black Jews*, Jacobovici had become acquainted with several senior Cineplex executives, including Jeff Sackman and Robert Topol, and had sent them the treatment. Both reacted positively, but noncommittally; after all, making esoteric documentary films about the byzantine politics of the Middle East was not exactly a corporate priority. To flash the green light, Sackman and Topol knew they would need the approval of then Cineplex CEO Garth Drabinsky.

As it happened, Drabinsky was about to fly overseas to be honoured by a Jewish fundraising organization and to deliver an address. More as an executive summary on Arab–Israeli relations than as anything else, Topol decided to give him Jacobovici's treatment to read en route. Apparently, he was impressed. Some of its political analysis later made its way into Drabinsky's speech. More importantly, when he returned to Toronto, Drabinsky instructed Topol to put up $300,000 as an advance—this was, it must be remembered, still the spend-free 1980s—and to buy world rights. It was only then, Halpern says, that the film began to acquire a life of its own. "Then you could see what happens when someone with a lot of power really wants to get something done." Indeed, it was Cineplex's improbable support that provided the fuel needed to propel *Deadly* out of the overpopulated land of In Development into the far more rarified region of In Production. When the project later ran into a series of regulatory problems at Telefilm Canada, it was Cineplex that found a way to break the logjam and sustain the momentum. And when the film needed more funds to finance a second-unit shoot, it was Cineplex that—uncharacteristically for distributors—invested more money.

The rationale for Cineplex's interest could be summed up in one word: Garth. To be sure, there were legitimate reasons for believing that *Deadly* had a decent shot at finding a mainstream audience. The topic itself was hot, and getting hotter. Cineplex had a strong theatrical distribution network in the United States. It could package the film for foreign TV sales with other Cineplex products, more theatrical films like *The Grifters* and *Mr. and Mrs. Bridge*. The whole concept, Sackman says, "was extremely sound. We had Academy Awards envisaged." But without Drabinksy's approval, Cineplex would never have been involved. "The subject matter," Sackman concedes, "was very close to Garth's heart."

Given the distributor's enthusiasm, the producers initially believed that they could negotiate the Cineplex advance—if not to raise the dollar amount, then at least to keep a territory or two for themselves, for later sale.

"This is a very draconian deal," Halpern, a lawyer turned producer/screen-writer, told Topol and Sackman. "It gives you the world, forever, but it doesn't leave anything for us."

"That's right," Topol replied. "Get real, guys. This is a documentary film, not *Star Wars*. We're prepared to put a lot of money into your film. But this is the deal—the world, in perpetuity. Take it or leave it."

At which point, laughs Halpern, "we took off our little negotiating hats and we signed."

FINANCING With a signed distribution agreement in its pocket, commit-ting Cineplex to a five- and three-city release in the United States and Canada respectively, Associated Producers immediately filed applications for production financing with Telefim Canada and the Ontario Film Development Corp. At the latter, there was appreciation for the cinematic quality of Jacobovici's treatment, but initial concern about whether the proposal as drafted—to track the lives of six participants, Arab and Jew, in an actual riot—was credible and doable. "We challenged Simcha on that point," recalls Louise Clark, then the agency's head of production. "How are you going to identify and follow people out of a riot situation?" How would they know that the six would be truly representative of Middle Eastern types—an Islamic fundamentalist, a right-wing Israeli solider, a Peace Now activist. And how would they know that the characters followed would be interesting or willing to cooperate?

These were questions the producers themselves had already confronted. Jacobovici, in fact, dubbed Halpern 'Mr. Nyet' for his persistence in raising logistical problems with the concept. To the OFDC, Associated said the characters chosen would all have been identified before the riot. "Then, how do you know they'll be involved in the riot?" To that, says Halpern, there was really only one answer: "Trust us. We'll make it work."

Tecca Crosby, the OFDC's development officer, thought the proposal lacked feasibility on several grounds. The idea was nice, but Jacobovici could not guarantee delivery. Shooting in the Middle East was a dicey proposition at the best of times, the more complicated because Jacobovici himself was Jewish. How much access would Palestinians give him? On the other hand, there was no doubting either the director's knowledge of the issues, nor the merit of his objective—to make the conflict comprehensible to the average person. "With Simcha," says Crosby, "it really came down to his expertise on the subject, and a leap of faith on our part that, if he had to, he could re-tailor part of the way through." That faith was not misplaced.

At Telefilm, recalls Bill House, director of the Ontario office, "the most remarkable thing was how much support there was for the project immediately." House credited the treatment. "It was so well written, so articulate about the issue, and so clear, that if he could get the access, and we were prepared to accept that he could, it would be an extraordinary view."

So early on, *Deadly* developed very positive momentum—upbeat readers' reports of the treatment, approvals in principle from the agency cinecrats and the not unimpressive signature of Garth Drabinsky and his Cineplex orchestra. "At least perceptually," says Jacobovici, "everyone was in." Then, suddenly, a snafu: as a feature documentary, the film was simply ineligible for funding under the policy guidelines of Telefilm's Theatrical Fund. Documentaries, by definition it seemed, could not be feature films. In order to receive production financing, Jacobovici *et al.* were told, they would have to apply under the Broadcast Fund. "They were very apologetic about it," Halpern recalls. "Very sympathetic. But those were the policy guidelines."

It was Jeff Sackman who suggested the project then be taken to his friend, Jay Switzer, head of business affairs at CITY-TV. Given Switzer's support, Associated thought the solution was simply paperwork—refile the applications under the Broadcast Fund. But that avenue, too, appeared closed: yet another policy criterion stipulated that in order to qualify for Broadcast Fund dollars, 25 percent of the film's production financing had to come from a Canadian broadcaster. (The requirement today for documentaries with budgets over $500,000 is only 15 percent.) "Now, we were really over a barrel," Halpern says. The budget for the film was over $900,000. What Canadian broadcaster would agree to put up $225,000? "And yet," says Halpern, "it was simply impossible for us to conceive that with that kind of financial commitment already on the table from Cineplex, there would not be a way in which we could satisfy the policy requirements and still make the film."

In researching and filming Deadly Currents *filmmaker Jacobovici worked closely with both sides to achieve a balanced portrayal of the Arab–Israeli conflict.*

Then, at a meeting with Telefilm, it was suggested that the project adopt the model widely used by London's Channel 4 TV to launch many British film ventures—having the broadcaster buy the entire license and then sell off theatrical rights. In this instance, CITY would acquire all rights to *Deadly*, retain first broadcast rights, and sell the theatrical rights back to Cineplex–Odeon. Switzer was receptive to the idea, provided that Telefilm and his own legal affairs department sanctioned the paper flow. The *Deadly* deal, Halpern concedes, "was worked out among people who knew and trusted each other extremely well. We would never have been in a situation to do this on our own."

At first, however, Telefilm equivocated, saying it would have to study the new structure. Associated pressed the issue. "This requires an enormous amount of work, and the goodwill of many people," Halpern argued. "We won't do it unless you can say now that in principle, it can fly." Eventually, Telefilm gave its blessing, although not without a healthy internal debate and a protracted delay. In fact, during that period, the agency went through one of its periodic upheavals; the film's strongest backer, Bill Niven, went to Paris; a new team arrived; and the film slowly crept up the new-projects agenda. In March, Jacobovici cancelled plans to attend a month-long shoot in Africa on another film because Telefilm was finally ready to consider the *Deadly* proposal, and would need him for possible questions; the issue was not raised by the agency until the crew returned from Africa.

The delay was all the more frustrating because, in the interim, Jacobovici was turning away other work and facing mounting financial pressures. "I was desperate," he recalls. "In the six months' lag, there was no income for me." In a sense, the documentary proposal had become a victim of its own success, trapped between the unofficial approval and the formal green light. When it finally flashed, in the spring of 1989, the producers told the agency that they would return in seven days with newly written agreements. Virtually nothing happens in the film business in one week, let alone the redrafting of complex distribution agreements, so the odds of fulfilling that pledge must have seemed utterly absurd.

Redrafting the agreements involved a series of complex considerations, including liability, responsibility to the production, tax implications and cash flow. To accelerate the process, Halpern dusted off his corporate law books and took first run at drafting the wording. Jacobovici "rushed around on my bicycle with documents. I couldn't wait for the couriers." The entire package was restructured, with all the legal approvals, within a week.

Then, another snag surfaced. The agreements gave CITY the right to air the film in prime time for a bargain price of $40,000. That, Cineplex argued, would impede its attempts to sell the film to a national broadcaster like the CBC, for a much higher license fee. As a result, another set of amendments was prepared, under which CITY agreed to claim the second window (five showings over a five-year period), reduced its investment, and left the first window open. Cineplex later sold the film to the CBC for $120,000.

So the financing architecture was as follows: CITY bought all domestic rights for $315,000, and then immediately sold them to Cineplex for $275,000. There was a separate sale of foreign rights alone for an estimated $25,000. Cineplex also agreed to repurchase first-run TV rights for $15,000, reducing CITY's ultimate investment to $25,000. Since Telefilm funded 75 percent of Cineplex's advance, the distributor stood to recoup its minimum guarantee with the sale of the first-run broadcast rights to the CBC. CITY actually kept an option to reacquire the first window, an option it might have exercised. "We could have and should have exercised that option," says Switzer. "If we were sharks, we would have. But the idea is to let as many people see these films as possible, not to traffic in other's people's films." Sackman agrees: "CITY was very conciliatory and very helpful. They could have been a lot more stringent."

Even with all the paperwork in place, Telefilm stalled the final approval. In meeting after meeting, *Deadly* got bumped from the agenda. Desperate, Jacobovici phoned House and Peter Katadotis, head of English-language production in Montreal, and "appealed to their sense of fairness. I said, 'it's one thing if you say no. It's another thing if it never gets raised. Because in the meantime, we're swallowing water here. We can't proceed; we can't let go. We're in limbo.' " In the end, House and Katadotis conferred privately by phone and then issued the agency's blessing.

The final production financing picture was:

Telefilm:	. . . .	$404,000
OFDC:	. . . .	$225,000
CITY-TV:	. . . .	$25,000
Cineplex:	. . . .	.$290,000
	Total	$944,000

PRODUCTION Although he was a native Israeli, Jacobovici was under no illusions about the welcome he would receive from Israeli officials. With the *Intifada* in full flower, the army was not likely to embrace the prospect of an independent film crew wandering through the riot zones of the West Bank. But the Israelis, in a sense, were the least of his problems. They represented the kind of logistical hurdles that any documentary filmmaker might encounter, and he had enough friends, contacts and resources to facilitate the leaps. The real difficulty, apparent from the outset, was the Palestinian side of the equation. To make the film work, he would not only have to give equal time to Palestinian viewpoints; he would have to get beyond the glib rhetoric of 15-second sound bites typically given to American network TV correpondents. If he showed the impact of daily life on Israeli society, he would have to do the same in the Arab community. If he showed how the Israelis dispensed justice to Palestinians, he would have to show how Palestinians meted out justice among themselves. He would, in short, have to penetrate the lives of ordinary Palestinians. But how exactly would he do that? How would he—an observant Jew and a former member of the Israeli armed forces—find them, approach them, gain access, win their trust?

There were several answers, including, says Jacobovici, a budget generous enough to buy enough time to be able to follow all leads, some of them false. His own knowledge of the factional nuances of Palestinian politics won him respect from revolutionaries. And some nine weeks before the start of principal photography, in August 1989, his associate producer Jane Logan began making the rounds of the Palestinian community—writers, artists, acolytes, press agents. Sometimes, Jacobovici would accompany her—and be introduced as "Sim," a Canadian filmmaker of Romanian extraction. Often, she went alone, presenting the case for a documentary that, as fairly as possible, would explain both sides of the Arab–Israeli dilemma. It is tempting to think that the Palestinians agreed to cooperate on the strength of the proposal itself. Perhaps some did. But it is also true that many of them simply were responding to Logan herself—an attractive, blue-eyed blonde who spoke fluent Hebrew (having lived on a kibbutz in the early 1980s) and had a master's degree in Middle Eastern studies. Jacobovici acknowledges that without Logan, *Deadly* would have been a much different film.

Their conversations with Arabs were always conducted in English. In fact, Jacobovici disguised his knowledge of Hebrew as well as his Jewish identity, by ignoring all Hebrew spoken in his company, even when it was directed expressly at him. At least one Palestinian interviewee eventually surmised the truth, noting that the crew always shut down early on Fridays, in time to prepare for the Jewish sabbath at sundown, and worked all day Sunday.

They got their first real break even before the arrival of the film's crew. For dry-run purposes, Jacobovici had hired a local camera operator and sound man and had won Palestinian permission to take them into the *casbah*, the labyrinthine Arab market in Nablus. The footage was excellent, but time was short: the Arabs had invited the crew to lunch. It would have been both ungracious and impolitic to refuse the invitation, but Jacobovici, who has never been good at hiding his emotions, was visibly upset at having the day's work short-circuited. Recognizing his concern, his Palestinian contact suggested that he return the next day, broadly hinting that he would not be disappointed by the results. They were right. Jacobovici's cameras arrived in time to catch a gang of hatchet-wielding Palestinian youths, masked in *kaffiyahs*, marching through the narrow alleyways in search of a shopkeeper suspected of collaborating with the Israelis. The crew was unaware of—and, on ethical grounds, would not have filmed in any event—the denouement: the vicious beating of the suspect, who later died in hospital.

The production scored some cinematic coups on the Israeli side as well, many of them arranged by producer Ric Bienstock. A Canadian friend, Gordon Wiseman, was working as an army lawyer. Normally, film crews of any kind were never allowed inside the courtroom, but Wiseman suggested one West Bank judge who was persuaded to sanction the shoot—providing a rare glimpse of how justice is administered in Judea and Samaria. Later, Jacobovici saw a newspaper article about a bizarre and provocative perfor-mance artist named Juliano Mor, and spent days trying to find him. Half-Arab and half-Jew, Mor's schizoid routine, complete with a self-ad-ministered paint-splashing, served as a kind of metaphor for the nation itself.

But *Deadly*'s most riveting sequences—so compelling and so novel that some thought they had been staged—were two scenes in which a cadre of young Marxist Palestinians first plot the capture of, and then interrogate, another youth suspected of working for the Israelis. The arrangements for this shoot—code-named Operation Sunset—were carried out over several weeks in elaborate secrecy, one contact leading to another and then to another. But even when Jacobovici and his cameraman Mark Mackay finally set off for their late-night rendezvous with Palestinian intermediaries, they had no firm idea of who exactly they were meeting, and where exactly they would be taken.

The two men drove to the appointed spot, about an hour from Jerusalem, exchanged the agreed-upon code words with their contact, and then sat blindfolded in a van for several long minutes. Waiting, Jacobovici wondered whether he had made a fatal mistake, putting his life and Mackay's in the hands of people capable of killing without compunction. It was a classic paradigm of the symbiosis that sometimes governs the political documentary—the filmmaker implicitly asks his subjects to trust what will ultimately be done with the footage, but first he must show his own good faith, by implicitly entrusting his life to them. And what if he encountered an execution? He knew he could not film it—he considered that immoral—but would he try to intervene, risking his life? Fortunately, it was a question he did not have to answer. The clandestine shoot went off without incident.

Like every documentarian, Jacobovici also confronted more mundane concerns, including how to stretch his budget in order to put as much of the available money as possible on the screen. To that end, the production team traded its dollars on the black market, negotiated with airlines for free excess-baggage shipments, rented an apartment in Jerusalem (instead of hotel rooms) and, rather than leasing, decided to purchase a van, and then sell it back to its original owner at the end of the shoot. The final cost of the vehicle, Jacobovici estimates, was $400 for six weeks. "It sounds ridiculous," says producer Bienstock, who, among other things, oversaw the film's expenditures. "But you nickel and dime wherever you can nickel and dime."

Even with these economies, it was clear early on that the initial production budget of just under $1 million would not be enough. For one thing, Jacobovici was using up miles of raw stock—an estimated 200,000 feet of film by the time he was finished. It was not that he was unaware of the constraints; it was simply that he would never allow those limits to alter his judgement of what he deemed essential footage. Inevitably, this tension between the imperatives of prudent finance and the imperatives of creative filmmaking provoked more than one argument with Bienstock. "I did have a concern that we were shooting too much," Bienstock says. "But it's a balancing act. Because it's one thing to say, 'don't shoot too much,' and it's another to say what you shouldn't be shooting. The fact is, sometimes you roll the film just to loosen somebody up."

The balancing act was all the more difficult because of personal chemistry. Jacobovici, Bienstock explains, is capable of immense charm. But he "is also a perfectionist. He knows what he wants and will stop at virtually nothing to get it. Sometimes, he is abrasive, not only with his colleagues, but with people whose cooperation he really needs to achieve what he wants." In this, Jacobovici saw no inherit contradiction. He was always willing to try Nice; if Nice did not work, he would try Less Nice, and Less Nicer Still, always pushing, always focussed on his objective—permission to shoot here, gain access there. With a background in student activism, he knew that some people respond well to sweet diplomacy, others to blunt intimidation. He could play both those notes, and all the notes in between. Indeed, he was quite prepared to invoke any strategy that delivered the permissions he was seeking, even at the risk of losing. In most cases, he succeeded.

In much the same way, Jacobovici refused during filming to say whether he agreed or disagreed with the positions taken by his subjects—a conventional interviewing technique. Even when he did agree, he says, he remained silent, convinced that the subject would think his opinion false, and would lose respect for him. In fact, it was better to let subjects think he disagreed, because psychologically they would then go further than they might otherwise, seeking to persuade him of the validity of their argument. Whether his subjects liked or hated him was irrelevant; it was only important that they expressed themselves honestly and passionately.

Stylistically, Jacobovici's goal was to make *Deadly* feel and look like a real, big-screen feature film. Its content might be purely documentary, but its form would be as dramatic as possible—hence the crane shots, the grainy, black and white footage and the post-modern awareness of the camera's constant presence.

Returning to Toronto in December 1989, the producers set out to raise money to finance a second-unit shoot. Their first stops, predictably, were at Telefilm and the OFDC, but the agencies were not sympathetic. They were already standing behind Cineplex in terms of recoupment (on the optimistic, if not altogether naive, assumption that there would *be* recoupment); and they were not about to burden themselves with any additional debt. Recalls Louise Clark: "So the producers said, 'Okay, we'll go back to the distributor.' And our reaction was like, 'We won't hear from them again.' I mean, no one goes back to a distributor in the middle of a shoot for more money. And the next day, the letter came from Cineplex, stepping to the plate and putting in another $30,000, and we went, 'Oh, my God.' " Indeed, not only had Cineplex agreed to finance the second shoot; it agreed that this supplementary investment would stand behind the agencies in terms of recoupment. Later, Associated made Sackman and Topol executive producers of the film, together with David Green.

In August 1990, shortly after Saddam Hussein decided that Kuwait should become his nineteenth province, the second unit of *Deadly Currents* returned to Israel. The Iraqi invasion represented a critical turning point in the modern history of the Middle East, with geopolitical implications for every state in the region. Jacobovici's challenge was to weigh the impact of the Iraqi move on Israel without losing sight of the bigger picture: the Arab–Israeli conflict had been around for centuries before Saddam Hussein and, in all probability, would be around for centuries after the Kuwaiti adventure had become an inconspicuous blip on the time-line of history. The crew stayed six weeks, mostly doing interviews with various Palestinian and Israeli intellectuals, a series of talking heads that helped put the action of the film—the riots, the executions—in some context. Jacobovici shunned politicians "like the plague," convinced that all they ever delivered were predictable party lines, devoid of insight or fresh analysis. By November, he was back in Toronto, ready to resume editing.

POST-PRODUCTION From the beginning, Jacobovici was determined to make his film without the documentary convention of narration. "If you're listening to the narrator," he told one interviewer, "then you're not drawing your own conclusions. You're measuring your beliefs against an off-camera voice. I don't want to let you off the philosophical hook that easily." But abandoning narration always imposed a huge challenge—making the film's disparate stories and several themes seamlessly connect. Resolving those editing problems, figuring out what Jacobovici calls "the giant Rubik's Cube" of the film, took him 16 months.

His editor was Steve Weslak, who at the time was just beginning to make a name for himself among American producers working in Canada series. "Although I have no interest in Israel or Jewish issues, the project sounded really interesting," Weslak says. "I figured, 16 weeks. No one's going to forget me in 16 weeks." Like Jacobovici, he would be at work for the next 16 months.

Signing on at his standard documentary fee— $1,100 a week, plus $200 a week for the editing suite—Weslak started work December 6, 1989. "Right away, I could see that the footage was fantastic. The very first reel had these Palestinians in Nablus running around with their axes. It was amazing material." Weslak deliberately did not read the film's treatment. "Everybody else—director, producer—they're all working to a particular vision," he says. "The one thing I can bring to it is some kind of objectivity, look at the film the way an audience would, saying 'this is interesting, this is dull, this is redundant.' " Only late in the editing process, when others were often feeling overwhelmed by the material, would Weslak read the initial treatment. At that point, he says, it "really helps to put things back into a kind of focus."

It took Weslak and Jacobovici several weeks just to screen the raw footage. The scope of the project was mammoth—but not overwhelming. "It's like building a house," Weslak explains, of his approach to editing. "You don't ever want to think about the whole job, so you think about the pipes, the kitchen cabinets, the windows, the trim. You break it down into bits and pieces. If you try to conceive of the whole thing, then it's impossible." It was soon clear that the project would take much longer than anticipated, and Weslak was forced to turn away more lucrative work, including an Australian TV series. He was not, however, resentful of missed opportunities. "What's the point of whipping yourself? I had gotten into the project, and I really liked it. It just went on too long."

What bothered him most were what he calls Jacobovici's "obnoxious work habits," showing up two hours late, taking long lunches, spending an hour and a half on a single telephone call. Their schedules were never in sync. Weslak preferred days; Jacobovici seemed most productive after dark. But as the weeks passed, it also became clear to Weslak that Jacobovici had developed some kind of mystical connection to his film—"that he was destined to make it, and everything he had done before had prepared him for this this occasion." Given that attitude, it seemed to Weslak that "all ordinary constraints—of time or money or deadlines or even personal relationships—became absolutely irrelevant."

At the time, Jacobovici was facing enormous personal pressure. Under the auspices of Ontario's Small Business Development Act, he was trying to raise financing dollars to shepherd a variety of future film projects to completion; the offering would later collapse for lack of investment. Simultaneously, he was going through both a painful marital separation—the marriage, his first, had lasted less than a year—and a spiritual reawakening, complete with strict observance of the Jewish sabbath. Always exhausted and often depressed, he spent many nights shuffling and reshuffling colour-coded notecards of the film's sequences on his office floor, trying to make the Rubik's Cube work. I always knew where I wanted to go," he says. "But I was often stumped. I didn't know how to get there." Weslak, growing impatient, urged him to use narration. Jacobovici refused, arguing that narration was the easy but the wrong solution.

One central problem was length: Weslak felt that any film on this subject longer than 90 minutes would tire audiences; Jacobovici, he laughs, kept talking about the five- and six-hour films he admired. Of course, Associated was contractually committed to delivering a film under two hours. For Jacobovici, the problem was how to develop pace without sacrificing depth

There were many full and frank exchanges of opinion, but no shouting matches. About a week into the edit, Weslak told the director, "Look, if you yell at me, I'm just gonna walk out of here." If they argued at all, it was about the film's editorial balance. Weslak nursed a preference for strong point-of-view documentaries, films that "grabbed me by the lapels." By meticulous design, Jacobovici was striving for a film that, as much as possible, would be faithful to the two competing visions of Middle Eastern reality—Arab and Israeli—without explicitly endorsing either one. "I also wanted a film that grabbed me by the lapels," Jacobovici insists. "But it had to be seductive. It had to sneak up on the viewer. I wasn't interested in presenting a lecture with pictures." So Weslak kept saying, "It's too wishy-washy. Who knows what the hell it's even about?" And Jacobovici would say, "No, no. If we reveal our point of view, I instantly lose my effectiveness."

Eventually, Weslak concurred, converted by the test screening process. Separate and mixed audiences of Jews and Arabs would attend rough cuts at Film House in Toronto and be invited to offer comments afterward. Invariably, the Jews would cite certain scenes as "big scores" for the Palestinians; the Arabs would cite other scenes as big scores for the Jews. Sometimes, there would be agreement that the entire film was hopelessly biased in one direction; a few weeks later, with only the sequences rearranged (but no actual content changes), the same audience would say the film was now tilted hopelessly the other way. In a sense, says Jacobovici, their deliberate aim was to upset preconceptions about the Middle East: no sooner were the Palestinians portrayed as martyrs than they were shown as filled with anti-Jewish fanaticism; no sooner were the Israelis depicted as "the good guys," than they were seen in cavalier mistreatment of Arabs. "Your sympathies keep shifting back and forth," Weslak says. "That's one of the things that gives the film its political balance."

There was also some heated debate about the film's extensive use of Arab and Israeli dance and music, as cultural subtexts of the ideological war. How much of this footage belonged in an essentially political documentary? Did any of it belong? What was this film about? Was it supposed to entertain, as well as inform? Was it supposed to teach, anger, amuse, incite? All of these questions, Weslak says, were variously on the table for discussion.

Initially, the producers were aiming to launch the film at Toronto's Festival of Festivals, in September 1990. In the end, it *was* unveiled at the F of F, but not until 1991. From June 1990 until the following January, Weslak says, "we were just struggling to find the right form and structure, moving things around, endlessly, trying to make different things work in different places." For Weslak, *Deadly* began to seem interminable. "I was totally exhausted, totally disheartened," he says. When Jacobovici returned to Israel for the second-unit shoot in August 1990, Weslak "actually tried to get off the project." By that point, he had been working on it for eight months. "When you work on something that long, you totally lose any sense of whether it's good or bad." he explains. Besides, the topic was "very depressing. Simcha was often very unsure about what he wanted. He was both the producer and the director, but nobody had control of him." All the self-imposed deadlines were fictional. And Weslak was under consideration by Gail Singer as a possible editor for her feature film, *True Confections*.

Weslak's misgivings were widely shared. Elliott Halpern was "concerned that Simcha had no distance from the film and by the length of the edit." Bienstock, in charge of the budget, was concerned about costs, and the lack of revenue to pay them. And executive producer Sackman thought the rough cuts were far too long. "I tried to get it to 90 minutes," he recalls. "I mean, c'mon: the conflict has gone on for millenia. What's ten minutes? But it was like asking Simcha to cut off his children's toes."

Dropping by the editing suite every week, Halpern thought Weslak "looked close to death." He wanted to be released from his celluloid hell, but he also wanted to finish what he had started. The conflict was tearing him apart. Halpern compares Weslak's relationship with Jacobovici to that between Cervantes' Sancho Panza and Don Quixote. "If Quixote is so crazy, why does Panza follow him? I think what Steve wanted was for someone to set him free. The door of the prison was open, and at any time he could leave, but he wanted someone else to pull him out."

With Jacobovici in Israel, Weslak finally went to Bienstock and asked to be relieved. His plan was to spend the six weeks of the Israel shoot bringing another editor up to speed. Unfortunately, Singer only confirmed her intention to hire him the night before Jacobovici returned from Israel—too late for him to abandon *Deadly*. Bienstock assured him that the edit could only last another eight weeks maximum, because the producers faced a Cannes Film Festival deadline. Instead, it lasted another six months. Ironically, for Weslak, the final months of the edit were probably the most enjoyable. The footage generated by the second-unit shoot provided a kind of through-line narrative that gave shape to what had been an amorphous structure.

For Jacobovici, the editing process was equally traumatic. The shoot itself had challenged his fundamental opinions about Israel. It was, says Halpern, "Simcha's one opportunity to make his definitive statement about that entity that he had spent a good part of his life thinking about and was in love with," the state of Israel. The film's riveting central character, performer Juliano Mor, says at one point about his Jewish mother, "That's not my momma, that's fascism." For Mor, Momma was a metaphor for Israel itself. Jacobovici, says Halpern, had the same problem "coming to grips with criticizing mom. If you're going to criticize mom, you'd better be careful and precise." And that questioning of Israel's very *raison d'être* was all the more agonizing because it was occurring in tandem with Jacobovici's own personal religious awakening.

Financial pressures were building as well. With the budget spent or committed, Bienstock was now working as a volunteer. Jacobovici, already deeply in debt, was living on credit. His personal life was in tatters. "My heart went out to him," says Bienstock. "I don't think he slept a lot. I don't know how he lived with the same footage, day in and day out, for all those months."

All of the tensions came together in the editing suite. "Everything," says Halpern, "was completely at sea." It took a long time to realize that the original scheme—the six characters in search of a story concept—would not work. "There had to be structure," Halpern saw, "but not one that took away from having an impressionistic feeling." It was a contradiction they somehow needed to make work. Eventually, they did—but eventually was a year later. Weslak was right. In the long run, a year meant nothing to Jacobovici. It was simply inconceivable to him that he would ever let go of a film that meant so much to him before—in his judgement—it was ready to be released.

Deadly's first rough-cut screening, which reduced some 100 hours of film to about four, was held in May 1991. Despite the length, no one walked out, and several people said they could easily have watched more. More importantly, the screening gave Jacobovici confidence in the process itself. Too many filmmakers, says Weslak, "hate to show anything to anybody, and don't want anybody in the editing suite. That's one of the reasons why a lot of films aren't very good. Directors forget that films are made for an audience."

In the end, *Deadly*'s marathon stay in the editing suite cut both ways. The final product was not only better; it was more timely. The first multilateral Arab–Israeli peace talks began in Washington only days before the film's opening in Toronto, putting the Middle East front and centre in public consciousness, and delivering an enormous promotional kick. On the other hand, it was during that year that the film's distributor, Cineplex–Odeon, began its long, tortuous descent into debtor's hell. In the ensuing corporate carnage, the film's key Cineplex backers—executive producers Jeff Sackman and Robert Topol—departed, leaving the project without an in-house champion. As part of its distribution agreement with Associated Producers, Cineplex had promised to open the film in five U.S. cities, with an estimated prints and ads campaign worth $100,000. Sackman, among others, believed that Cineplex's marketing muscle could make *Deadly* one of the rare documentary hits, crossing over into the filmgoing mainstream. Instead, as Jacobovici says, "we suddenly found ourselves going from having this amazing distributor with amazing clout to being a kind of orphan." The foreign distribution system, which would have allowed Cineplex to give it a grand theatrical opening in the U.S. and later market packages of six or 10 films (including *Deadly*) to Europe, had essentially collapsed. That, in turn, forced the producers to find a new distributor for the American market—just when the recession was beginning to squeeze out small films and independent producers, and just when fees for TV rights were beginning to plummet.

At the end of post-production, Jacobovici returned to the agencies yet again, requesting another $69,000 to pay for enhancements of the film's sound track. Again, they refused. "We spent a lot of time on it," recalls Judy Watt, head of business affairs at the OFDC. "But we did not feel it was really merited. 'If you hadn't taken so long on the editing,' we said, 'you would have had the money.'" At Telefilm, Bill House was in complete accord. "There's a limit to what theatrical documentaries should cost," he says. "It was not our responsibility to pay for the elongated editing schedules." Again, Jacobovici went to a distributor—this time to Alliance, which by now had tentatively arranged to market the film in the United States. Alliance agreed to a modified version of the sound enhancements. The producers also contributed the rebate due to them from their motion picture guarantor.

DISTRIBUTION Successful distribution of films, like good acupuncture, knows how to touch nerves. Many nerves, of course, will respond to a $10-million marketing campaign. The task for a distributor in Canada, where $100,000 promotion budgets are rare, and $1-million promotions are fantasies, is to find the nerves that respond to more subtle stimulation. This is all the more difficult when the film in question is a documentary—by definition, a less popular product to market.

By virtue of corporate upheaval, *Deadly Currents* was already a quasi-orphan of the Cineplex family. Logically, there were strict limits on how much cash-poor Cineplex would spend to promote the film. If the producers wanted their film to find an audience, it was starkly clear that they would have to do the lion's share of promotion themselves. "I told Simcha right at the beginning that we could not commit the time and manpower resources," Sackman says. "Cineplex had a lot of films, all of them more commercially oriented. If *Deadly* works theatrically, it'll be because of you, using good old-fashioned leg work." In fact, one of the only pieces of free publicity that the Cineplex promotion rep assigned to the film managed to generate was a photograph of Jacobovici in the fashion pages of the alternative Toronto weekly newspaper, *Now*. "Anybody who knows me knows I'm no fashion plate," he laughs. "I was embarrassed, but I did it." Promotion is promotion.

Complaining noisily about the lack of effort, Jacobovici persuaded Cineplex to pay the cost of a full-time publicist, Michelle Shulman, who would work out of his offices. But the campaign launched was a collective effort, in which all of the producers participated. The strategy, according to Jacobovici, was to build a critical mass of word-of-mouth on the film's behalf. "Nobody will normally say, 'Gee, honey, let's go out and see the *Intifada* on the big screen tonight.' But we believed if we could get past the first three weeks, then the film would build its own momentum. It would have its own legs."

The first stop was Toronto's Festival of Festivals. Organizers originally offered Associated a 400-seat theatre, arguing, logically, that filling a smaller house was far better than not filling a larger one. But Jacobovici was convinced he could fill the Varsity, an 800-seat theatre—and he did. The film's September 12 premiere was over-sold; another 800 people had to be turned away at the door. The producers were careful, however, to save the core of the publicity campaign for the weeks leading up to the film's actual theatrical opening.

Critics can and properly will debate the cinematic skills of Simcha Jacobovici. But when it comes to promotion, there are few doubters. The publicity campaign mounted for *Deadly Currents* was more nearly reminiscent of a military exercise than of anything else, and Jacobovici was its high-profile general. For a period of six weeks, it seemed almost impossible to pick up a newspaper or magazine, turn on the radio or watch a TV public-affairs show, without reading about, hearing or seeing Jacobovici recounting the story of the film's creation. These were not random or serendipitous events; Associated, acting as its own press agent, arranged virtually all of the interviews, orchestrating them with as much care as an opening tracking shot. "We did the film angle, the religious angle, the politics angle, the news angle," Jacobovici recalls. "We were climbing through every window. It was just a rolling, constant wave. It's not enough just to get reviewed. You've got to push the first audiences through the door, almost literally." To make sure the theatre was full, Jacobovici invited political science professors and high school teachers to bring their classes to the theatre, promising to attend the screenings and talk to the students afterward about his film. "They are not going to come on their own," he insists. "You have to literally go down there and talk to them, and then you are building your audience. And then they will go back to the schools and tell their friends about your film."

As a method of promotion, such tactics may seem obvious. But in fact, as Bienstock observes, "most filmmakers don't see themselves as promoters. They make the film and, 'there it is, folks.' " The reasons vary. Some directors simply are not good at promotion; others have no interest in it; others are simply exhausted and crave their moment in the sun of recognition. And most just cannot afford it. "Because any time you devote to promotion," Bienstock says, "you devote at a loss." Associated, already bleeding dollars, was prepared to take the loss. "You put two years of your life into something, you don't want to finish it and have it premiere and have it play two weeks," Bienstock says. "There is an intense desire to get it seen."

The media blitz was accompanied by poster and leaflet distribution at key target-audience centres—university campuses and the downtown core— courtesy of labour provided by dozens of volunteers. The poster, a vivid, red on black, all-type design, sparked sharp debate among the producers. For Jacobovici, a poster had one purpose: to draw attention to the film. He therefore wanted a graphic image that was first and foremost visible, a design that any myopic motorist, stopped at a red light, could read on a sidewalk construction hoarding five metres away. Postering, he firmly believed, was a form of guerrilla war. "If you glance over from your car, and you can't read it, that's a bad poster," he argued. Some of his colleagues thought the blood-red title, scrawled like graffiti across the top, was more evocative of a Friday the 13th horror film than of a sober political documentary. But none could agree on any of the still photographs taken during the shoot. And everyone wanted to avoid a choice that might be seen as skewing the film's editorial balance one way or the other—by showing only Israeli soldiers or Palestinian rebels. In the end, Jacobovici's view prevailed. The actual design was the work of Toronto's Robert Burns. Later, after Alliance acquired international sales rights, a new one-sheet was commissioned for use in film festivals and press kits. It showed three figures—a soldier, a masked terrorist and the film's cameraman, Mark Mackay, a statement about the media's role in shaping opinion about the truth in the Middle East.

It is a measure of the minimal expectations that accompany Canadian films that not many open simultaneously in two theatres in the same city. Certainly, very few documentaries do—Canadian or otherwise. And it is a measure of the enormously positive pre-opening hype that was generated for *Deadly Currents* that Cineplex, under steady pressure from Jacobovici, agreed to launch it at Toronto's downtown Carlton and mid-town Canada Square theatres. Jacobovici in fact had lobbied strenuously, but unsuccessfully, for a third screen, located closer to the city's Jewish neighbourhoods;

Cineplex refused. Still, to its amazement, the dividends of the public-relations investment began to be paid almost immediately at the box office. And, against all expectations (save, perhaps, the producers'), they continued to be paid. The film opened October 4, 1991 and stayed eight weeks at the Carlton, 11 weeks at the Canada Square—an extraordinary run for any Canadian film, let alone a two-hour, arguably depressing political documentary.

Associated wanted to take advantage of the national publicity it had received—on Morningside, The Journal, Canada AM and elsewhere—by opening simultaneously in Montreal and Vancouver. Cineplex was committed contractually to a three-city run, but there was no obligation to simultaneity and its faith was not that deep. After playing at the Vancouver International Film Festival in October, Deadly opened at the city's Royal Centre and stayed three weeks. In Montreal, there was trouble securing a screen. It was not until close to Christmas, hardly an optimum time to open any documentary film, that two Montreal screens became available—the downtown Egyptian theatre and the Côte de Neiges. Again, however, Jacobovici is convinced that only his relentless pressure on the distributor managed to secure the Montreal opening. "If I had sat back and waited for the system to work," he says, "we wouldn't have gotten Montreal."

In lobbying Cineplex, Jacobovici was pushing against a system not well suited to the release of documentaries. In essence, he was dealing with a competing agenda, one built on maximizing the commercial value of the property, regardless of venue. The logic is impeccable. Few Canadian feature films do good business at the box office, so few Canadian distributors are anxious to finance a generous (and probably wasted) prints and ads budget, even if it is federally subsidized. The only real money at the back-end is in television and perhaps video sales, foreign and domestic, and so the apparatus of distribution is largely geared to expediting the consummation of those deals. Theatrical release has no inherent monetary value; it is simply a vehicle for creating awareness, one piston in the publicity engine. Jacobovici's challenge, therefore, was to "to be an advocate for the film without alienating the distributor so much that they bury it, or say 'to hell with you.' I skated close to the edge." And if Jacobovici is prepared to concede that he skated close to the edge, it is a safe bet that most of the other skaters on the ice thought he was well over it. In total, Deadly played nine weeks in Montreal, a respectable showing, considering its Christmas release. "The word was out," Sackman says. "But people in Montreal just didn't go."

While Bienstock coordinated the Montreal opening, the filmmaker himself flew to Israel, to organize a special opening at Jerusalem's Cinematheque. The event, financed by Alliance and covered by the CBC and CTV national newscasts, brought an overflow crowd of Arabs and Jews together in the same room—every combination of Israeli and Palestinian hawk and dove. The film's actual theatrical release in Israel was less successful—largely, Jacobovici claims, because the sub-distributor, Erez Films, failed to support it. "The distributor thought, 'all of these people came to the Cinematheque, all he has to do is stick it in the theatre.' I told him, 'all of these people came together because we spent two months getting them here. You have to work.' " *Deadly* played only two weeks in Tel Aviv. However, it later received regular screenings at the Cinematheque, and was accepted by the Ministry of Education for use by Arab and Israeli high school students.

In aggregate, *Deadly* yielded about $100,000 in Canadian box office revenues—"not bad," says Sackman, "relative to expectations and the cost [in prints and ads] of achieving it." "*Deadly*'s gross in Toronto was fantastic," Sackman says. "There was an inherent quality in the film that stimulated positive word-of-mouth. Eleven weeks is incredible." In the end, its success rested on a combination of factors. Among them:

1) Vigorous promotional effort. "Simcha," says Elliott Halpern, "is a near-genius on how the media operates." Telefilm's Bill House agrees: "The producers did a great job of gathering that marketing momentum. There was a lot of hype." The campaign kept rolling even after the first month had passed, to remind viewers that the film was still in the theatres.
2) Excellent reviews by the critics.
3) Home-town advantage. "There is such a thing," Halpern insists. "There was greater receptivity by press and public in Toronto, a much warmer atmosphere."
4) Good timing. The Middle East peace talks kept the issue on the front pages.
5) Sheer luck. It was a weak autumn for feature films, generally. As a result, exhibitors were content to keep a Canadian film doing respectable business in the theatres.

U.S. OPENING For a variety of reasons, commercial and artistic, Associated Producers wanted to secure a U.S. theatrical release for *Deadly*. This peak is not easily climbed at the best of times; it is even less easily scaled in the middle of the steepest economic downturn since the Great Depression, when the film is a tense documentary about a seemingly insoluble problem in a country that causes few Americans to breathe deeply. The major U.S. distributors were never interested, because there was not enough money attached to the project. The minor distributors were disinclined to offer any sort of minimum guarantee. A year earlier, says Sackman, a company like Miramax might have been interested in buying *Deadly*'s U.S. rights. By the time the film was ready for screening, Miramax had reached the point where it was no longer deemed expedient to apply its marketing resources to films with a profit potential of less than a quarter of a million dollars.

Sackman did hold extensive discussions with Miramax's Prestige division, and these seemed promising—so much so that other avenues were not pursued. Prestige had already acquired rights to *American Dream*, Barbara Koppel's documentary about a bitter labour dispute in Minnesota, which later won an Academy Award. But suddenly—sign of the times—the Prestige division was closed, out of business, leaving *Deadly* in what Jacobovici calls "the distribution twilight zone."

It was at the Festival of Festivals in Toronto that Alliance Releasing agreed to act as Cineplex's sub-agent for international rights, taking a commission of about 32.5 percent. Meeting at Alliance's Sutton Place Hotel hospitality suite, Victor Loewy reached a non-binding agreement with Sackman, Topol, Jacobovici and Cyril Drabinsky of Film House, to distribute the film in return for covering *Deadly*'s post-production costs. The agreement was non-binding because, although Cineplex–Odeon had been invited to send a representative, no one still officially connected with the organization actually attended the meeting; it was simply assumed that Cineplex could be persuaded to consent. It was, but the final contracts were not signed until a year later, when Alliance consented to put up a modest minimum gurantee on foreign sales.

Once again, the film's life—in this case, the transfer of foreign rights—was secured on the strength of personal and professional relationships, based essentially on trust. "Nobody likes to be told you have to do something," Sackman explains. "But basically we went to Victor and said, 'You've got to take this film.' And he did. But it took Alliance a little while to get comfortable with the idea that it was their film. They didn't have the same emotional commitment to *Deadly* that we did. You can't just pass that on."

For Associated, the new agreement was problematic. Jacobovici remained convinced that if he could mount the picture in Manhattan, dividends would accrue. Their faith was based in part on its remarkable box-office performance in Toronto; in part on Jacobovici's serendipitous success with *Falasha* in 1984. Amid similar skepticism about its chances, he had managed to a secure a one-week lock date at the Film Forum II, only three weeks after Operation Moses, the dramatic Israeli airlift of Ethiopians Jews from the Sudan. The film grossed a respectable $24,000 for the week.

Alliance had little appetite for a theatrical release in the U.S. On the strength of the film's success in Canada, the odds were good that it could score a healthy, first-window TV sale to Home Box Office, perhaps in conjunction with other Alliance-distributed films, including *Black Robe*. A U.S. theatrical opening was likely to lose money. And it would make pay–TV a second-run affair, discounting its sales value. Jacobovici's response to this, delivered to Rola Zayid, Alliance's vice president of TV sales, was "show me. Make the HBO deal. It's not what I want. I want a theatrical release. But convince me—by doing something. Because you can't sit on this film for two years. It has a certain timeliness."

Both Zayid and Charlotte Mickie, Alliance's director of foreign theatrical sales, finally surrendered and said they would recommend it to Victor Loewy. Loewy was less impressed. First, he was not convinced that Toronto was a useful model for New York, a prescient observation as it turned out. New York, Loewy told Jacobovici, was a much tougher venue for films. Advertising was too expensive to buy; and the free publicity tap was much more difficult to turn on. Yes, there were four million Jews—the film's core demographic—but they were scattered through the boroughs, Long Island, the suburbs; there was no guarantee they would be motivated to come downtown to see this film. In the end, Loewy argued, *Deadly* would appear "on an inappropriate screen with a big house nut, nobody would come, and you'll burn bridges because it will be perceived as a flop. And who's left holding the bag? Me."

Jacobovici had counter-arguments, but was having trouble getting through to Loewy. Finally, on a Sunday afternoon, the same day he was scheduled to fly to Spain on another shoot, the director decided to call Loewy at home in Montreal. Because he felt uncomfortable doing so, he wanted a light-hearted way to break the conversational ice. When Loewy answered, Jabobovici started speaking Romanian—Loewy was born there, and Jacobovici, whose parents are Romanian, is fluent in the language.

"I assumed he wouldn't know who it was," Jacobovici says. But right away, Loewy said, "Simcha, why are you calling me at home? I have guests. I don't have time to talk."

"Victor, I'm going away for a month to shoot and . . ."

"That's wonderful. Have a good time."

"Victor, you've got to give me five minutes."

"I don't have five minutes. We know what we're doing. Go and shoot your film."

"I know you know what you're doing," Jacobovici insisted. "But if you sit on this film too long, it won't be worth the stock it's printed on. Whereas if you release it theatrically, it will act as a showcase, and its value for television will be raised, not diminished. If we hadn't released it theatrically in Canada, the cassette would still be sitting on a desk at the CBC."

Instead, the director argued, its box office results had yielded a $120,000 fee from the CBC and a prime-time broadcast date. Jacobovici barrelled ahead. "People don't understand a documentary they've never heard of. But if we open in New York and are reviewed well in the *New York Times*, the *Village Voice*, people will know about it, and we'll be able to build on that. And if we don't, we're going to wind up with a film that nobody's going to want."

Jacobovici then explained that he had managed to raise $50,000 from a private investor to stage a New York opening; that Normandie Productions, a small independent company would act as the sub-distributor; and that Mark Lipsky and Adam Rogers, former publicist and booker respectively from Miramax's Prestige division, were now available on a freelance basis. Alliance would not have to invest a single dollar.

"There's no minimum guarantee," Loewy observed. "I'm not selling it to anybody who doesn't give me a minimum guarantee."

"Then you won't be selling it to anybody, and it'll soon be worth nothing."

"That's all very nice, Simcha," Loewy said, "if the *Times* says it's wonderful and millions of people see it. But what if nobody comes and the reviews are shit? You never know. Some of the greatest works of art have been called shit. So then nobody will touch it. My way, I have a film that's a little mysterious. Your way, I'll have a film that's flopped. Tell me," Loewy asked at last, "are you prepared to put your money where your mouth is?"

There was a long moment of silence at Jacobovici's end of the line. He knew exactly what Loewy was asking—if *Deadly* bombed in New York, and Alliance was never able to recover its minimum guarantee to Cineplex, would Associated Producers agree to share in the loss? All along, he had insisted that the film would do well in New York; now, Loewy was testing that faith—challenging him to either risk some real money or see his film buried. He had no money, but he did believe.

"Okay," he replied, tentatively. "I'll risk . . . How much?"

At that point, Jacobovici recalls, Loewy started laughing. The challenge was a bluff. "Okay," he said, "go and release it in New York."

As a result of that conversation, a sub-distribution agreement with Normandie was signed. Mark Lipsky's Spotlight Films was hired to promote the film. Adam Rogers was hired to book theatres and track the results. And the first of a long series of overtures was made to Telefilm Canada, to access its Production Marketing Assistance Fund, a pool of money set up to facilitate the launch of Canadian films in both Canada and foreign markets. Under the terms of that fund, Telefilm would inject up to 50 percent of the costs of the U.S. prints and ads campaign. Having raised $50,000 on their own, the producers were expecting Telefilm to match that amount with another $50,000 to finance openings in Los Angeles, Boston, Chicago and elsewhere.

Among the producers, there was a high degree of optimism about the film's chances in New York. A few months before its release, Sackman said, "I don't know why this film can't do a million dollar box office in the U.S. Hit just one percent of the Jews in New York City and you've got a quarter of a million dollar gross right there." That, he predicted, would lead to someone bigger taking the film for the rest of the country, and translate into enhanced television and video sales. Jacobovici concurred. "The theory," he maintains, "wasn't off the wall." But it was skewed by history, by his 1984 success with *Falasha*. "I was naive," he says. "I felt I could do it again."

A month before the film's scheduled U.S. opening, Jacobovici and Beinstock went to New York to prime the media pump. Publicist Lipsky gave them an office and telephones, and they started making calls to newspapers, radio and TV stations, magazines—just as they had in Toronto a year earlier. After rejection by Karen Cooper at the Film Forum, a second choice was the Angelika, which caters to a student crowd. But it, too, rejected the film. The fall-back plan was to open at two locations, the small, uptown Carnegie Cinema, which had the virtue of being physically close to the city's Jewish community, and the downtown East Village, a multiplex arrangement in which the film would be competing with such movies as *1492* and *The Mighty Ducks*.

The publicity campaign seemed to work everywhere, except at the box office. On its October 17 opening, six major dailies reviewed *Deadly*, all with good to excellent notices. In the *Wall Street Journal*, Julie Salomon called it a vibrant portrait of the madness of the Middle East. In the *Times*, Stephen Holden described it at "an elegantly interwoven sequence of words and images." *Newsday* gave the film its only "money review" in New York, awarding it 3.5 stars and urging readers to see it. The sole discordant note was struck by David Denby in *New York*, who said the film had too many evocative images and not enough illumination.

Still, given the general reaction, a film about cabbage-growing should have sold out the first weekend, Jacobovici concedes. Instead, *Deadly* recorded a poor opening weekend (about $1,700 gross in each theatre). And while it built steadily through the week, it was not strong enough to resist the competition. Had it been able to survive four weeks, Jacobovici believes it would have survived three months. But bottom-line exhibitors do not wait four weeks, not with a new Hollywood release available that can deliver better numbers instantly. Opening a film in New York, Jacobovici concluded, was "like being in a room with 10,000 people talking at once and you're whispering. Unless you have a big microphone—that is, a lot of money—it's extremely difficult to be heard above the din."

In a city subjected to a constant avalanche of shows, movies, concerts, exhibits, Bienstock found it "tough to get the word out, tough just to get reviewed." In part, timing was against them. In the countdown to the U.S. presidential election, most major media organizations were not focussed on the politics of the Middle East. And a flood of new Hollywood releases made exhibitors unwilling to tie up precious space with Canadian-made documentaries, however well reviewed. Among national film reviewers, only the *New Republic*'s Stanley Kauffman reviewed the film. Bienstock left daily voice-mail messages with *Time*'s Richard Corliss, finally reached him, and asked what was the best way to get him to see the film. "You can either send me a videotape," Corliss said. "or stake out the Time–Life building and kidnap me." Corliss never reviewed the film. If she were doing it again, Bienstock says, she would go to New York earlier, spend more time seeding the ground for the first two weeks of the run, and "paper the hall to keep it there" until word-of-mouth developed.

Summarizing its New York showing, Jacobovici believes that several factors contributed to *Deadly*'s disappointing box office performance. The city's Jewish community, which he misread, is more stratified and less homogenous than in Toronto. "New York," he became convinced, was "an optical illusion. It's a community of communities," broken into little pieces, each loyal to this cinema or that organization. "Either you penetrate one of those islands or you make yourself heard with ads." The latter was never possible; even a postage stamp-sized ad in the *Times* cost $3,000 and the entire campaign—for publicists, prints, trailers, posters, flyers and ads—was $50,000. In terms of free publicity, the U.S. election "blew us out of water." And Jacobovici never managed to appear on TV, or defeat a certain *Intifada* weariness that had set in.

Despite the numbers, the producers did not regard New York as a complete failure. The reviews were good enough to start winning calendar dates in rep house cinemas in smaller U.S. centres. "If we hadn't played New York," Jacobovici maintains, "we wouldn't have had the reviews to get into Minneapolis and Charleston and other places." Still, New York did persuade the producers to delay the film's planned Los Angeles opening until January 1993. Even then, Los Angeles was only possible if Telefilm agreed to make *Deadly* eligible for matching fund dollars, and Telefilm was suddenly raising objections. The agency already had made a $400,000 production investment in the film, and it was now declining to put any more money at risk. For Jacobovici, this position was puzzling. The basic premise of the U.S. theatrical release was to raise the film's value to television, from which sale Telefilm would receive its pro-rated share. Having backed the making of the film on cultural grounds, how could Telefilm suddenly refuse to inject a relatively small additional sum for pragmatic, sheerly commercial reasons?

Reflecting its new commitment to commercial priorities, Telefilm insisted, as a condition of granting launch fund dollars, that Alliance agree to cross-collateralize any debt. In other words, if Telefilm committed $50,000, and the film only returned $20,000 at the box office, the agency wanted the right to recoup from the revenues of TV sales and other ancillary sources as an equal partner. Not surprisingly, Alliance balked. Suddenly, the launch fund money was no longer a grant, but a loan against future revenue. Suddenly, Telefilm seemed less interested in simply helping Canadian distributors penetrate the American theatrical market, and more interested in behaving like a distributor itself. "So I set sail," Jacobovici says, "believing that I have access to $100,000, and find midstream that Telefilm and Alliance have irreconcilable differences and I'm drifting out there."

Nor did he have any remaining moral leverage with Victor Loewy at Alliance. Against his better judgement, Loewy had agreed to the U.S. release, and had played along hoping to raise the value of *Deadly*'s TV sale, only to find that Telefilm wanted a share of the spoils. For Jacobovici, there was no room to manoeuvre. In the end, Alliance agreed to let both Telefilm and Normandie Productions be cross-collateralized from TV, video and non-theatrical revenues in the U.S.—but only after Alliance had claimed both its distribution fees and its expenses, and recouped its minimum guarantee. Telefilm agreed because Alliance would also be recouping its advance from worldwide sales, so that by the time an American TV or video sale was completed, it was conceivable that the distributor would already have been recouped. Normandie waived its normal up-front distribution fees, but in return was allowed to participate in other revenues. By Hollywood standards, the parties were arguing about a trivial amount of money— $100,000—but the accord nevertheless required a substantial commitment of time on all sides.

The film opened on January 22, 1993 at Los Angeles' Fairfax Theatre, a setting Jacobovici considered inappropriate because of its size (300 seats). Still, it played to enthusiastic reviews and stayed three weeks. Across the United States, *Deadly* played in more than a dozen American cities, including four weeks at the Lumière in San Francisco, and good runs in Washington, Boston and Chicago. Its estimated U.S. theatrical gross: $30,000.

One day at the theatre, Jacobovici met Steve Okin, a promotion rep for Columbia–Tristar Video, who voiced interest in acquiring the video rights. Later, the company did solicit the rights, but without offering any advance; the prestige of the company's name, Okin argued, and the broad video release it could underwrite, were sufficient. By the summer of 1993, Columbia–Tristar had taken an option on the video rights; RKO had replaced Normandie as sub-distributor; New Yorker Films had acquired non-theatrical rights; and both PBS and the Discovery Channel were reviewing the film for possible purchase.

Elsewhere, there were Canadian television sales to Radio–Québec ($18,000); and to French-language TV Ontario for $3,000. Abroad, Alliance sold 90-minute versions of the film to Bavarian Dutch, British (BBC—an estimated $30,000) and Swiss/French television. The Jordanians, allegedly, were also interested, but only wanted one hour—a version with all the Israelis edited out.

From *Variety*'s point of view, Halpern concludes, "*Deadly* wouldn't be a commercial success. But in the world of Canadian cinema, it was a terrific success. It had a long run by any standard for a Canadian feature." In recognition of its merit, the film won a 1992 Genie award for best documentary, the Gold Award at the Houston International Film festival and the Grand Prize at the Nyon International Film Festival, the world's most important forum for documentaries.

FINAL TAKES Simcha Jacobovici: "Nobody is going to get behind a small film, a documentary, if the filmmaker doesn't. And the question is, do you want to make films? Or do you want to make films that are seen? I'm not a distributor, but our understanding of the filmmaking process from A to Z—festivals, funding agencies—it's been a tremendous education. And at each step of the way, it was like manoeuvring through icebergs."

Ric Bienstock: "People ask me, 'how did you get that footage. How did you get so close to them?' It's not magic. We had great contacts on both sides and they were nurtured. We hung out there for four months, in cafes, talking, meeting. It wasn't just Simcha's vision. It was a systematic effort to find what we needed."

Elliott Halpern: "It's very hard to release a documentary theatrically. The producer has to remain involved, because distributors aren't set up to promote it. They don't have the pre-packaged U.S. campaigns. And the returns aren't there. In the U.S., producers think their job ends when the film is finished, and that makes perfect sense. In Canada, if you want your film shown, you have to be completely obsessed."

10
The Big Chill with a Ph.D.

Le Déclin de
L'Empire Américain
(The Decline of
the American
Empire)

DIRECTOR: Denys Arcand	Dorothée Berryman, Louise Portal, Geneviève Rioux,
PRODUCERS: Roger Frappier (NATIONAL FILM BOARD); René Malo (CORPORATION IMAGE M&M LTEE)	Pierre Curzi, Rémy Girard, Yves Jacques, Daniel Brière, Gabriel Arcand
ASSOCIATE PRODUCER: Pierre Gendron	**DISTRIBUTOR:** LES FILMS RENÉ MALO (CANADA);
WRITER: Denys Arcand	CINEPLEX–ODEON (USA); NEW WORLD
DIRECTOR OF PHOTOGRAPHY: Guy Dufaux	MUTUAL PICTURES (world)
SOUND: Richard Besse	**RELEASE DATE:** June 20, 1986
EDITOR: Monique Fortier	**RUNNING TIME:** 101 minutes
ACTORS: Dominique Michel,	**BUDGET:** $1.8 million

---

*"Strangely, the best things that you do sometimes just happen to you, without precon-
ceptions. It just flows out of you. It's an even better film than I thought. I found something that echoed the life of thousands of people, everywhere. Once, in Brazil, some
professor came to me after a screening and said, 'how do you know this? This is my life
here. It's all our lives.' I struck the right chord, I guess."* — Denys Arcand, director

"The most difficult part of Le Declin *was to write it. It's a great piece of literature.
So it was very easy to put the money together, because the script was really great. This
is something we always forget. Movies have to be written first. That's where it starts.
With [Ingemar] Bergman, with [Woody] Allen, and with Denys Arcand."*

— Roger Frappier, producer

SYNOPSIS Eight history professors, four men and four women, gather
for an autumn weekend on the shores of idyllic Lake Memphramagog,
Quebec. The women exercise and talk about sex; the men prepare the food
and talk about sex. Apart from a few flashbacks, almost nothing happens,
and yet the film manages poignantly to address the most important questions about love and relationships that confront men and women.

ORIGINS In an age when it is considered almost obligatory to rush
children into reading at an early age, it is perhaps instructive to learn that
Denys Arcand did not pick up his first book until the age of 12. Thirty-four
years and several hundred books later, Arcand wrote and directed *Le Déclin
de l' Empire Américain*, arguably the most interesting, unconventional and

Denys Arcand, director and writer, Le Déclin de L'Empire Américain.

successful Canadian film of the 1980s. Among its many honours and accolades were eight Genie awards; the international critic's prize at the Cannes Film Festival, an Academy Award nomination for best foreign film, the Toronto Festival of Festivals' most popular film award, the New York critics' award for best picture, the Chicago film festival's silver Hugo award, the Italian film festival's press award, and the Golden Reel as the highest grossing film in Canada.

Of course, Arcand had some help—the production genius of Roger Frappier, perhaps the most talented of the Quebec school of producers; the distribution savvy of René Malo and his associate, Pierre Latour; and a remarkable piece of naturalistic, ensemble acting.

In English Canada, scores of writers, directors and producers are daily engaged in the attempt to make the great Canadian film—a low-budget, crossover movie that somehow combines the box-office drawing power of *E.T.* with the critical acclaim of *Citizen Kane*. *Le Déclin* did not soar quite that high, but its overall performance, critical and commercial, has still not been matched by any film produced in English Canada, not even by *Black Robe*, the lavish, $14-million, 1991 Canada–Australia co-production. And not the least of the many ironies associated with *Le Déclin*'s creation is that its unparalleled international success (for a Canadian film) was achieved by a largely unknown director, with a largely unknown cast (outside of Quebec), appearing in a sub- titled—and therefore less accessible—film in which, as in a Seinfeld sit-com, almost nothing happens.

How was that possible? From what creative matrix did this film spring? What confluence of factors managed to bring together Arcand, Frappier and the others at precisely that moment in the decade? And with a script that clearly spoke, with humour and affection, to a generation's concerns about the cold emptiness at the heart of cultural hedonism? These questions may not in the end be answerable, but if *Le Déclin* is to serve as any sort of model for aspiring filmmakers, they are surely worth exploring in some detail.

The eldest of four children, Denys Arcand was born into a working-class family in Deschambault, a small village near the St. Lawrence River between

Quebec City and Trois Rivières in 1940. He seldom went to movies—his father viewed cinema as a lower-class form of entertainment and associated it with the Depression, during which film was a kind of narcotic for the unemployed. But his neighbour, an uncle, was an agronomist who owned a 16MM projector. On summer nights, Arcand remembers, his uncle would rent a concert film from a distributor in Quebec City and hold outdoor screenings for the village; Arcand went—without his parents. And while they were naturally proud of his subsequent success, they were "never really convinced," he says, that film was a legitimate form of artistic ecxpression. His father never saw *Le Déclin*—his mother did. "I warned her against it," he says. "Of course, she was quite scandalized."

His father, a river pilot who had never finished high school, wanted his four children to get a formal education and become professionals. As a result, the family moved to Montreal when Arcand was 12. Attending a Jesuit college, he inclined naturally to literature, theatre and the arts. But with few obvious career opportunities in those fields—in film, there was only the National Film Board and every aspiring filmmaker was knocking on its doors, usually in frustration—Arcand decided to study for his master's degree in history at the University of Montreal. He had no taste at all for law, medicine or any more conventional profession; history was the only field he found "somewhat interesting." But even then, he made his decision "more to please my parents than anything else."

It was during his post-graduate years that Arcand, always active in university theatre, became involved as an actor in his first cinematic venture—a largely-improvised student film to which the National Film Board had loaned some talent, including Michel Brault and Claude Jutra. "I was completely seduced by them," Arcand recalls. "By the way they lived, by the fact that they travelled all over the world and knew about things like jazz music, which I knew nothing about." It was the filmmakers rather than the art of filmmaking that lured Arcand. "I wanted to be like them." After graduation, in 1962, he approached the Film Board for a summer job and found that "his history connection paid off." The NFB had been contracted to prepare a series of 30-minute educational films on the history of Canada, in preparation for the country's Centennial celebrations. Arcand started as a researcher, but soon was promoted to scriptwriter and then, largely by default, to director. But as a harbinger of his future conflicts with the NFB he found his interpretation of history completely at odds with the traditional views held by the powers at the Film Board, including its powerful head of French-language production, Pierre Juneau. "I had enormous problems with censorship," he says. "I was forever rewriting the voice-over commentaries. There were six or seven versions before they were accepted. Eventually, they dropped the series. I was perpetually creating problems for them."

By then, however, he was on staff—drawing a regular paycheque but

Poster art created for the release of **Le Déclin de L'Empire Américain** *in France, where the film drew more than 1.5 million moviegoers.*

without an official assignment, and spending hours in the Film Board's cafeteria, the unofficial nexus of Quebec cinema. It was Michel Brault who finally suggested that Arcand try his hand at writing a screenplay. The result was *Entre la Mer et L'Eau Douce*, a film about a rural folksinger who comes to Montreal and becomes a success; although it was not made for several years, the film starred Geneviève Bujold—her first feature. Arcand left the NFB in 1966 to make films for Expo '67, but returned as a freelancer in 1970, and directed the film that virtually overnight vaulted him into the first rank of French Canadian filmmakers—*On est au Coton*, his landmark, three-hour documentary on the Dickensian working conditions in Quebec textile mills. Scheduled for release amid the turmoil of October 1970—the month of the FLQ crisis, the James Cross kidnapping, the Pierre Laporte murder, the *War Measures Act*—the film was shelved by then NFB Commissioner Sydney Newman. "There I was, a complete unknown filmmaker," Arcand told the *Globe and Mail*'s Christopher Harris. "Nobody thought I was a filmmaker of any importance and out of the blue came this censorship. If they hadn't done anything, the film would have died, because it's a very difficult film, a rambling film that goes on forever and in every direction at the same time. It's not such a masterpiece." The censorship, he said, "was the best thing that ever happened to me."

Even before the controversy over *Coton* had erupted, Arcand had embarked on another political, and equally sensitive subject, a frankly pro-separatist documentary (*Duplessis et Après*) that explored the lingering impact on Quebec society of Maurice Duplessis' long reign as premier. Again, there were censorship problems with the Film Board. "They didn't know what to do with it," he says. "So they didn't promote it; it was never shown; they just ditched it."

Fed up with petty functionaries, Arcand left the Film Board in 1971 and, in three years, directed three feature films, *La Maudite Gallete*, *Rejeanne Padovani* and *Gina*. None was a major box-office hit, but all were reasonably well-received. In fact, *Galette* was entered into Critics' Week at Cannes, and *Padovani* was in Cannes' Director's Fortnight. Of the three, the most impressive perhaps was *Padovani*, which *Village Voice* critic Andrew Sarris called "a dry, austere, almost obscure contemplation of corruption" in the Montreal construction industry. For the next several years, Arcand worked mainly in television, not always of his own volition. There was a hit series on Duplessis, three episodes of a dramatic series (*Empire Inc.*), and *The Crime of Ovide Plouffe*—what Arcand now calls "a shlock sequel to a sequel. I was aimlessly waiting," he told the *Globe and Mail*'s Jay Scott of this period. "I'm so pessimistic about filmmaking in general. I tried not to have any desires at all. It was work. It was helpful." His sole excursion into film between 1974 and 1985 was a documentary for the National Film Board on the 1980 Quebec referendum, *Le Confort et L'Indifference* (a title that might well have applied to the *Le Déclin* script). The work was significant on at least two counts—it seemed finally to have exhausted Arcand's interest in politics, at least as a subject of films, and it brought him together for the first time with producer Roger Frappier. In fact, it was Frappier, then with the NFB, who had approached Arcand after the election of the Parti Québecois in 1976 and suggested making a documentary on the referendum.

The son of a welder, Frappier was born in Sorel, 40 miles south of Montreal. He moved to the larger city at the age of 17, shortly after the death of his father, and put himself through college with a waiter's job at the Queen Elizabeth Hotel. In the early 1960s, he recalls, Montreal movie theatres opened doors at 9 A.M.; Frappier was there every morning, supplementing his academic studies with an intense, self-administered course in cinema. "It was fantastic," he says. "I saw 12 to 15 films every week." After working at Expo '67 as a projectionist (no doubt screening films made by Denys Arcand), Frappier applied for work at the National Film Board and local production houses. Rejected, he went to London in 1968, "speaking about four words of English," and enrolled at the London School of Film Technique. The school itself, he concedes, did not deserve its reputation, but there were ample compensations, including access to the movie sets of their teachers; Frappier watched Lindsay Anderson direct parts of *All the King's Men*.

A year later, his savings exhausted, he returned to Montreal and began to work in documentaries, both as a director and a producer. He also did some acting, and had a small role in Arcand's *Rejeanne Padovani*, playing a student who is beaten during a demonstration. But by 1979, Frappier was tired of the chronic indebtedness that accompanied the documentarian's life. "I don't regret anything. But my daughter was five months old, and I had to do something with my life. I couldn't sit in the living room and say 'No, I won't do this, I won't do that, I'm too pure.' " One night, during a trip to the corner store, he bumped into a friend in the advertising business.

"What are you doing with yourself,' his friend asked.

"Nothing," Frappier replied. "I haven't worked for months."

"Would you do advertising—commercials?" A week before, the answer to that question would have been a firm and immediate No. Now, Frappier said:

"Do you think I can do that?"

"Of course, you can."

When he went home, he said to his wife, "you'll never guess what I found at the store."

"What,' she said.

"A job."

Days later, Frappier was behind the cameras, directing a commercial for the Ministry of Education. He spent the next three years in a world he once considered alien and hostile. "It saved my life," he confesses. "Psychologically and financially." Now, he has "a lot of respect" for the art of making TV commercials, and much of what he continues to apply in feature films derives, he says, from that experience. "First, you have to communicate an idea—understand it and communicate it, in a form that is nice to receive. Second, everything must have a reason. Why is the camera here and not there; why this lens and not that one? Third, because so many people are involved, even people you don't want to deal with, you must learn to negotiate your own space. And fourth, I learned everything about how to launch a product. To be on a set one day a week is the best school for learning to deal with stress and deadlines. After that, everything in feature films seems normal."

But after three years, Frappier had learned as much as he wanted to learn. One night at 3 A.M., struggling with a problem-plagued commercial for Stay Free, "I decided I'd had enough. You make $27,000 for a month and then you don't work for three months. You're always pitching, pitching. It's tough on the ego. One day you're hot and then you're not."

His decision was doubtless made easier by two attractive job offers in the feature film industry—one with the National Film Board as executive producer and head of Studio C; the other with the province's film development agency, the Société Générale des Industries Culturelles du Québec (SOGIC), as head of production. With two invitations—"it had never happened in my life, before or after"—Frappier had time and space to negotiate. The NFB position, however, was clearly superior because the Film Board was a genuine studio—with sound stages, editing, mixing and all the other facilities required to see a film through to completion. "The only thought I had was that, if I went back to the NFB, I would produce differently, and work with filmmakers I liked, and go into production in a relatively short period," Frappier says. "I had not succeeded as a feature film director. So I wanted to become the kind of producer I would have liked to have had. I had good ideas, but I needed people to trust me, give me money, and time to develop them, organize, market and promote." Before taking the job, Frappier insisted on several conditions—budgets generous enough to make several small (under $1 million) features, the right to hire filmmakers he wanted to work with and, most critically, sole decision-making power to green-light film projects. Then NFB commissioner François Macerola agreed. Among the first group of directors: Denys Arcand, Lea Pool, Pierre Felardeau, Bernard Gosselin and Jacques Leduc.

Within the group, there was a tacit understanding that the films made by Studio C would deal with contemporary issues, "with the problems that we were living," Frappier says. "A lot of things were happening to us that we never saw on the screen. Most of us were plus or minus forty years old, and all the movies we were seeing we could not relate to, especially French Canadian films, which at that time were all period pieces."

DEVELOPMENT For Denys Arcand, the invitation to join Frappier's circle suited his needs almost perfectly. Most producers, he says, expect directors to approach them with scripts, treatments or outlines. "But usually, I don't have projects," he confesses. "I never have any interesting ideas. I have areas of interest, and I need a producer who will go along and sign contracts on the strength of that. Even on *Le Déclin*, I did not know where I was going. I said to Roger, 'I think I might do a film about conversations.' And he said, 'Yes, fine. Here's the contract. I'm going to give you $30,000. Go home and write.' So I was financed while I was groping in the dark. Frappier was willing to do that. It was a good offer, because it was an open offer." The precise origins of the *Le Déclin* script are not clear. According to Arcand, it began with his search for a film that could be contained within Frappier's projected cost (about $800,000). "You don't go very far on that kind of budget in a feature film." Arcand says. "So I was trying to think of a way . . . . And the cheapest and still interesting film I could think of was Louis Malle's *My Dinner with Andre* . . . . What kind of film could I do like that? Probably the most interesting kind of talk is always about sex lives. If you were in a restaurant and you overheard people discussing their sex lives, you'd immediately stop and try to listen to the conversation. There's an element of voyeurism in every one of us that you cannot escape." In the late summer of 1984, Arcand started writing a script based on overheard conversations. That became the first draft. The original title was *Conversationes Scabrouses* (Racy Conversations).

Frappier, however, also lays claim to some credit for the concept. For some time, he says, he had been contemplating a movie that would be focussed around a restaurant meal. The first course would feature a group of men talking about women; for the second course, women would join the men; then the men would leave; by dessert, only the women would be left, to talk about the men. "We were looking for a way to break cinematic conventions," he says. "A year and a half later, *My Dinner with Andre* came out." That idea provided the essential structure of Arcand's first pass at the script—"people sitting at a table and talking about sex." He wrote the first draft as he always writes, by hand, in genuine ink, on plain white paper, working from about 10 in the morning until 2 P.M. "I'm a very slow writer," he admits. "And I always start with more than I need, and then cut. The first script was like a novel—250 pages, very, very verbose."

When he had Arcand's first draft, Frappier immediately took it to his superiors at the Film Board, Macerola and Daniel Pinard, the head of French-language production, and said: "I want to tell you a year in advance that I have a text from Denys, and it will be a discussion about sex for an hour and a half." Both men read the draft and gave their approval. Within Studio C, Frappier had organized a series of workshop discussions to evaluate the scripts. In advance of the meeting, the screenplay would be circulated to each member. When they met, the entire morning would be given over to hearing detailed assessments of the script. Each assessment, Frappier says, was delivered without interruption. After lunch, they would return and open the floor to all participants. Later, Frappier and the director would review the critiques and decide what was worth changing. This collective approach, he believes, had several advantages, not the least of which was that it accelerated the process. "It's so tough to write when you wait months for a reaction. And I think the writer can take the criticism more easily in a group situation."

Arcand says the NFB group was always very supportive, but did not provide many specific suggestions for the script. What did help, he says, were interviews he conducted with friends, men and women, about their sex lives. "My method of working was totally unorthodox. I read a great deal about sex, and talked to basically anyone who wanted to talk to me." Arcand took no notes; he simply listened, getting a feel for character and background, "for how people were living." Because it was a film based almost entirely on talk, the talk, he knew, had to be of particularly interesting kind. "You needed a certain eloquence," Arcand says. "You almost had to have educated people. People who liked to talk and could play with words easily. The sexual life of a trucker might be as interesting or maybe better. But he won't be able to express it. To see that life you'd have to film it, and that would take a higher budget. But university professors, they talk all the time; that's their job."

In choosing the well-spoken and well-heeled community of academics, Arcand had other considerations in mind as well. One of them was the potential foreign market for the film—specifically, France. For years, Quebec filmmakers had to have their films sub-titled or dubbed into Parisienne French, to eliminate what Arcand once called "the monstrous problems" of *joual*, the language of the street in Quebec. So "I was vaguely aware," he says, "that if it were to be understood abroad, then the superior French spoken by university professors would allow it to be seen."

And there was something else. In a 1986 interview with Michael Dorland in *Cinema Canada*, Arcand addressed the thematic heart of *Le Déclin*. "What Canadians seek above everything else is comfort," he said. "You see that on the economic plane. Anybody who starts up a company immediately wants to sell it to the Americans, so that he can get together three million bucks to go and build a villa in Palm Beach or Palm Springs and end his life playing golf. That's the fundamental Canadian sense of comfort. So I wanted people who were comfortable, people in their forties who were happily installed in comfort and won't budge until they retire."

Still, it was only after Arcand had written three-quarters of the script that he erected the script's metaphorical scaffolding—an empire's decline. As he once told critic Jay Scott, "I had to invent a thesis and justify all the blue language I'd written. It's not a real thesis. It's a thesis for movie purposes." The concept was rooted in the notion of leisure. University professors,

Arcand discovered, had "enormous amounts of leisure," he told Dorland. "They're not working very hard." That lifestyle is essentially parasitic; "they're living off the crumbs of the American table. This country is rich because America is rich. And their destiny is linked to that of the American empire. I felt there was some truth to that." Canada was to the United States what the Etruscans were to the Romans, a nation on the margins. "Here," he told Dorland, "we're just spectators. And all of Canadian policy at bottom is a reflection of that: always trying to demarcate ourselves a little."

Despite their hedonism and their egocentricity, Arcand retained an essential affection for these characters, "because those characters are also me. I can't bear people who don't want to see what appears to be reality," he said in another interview. "That's why I make films, for those who cannot see what is there: to say to them, look, I'm showing you what is . . . They're not insects I'm looking at, not at all. They're my friends. They're me. So I can only attempt to look at them with lucidity. After all, what can they do? They cannot change history. They are lucid enough to know that history is a kind of blind force that advances like a glacier . . . whether you're conscious of it or not."

The script took him about 10 months to finish, working from August 1984 through May 1985. There were four versions, which he rewrote completely four times. At one early stage, he recalls, Frappier seemed to think the film had more potential than he had originally envisaged, and that it would require a bigger budget to open it up. It was at that point that Frappier decided to approach Montreal producer René Malo about possible co-production. Malo liked the script and readily agreed to participate and raise production financing. According to Frappier, the financing package was put together in record time—four days. "That doesn't happen at all, anymore," he says ruefully. "It took four days to finance the first film, four weeks for the second; now it takes four months. Financing gets tougher and tougher all the time."

The participants in Le Déclin were the NFB ($500,000); Telefilm Canada ($850,000); SOGIC (350,000); and Radio-Canada ($100,000), for a total of $1.8 million. With a bigger budget, Arcand felt free to bring new elements to the film, adding flashbacks from the characters' past lives, as well as the Lake Memphramagog weekend setting. Not everyone, however, was equally taken with the script. Even after they agreed to invest, Telefilm officials told the producers that they thought the film was elitist, and doubted that it could work commercially. And two foreign sales agents in Canada, on seeing the finished film, pronounced themselves fortunate not to have acquired the rights to Le Déclin because "Malo wouldn't be able to make a penny on it.") Afterwards, says Frappier, the naysayers attributed the movie's success to its obsession with sex.

But Malo himself also lobbied for script changes. "He wanted it to end on an up note," Arcand recalls. " 'Do it light,' he kept saying. 'Do it light.' At one point, Malo even arranged for Arcand to view *The Breakfast Club*, a Hollywood film the distributor thought typical of what audiences wanted to see. "I was at the time puzzled about why I was being shown the film," Arcand says, "but later I agreed that it's a good idea not to finish on a sombre note." On the other hand, he concedes that his outlook on life in pessimistic. "I'm not gloomy, but I generally think life is not that rosy, and I see no reason to change."

PRODUCTION In casting his film, Arcand decided for the first time to invoke video technology, inviting each of the candidates to read portions of the script for the camera. The video audition followed private meetings in which he simply talked to the actors, "to see if we see along the same lines, if we can work together, if the chemistry is right." He tested four or five actors for each role, edited the videos together, and ranked them in his order of preference before showing them to Frappier and Malo. There was no disagreement from the producers. Casting was complete by the end of July 1985. He has used video auditions on all his subsequent films. "If it works," he says, "don't break it." One Sunday in August, the cast gathered in a Montreal office building for a slow read-through of the script. A number of changes were suggested, especially by the women. "The original script for the women's roles was more discreet and less raw than what's in the film," Arcand says. "But the women said, 'You should see what we say about our boyfriends. We're worse than the men.' So the women characters became, at their own suggestion, more audacious."

The seven-week shoot began in Montreal in late August, then moved to Lake Memphramagog in the Eastern Townships. According to Arcand and others, "it went like a breeze. I hear other people have problems. I haven't had that experience. The weather was absolutely gorgeous. We were living in condos and could walk to the set every day. It was a beautiful autumn. There were no technical problems. It was an enchanted experience." Frappier's recollection is much the same. On weekends, he recalls, the cast and crew chose to stay by the lake rather than return to Montreal. A rare sense of fraternity prevailed. "People stayed and ate together and had big parties outside. And yet at the same time we were always wondering what the result would be. We did not know if the film would appeal only to intellectuals or to a broader audience." Looking at the daily rushes every evening in a local hotel, "we had a sense of what we were doing. But we did not know how it would touch the people."

Principal photography was complete by early October and, by Christmas, the film had been edited. Arcand nursed few illusions about its success. "I didn't expect much," he says, "because although people liked the film, they were a little bewildered. The people in the NFB lab and the head of French-language production—they thought 'that's a weird film. There's no action. All these people are talking.' They weren't negative, but they weren't convinced. And I was completely lost, as I always am. I had no opinion, no idea whether it was good or bad. I expected it was okay. I had absolutely no hopes. Frappier and Malo were a little more hopeful than I was. We thought we had an okay little film."

Seeing the fine cut of the film at the NFB, Malo's associate Pierre Latour thought it would be difficult to release theatrically. "I never thought we could capitalize on the humour," he says, "because I found it to be a very dark look at society, a sad film with a pretty sad ending, a group of friends collapsing. I thought it was a profound film, and a clever look at contemporary society. But the undertone is consistently dark. A long time before *Sex, Lies and Videotape*, this was *Sex, Lies and Cooking*, or *Teaching*. So I was amazed." Indeed, after *Le Déclin* opened to sold-out audiences in Montreal, Latour went to the theatre more than 30 times, just to verify that audiences were continuing to enjoy the film. Malo, Latour says, was always more confident, although he, too, found the ending sombre.

CANNES Early in 1986, a cutting copy of *Le Déclin* was sent to the selection committee for the main competition at Cannes. The Cannes representative emerged from a screening with eight pages of suggested editing changes. "They were worried about its reception," Arcand recalls. "They thought it was too racy." Frappier traced the problem to isolation. "It's always the same story," he says. "People from festivals look at films alone, by themselves, in small rooms, without a crowd. It's like going to a concert alone; there's something impossible in that task, because you don't get the reaction of the audience, and you're not receiving the film as an audience receives it in a theatre. That's why they sometimes make mistakes. Films, especially comedies, need an audience." The problem was compounded at Cannes, where officials are always "looking for something that does not exist. Cannes is a tough place to take movies, because people want it to be the end of the world."

Still, the producers were now faced with a critical decision—whether to make the suggested editing changes on *Le Déclin* in order to win entry to the main competition. A few months before Cannes, Frappier and Malo organized a private screening for about a dozen people in Paris. Nobody laughed, Frappier remembers. "Or if they did, it was in the wrong places. Everything went badly. I could see all the mistakes in the film. I was completely shaken." Afterwards, he and Pierre Gendron, *Le Déclin*'s associate producer, strolled on the Champs Elysées, "one of the most beautiful streets in the world, completely oblivious to our surroundings, utterly depressed, asking ourselves, could we have been so wrong? We came out with our hearts in our hands, not disappointed, but wondering—because we liked the film a lot more than did the people in that screening."

At that point, Frappier and Gendron phoned Arcand and explained the situation. "And all of us agreed on the phone that that was the movie we had made, that we weren't going to change it, and that it would live or die that way. We were going to stick with it." So *Le Déclin* was rejected for the main competition, but was accepted for the Director's Fortnight.

The cool reaction to the film at the private screening in Paris was more than offset by the undiluted praise issued by the 70-odd journalists who saw the film a few weeks before the Cannes festival opened. Arcand knew nothing of that reception. He was incommunicado, having attended a seminar in Belgium and then taken a long, leisurely train ride to Cannes, via Luxembourg, Switzerland and Italy. "Nobody knew where I was. I remember walking into the Carlyle Hotel in Cannes with my suitcase and the secretary from the Telefilm office saw me in the corridor—I was going to find out where they had booked my room—and she started screaming at me. 'Where were you? You've got a monster on your hands. It's going to be so big you can't imagine.' I was utterly dumbfounded."

To promote the film in Cannes, Malo and Pierre Latour created handbills based on a fake *Time* magazine cover. The central image was the film's provocative poster, designed by Montreal artist Yvan Adam, which showed the bodies of a faceless, well-dressed couple; onto the woman, a pair of breasts had been drawn, like graffiti; onto the man, an erect penis. "None of us," confesses Latour, "had any idea about the poster or how to sell the film. It was René's idea to bring in Yvan. And when we saw it, we knew immediately that this was the right image. It was unanimous. Of course, they had to lobby *La Presse* to run the poster. The breasts weren't the problem; the erect penis was." This aggressive positioning was designed to counter the effects of the title, which Malo had never particularly liked, on the grounds that it was both too long and made the film sound too much like a documentary. Indeed, as late as March of 1986, Malo was still urging Frappier and Arcand to change the title.

On May 12, 1986, *Le Déclin* opened the Director's Fortnight at the old Palais theatre, since destroyed. Arcand remembers a mob scene, with an overflow audience and patrons scrambling to get in. After the screening, he says, "people applauded for like 20 minutes solid. And you don't know what to do. You're just standing there. It was really awesome. It was the first time in my life that I've been hit by success. You don't understand it. You're very happy, but at the same time, it's sort of overwhelming. It's beyond you; you don't know what you've done." Arcand took his bows with Dorothée Berryman, the only member of the cast to attend the festival—a measure, no doubt, of the generally low expectations for the film.

Even Frappier did not attend. Only 14 months after joining the Film Board, he had quit to join Pierre Gendron in Oz Productions. The company was just getting started, and he "did not have money to go to Cannes." Frappier's premature departure from the NFB was also caused by a power struggle. In 14 months, he had produced 12 films, all on or under budget, including Lea Pool's *Anne Trister*, made for $1.4 million. But now his superiors proposed to recreate a program committee with final authority over movie projects. Frappier balked. "I said, 'I'm a responsible producer. Judge me by what's on the screen.' I don't believe in committees. These people receive a script on Friday, read it over the weekend while they're gardening, fishing and going to store with their kids, and then arrive on Monday morning and say, 'well, I didn't really like it.' I don't believe in that. You have to trust the filmmakers. And you have to trust the producers. A movie is a total impression. You have to read the whole script. If I do it properly, it takes me a whole day." Arcand's analysis of Frappier's resignation from the NFB is more prosaic. "He just couldn't stand being in meetings all day."

Attaining overnight international stature did not, Arcand believes, have much effect on his professional life. He was already working on his next film, *Jésus de Montréal*; it had a slightly larger budget, but was otherwise a picture of similar scale and ambition. But on a personal level, the success of *Le Déclin* allowed Arcand to stop being afraid of ending his life at the Salvation Army. "That was always my main concern," he insists. "All through these years, I was worried about ending up on the streets. I made no money. I had no savings. I was incredibly badly paid. I wasn't starving, but I had to work all the time. And then suddenly I knew that after this, I would have job offers and producers would ask me to do projects. It was an immense relief."

For René Malo, it was an immense profit. On the morning after the Cannes screening, buyers from Israel were on the phone, followed quickly by Britain (Artificial Eye), Germany (Tobis), Switzerland, New Zealand, Spain, Holland, Norway, Denmark, Argentina, Brazil, Sweden and Australia. Said Malo: "Some producers are in business for a day like this." Not including France, Malo left Cannes with minimum guarantees worth more than $600,000 and sales to more than 20 countries. The film, of course, left with the prestigious Critics' Prize. And there were some 11 American buyers bidding for the U.S. rights, including Orion Classics and Samuel Goldwyn. The prices being offered Malo told *Variety*, were "in the highest range for pictures of this kind." He was in no particular hurry to complete the U.S. deal. "If the picture survived the festival like this," he said, "it can survive a few weeks more."

DISTRIBUTION The enormous buzz created by *Le Déclin* in Cannes confronted René Malo with a crucial decision—whether to open immediately in the theatres or wait until after the Montreal Film Festival in late August. Technically, it should have opened the Montreal gathering because that year, festival director Serge Losique had arranged to import the entire catalogue of films appearing in the Director's Fortnight at Cannes. More to the point, opening *Le Déclin* in June would put it in direct competition with Hollywood's annual outpouring of family-oriented summer films, with their extravagant promotional campaigns. "So waiting," says Pierre Latour, then Malo's assistant and now head of distribution for Frappier at Max Films, "seemed the natural thing to do. Even films that score big at festivals in the spring are usually shelved for the summer, in order to be released at the Montreal and Toronto festivals. Once in a while, a film is strong enough to resist that pressure. But usually, nothing else has any chance."

According to Latour, Malo "had mixed feelings about it. It was a big gamble for him." If the film bombed, there would be no recovery, at least not theatrically. And a poor performance in Canada would doubtless have complicated his negotiations for U.S. distribution. Both Latour and Frappier were pushing hard for a June release. It was not only a case of "striking while the iron is hot," Latour says. "There were no other quality pictures available for that summer, only the usual Hollywood schlock. I thought we should position *Le Déclin* as both serious and humorous, a quality movie, and open in one theatre in Montreal." By the end of the summer, he predicted, it would gross a very respectable $250,000 in box office revenues (a 10-week average of $25,000).

Finally, Malo agreed. After a gala premiere at the Place du Canada, the film opened on June 20, 1986 at the Crémazie, a 650-seat theatre in the north end—close to some of the city's upper-crust neighbourhoods, but not too far from the more working-class north shore. The film, it turned out, appealed to both demographic categories; the elites identified with its intellectual angst; blue-collar viewers laughed at the folly and pretensions of the academic set. The first week's gross: more than $57,000.

Because of the theatre's small lobby, moviegoers had to line up outside, a twice-nightly advertisement of its popularity. Not surprisingly, press coverage was relentless, with weekly articles in the French and English-language media. Other newspaper stories, unrelated to the film itself, also seemed determined to promote it. Recalls Latour: "In all the headlines, there was the decline of pulp and paper, the decline of the textile industry, the decline of everything." Even the weather cooperated; it was one of the rainiest summers in memory, and indoor entertainment was in demand. By the time it opened Toronto's Festival of Festivals in September, paired with Leon Marr's *Dancing in the Dark*, it had played to sold-out Montreal audiences for 11 straight weeks. At the Crémazie, a good week was $15,000-18,000. *Le Déclin* averaged more than $50,000 in its first eight weeks, eclipsing the mark set by *Out of Africa* ($43,000) and setting precedents once considered unthinkable for a Canadian film. Says Latour: "It was *the* film of one summer."

By September, of course, it had opened elsewhere in Quebec. In tiny Ste. Adèle, in the Laurentians north of Montreal, it grossed $14,000 in its first week, breaking a record previously held by Steven Spielberg's *Raiders of the Lost Ark*. In suburban Longeuil, it broke records too, grossing almost $160,000 in seven weeks; a third of that figure would ordinarily have been considered quite successful. By December, *Le Déclin* had grossed $1.54 million in Montreal alone, and $2.43 million in Quebec. By March, it had earned $3 million, passing *E.T.* to become the highest grossing French-language film in Quebec history. In its initial run, it ultimately played for almost an entire year in Montreal. In fact, it continued to play for three months after its release in video.

In Toronto, *Le Déclin* opened the Festival of Festivals. Interrupted four times by applause, its screening concluded with a five-minute standing ovation. Malo reportedly said he had never seen anything like it. Commercially, it opened in Ottawa on September 5, in Toronto on September 12 at two theatres, the Carlton and Canada Square, in Vancouver on September 26 and across the country in October. But the campaign for the film had to be changed to conform to English Canada's more puritanical mores; newspapers refused to run the poster with graffiti breasts and penis (although one edition of the *Globe and Mail* inadvertently carried it before it was caught).

Malo, for one, was outraged. "I believe it is ironic," he said, "that when this material has been approved by the Ontario Censor Board, that the advertising departments of Toronto's major newspapers would take upon themselves the role of censors and alter a significant work of art." Without the private parts, the poster made no sense; with it, most observers agreed, "it was a brilliant work of art that summed up the film." With no avenue of appeal, Malo was forced to devise a new campaign. An all-print advertisement was created. It quoted liberally from the critics; printed the words "sex, desire, passion, perversion, sensual, climax, and love" in large block type; and next to the word 'love,' asked the question: "why do they always treat it like a four-letter word?" In its first 13 weeks, the film grossed $523,188 in English Canada, more than half that amount in Toronto alone. Box-office receipts outside Quebec eventually reached $1 million, a new record that seemed unbeatable—until *Jésus de Montréal* grossed $1.5 million in English Canada. Arcand said at the time that he was "astonished by its success because for me, it was just another job. *Le Déclin* was about my private life, my private problems and trials with women, with other men and so on. Success is the strangest thing to explain because it was supposed to be a very small film."

Not surprisingly, the reviews for *Le Déclin* were almost uniformly positive. One of Canada's most insightful cultural critics, Robert Fulford (writing in *Saturday Night* under his then pseudonym of Marshall Delaney), called it "the most compelling Quebec film of the 1980s . . . . In its jolting frankness, its exploitation of sexual comedy, it is like no movie attempted in Canada before." Fulford saw *Le Déclin* as a "unique work of the imagination, daring and fresh." Arcand's professors, he suggested, were "Fellini characters trapped in a Bergman script." Their lives may have been futile, but they all remained "basically content," determined not to sulk or whine, but to enjoy life. (And Fulford cheekily noted the irony of an NFB production in which one character "drags off another for some S&M—perhaps not what Mac-kenzie King had in mind when he created the Film Board in 1939."

In the *Village Voice*, Andrew Sarris said that "what distinguishes [*Le Déclin*] is its charm and pathos . . . . I came, I saw, I was conquered, not so much by what was on the screen as by the deceptively simple strategy of Arcand's *mise-en-scene* . . . . The one homosexual is treated as sympathetically and as unself-consciously as any such character I have ever seen on the screen." In the *New York Times*, Vincent Canby said "Mr. Arcand has done something rare; he's made a movie in which intelligent characters define themselves entirely in talk." In the *Guardian*, film critic Derek Malcolm thought *Le Déclin* was "too jokey for too long, but when it gets serious, it becomes a great movie, a very original and quirky kind of film." In *Vogue*, Molly Haskell called it "*The Big Chill* with a Ph.D." Foremost among the dissidents, perhaps, was *New York* magazine's David Denby; Arcand, he said, had "reduced a group of intelligent men and women to a single set of preoccupations—sexual desire, sexual disgust, sexual loneliness and satiety . . . a tendentious little catalogue."

When movies begin to generate money, the question of profits inevitably arises. For Arcand, who had been paid writing and directing fees totalling about $100,000, the profit issue posed a legal dilemma. On paper, he was entitled to nothing more than what he had already received. He had been hired by a producer for the Film Board, and his contract expressly stipulated that all profits made by the film were the property of the Board, a standard waiver that until that point had been entirely academic. As Arcand says, "no NFB film had ever made this kind of money. The NFB was embarrassed. We were facing an unheard-of situation—a Canadian film that made money. Nothing in our experience had prepared us for this."

Arcand consulted lawyers, who examined his contract and told him, 'you're out of luck.' But, he pointed out, his work had also been done for the private sector—for René Malo, *Le Déclin*'s co-producer. If part of his labours had been effectively paid by Malo, surely he was entitled to part of the profits. That argument became the basis for an extended period of legal wrangling, out of which came a lump-sum settlement that Arcand calls "satisfactory. If I hadn't signed the original NFB contract, I'd be a lot richer."

Frappier was less fortunate. "I did it for my salary at the Film Board," he says. "I never had a penny from all the money the film made. I did 12 films in 14 months for $54,000, so I guess I made about $5,000 for *Le Déclin*. That was my salary. All the money made went to René Malo. That's life. What can I say? It was part of the rationale for setting up Oz Productions and later Max Films." Frappier has since been well rewarded, scoring box-office success, at home and abroad, with *Un Zoo la Nuit*, *Jésus de Montréal* and *Ding & Dong*.

Many observers have been struck by the generally superior box-office performance of Quebec-made films. But, as Frappier notes, Quebec's success is remarkable even by global standards. France, he points out, produces about 140 movies a year, of which perhaps 10 are sold around the world and three make significant profits. Quebec, on the other hand, usually makes less than one-tenth as many films a year, of which five are sold internationally, and three are solidly in the black—and all of that with an inside market one-tenth the size of France's.

Arcand is not surprised by the lack of commercial hits outside Quebec. English Canada, he says, is "facing an enormous talent drain" of writers, directors, producers and technicians. "If you were to repatriate tomorrow all the Canadians working in Hollywood, and said to them, 'come back to Toronto or Vancouver,' those cities would be booming with projects." In Quebec, with the exception of actress Geneviève Bujold and later director Yves Simoneau, "nobody ever thinks of going to Hollywood." Because of language, the culture of Quebec creates its own stars, who are "closer to the people than the stars of L.A. Law. The arts sections of its newspapers are full of stories about Quebec performers. Quebeckers don't watch David Letterman because they can't understand the jokes."

But in Quebec and elsewhere in the country, there would be no film industry without the financial support of government. Arcand is reconciled to it. "Canada is too small a country for it to be otherwise," he once said. "The TV networks don't pay enough for documentaries and the theatres don't bring in enough money for there to be purely private producers. So sooner or later, the state has to help. If the state is paying, it's bureaucrats who are going to pay and make the decisions. In the case of Canada, it will always be this way." Still, Frappier is not pleased about the more assertive role being taken by the funding agencies. "Now, they not only want the script," he says. "They want the marketing plans. They want me to tell them in advance how many countries the film will be sold in and for how much. I've never seen that in my life. In documentaries, they want a full script. This is why the cinema is getting more and more paralyzed in its styling and its way of expression, because these things are impossible to know."

For Frappier, it is the very ambiguity of film that gives it so much excitement. Why, he asks, did 21 producers reject the script for the French version of *Three Men and a Cradle* before it was accepted. Why did Cannes officials reject one of 1992–93's biggest movie—*The Crying Game*—as boring and uninteresting? "That's what is really great about the cinema," Frappier says. "There are no rules."

U.S. RELEASE Although almost a dozen major American distributors were bidding for the rights to *Le Déclin*, Malo leaned from the beginning toward an unlikely candidate—Garth Drabinsky's Cineplex–Odeon Films. There were several persuasive reasons for making that choice, not the least of which was a smooth, existing relationship between the two organizations. Moreover, Cineplex was at that point about to embark on the next leg of its ambitious corporate voyage—opening a U.S. distribution division to feed its own chain of American theatres. Drabinsky, who loved *Le Déclin*, badly wanted a Canadian film with which to mark the launch. And he was willing to pay roughly what the American distributors had already offered—$500,000 (US) for the rights and $300,000 in prints and ads, a substantial amount of money for an art film at the time. The only question was: would the film be hurt theatrically by Cineplex's relative inexperience? Drabinksy answered that question in part by hiring Jeff Lipsky, a vice president of sales at Samuel Goldwyn, to head his U.S. distribution division. "Lipsky was an established guy," Latour insists. "And there were other competent people there. Everybody was confident that this group could give it at least the same exposure other distributors would have. And they did good work. You must work with someone who believes in the film and Cineplex strongly backed it; they were proud of having a Canadian film. Of course, there is never a release that is not without fault at some level, but they did their best."

Although Drabinsky was at first reluctant to handle a sub-titled movie, *Le Déclin* was an extraordinary opportunity for Cineplex to establish its distribution profile in the American marketplace. Once the decision was made, the company put its full resources behind the launch, spending some $150,000 on the opening alone. The promotional budget was designed not only to build awareness of the film, but to set it for a possible Oscar nomination. The original release strategy was based on showcasing the film in festivals immediately prior to its theatrical opening. Hence, it played in the New York Film Festival just prior to opening at the Paris Theatre in late October 1986, and in the Chicago Film Festival before its opening in that city 10 days later. Malo had insisted on the Paris, a venue—managed by Cineplex–Odeon—at which every major foreign film had opened in Manhattan. Ideally situated behind the Plaza Hotel near Central Park, the theatre reflected *Le Déclin*'s European sensibility. "We needed to open in the right theatre, so that every critic would see it," Drabinksy told the Toronto *Star*. "We wanted the film to be seen as a classy, artistic venture."

The main promotional challenge, Drabinksy believed, was the film's title—which threatened to offend American nationalists and patriots. Somehow, it needed "an explanation, but not an academic one. We had to stress that it was a comedy, but also a sophisticated discussion of North American sexual and social mores." That immediately eliminated the use of Yvan Adam's poster. American newspapers were no more willing to run it than were publishers in Toronto. Three advertising agencies were retained to make proposals, but none of their suggestions appealed to Drabinsky. Eventually, he hired Los Angeles marketing consultant Tony Goldschmidt, who suggested softening the title by using an elegant, almost antiquated script.

The campaign also decided to exploit the film's critical success, by pushing quotes from reviewers and mentions of its awards onto the poster. But what made the final one-sheet work, Drabinsky maintains, were the use of highly suggestive words, like those used in the Canadian ads, "desire, sex, adultery, perversion, submission, embrace." these became darker and larger the closer one got to to the last word, "love."

Le Déclin became the Paris Cinema's most profitable film in many years, and continued to score box-office success at art theatres in Chicago, Los Angeles and elsewhere. After 17 days in those three cities, it had grossed $192,040. Already beginning to think about a possible Academy Award nomination, Drabinsky decided to lauch a second campaign, "to build momentum in the trade papers. We had to let the industry know Le Déclin was making real money," he said at the time. "There was no doubt in my mind that it was an Oscar contender. It had to be positioned properly and promoted carefully." The new campaign again relied heavily on choice quotes from the critics. But in place of choice, connotative words, the ads used still photographs from the film, designed to communicate that the film was a comedy and mainly about heterosexuals. By March, it was running on 23 screens in the U.S., and had earned $1.5 million at the box office. In the end, Le Déclin grossed about $2.5 million in the United States; had it not been a sub-titled film, Latour believes it would have made between $10-12 million. Films that are sub-titled rarely become runaway box office hits, and also tend to suffer from reduced earnings from video and television sales. Still, by March 1987, Le Déclin de l'Empire Américain had earned some $15 million world-wide, making it not only the highest grossing Canadian film in history, but one of the most successful sub-titled films ever.

After it was nominated for the Oscar in the best foreign-language film category, Drabinsky hired New York art film publicist Renée Furst to quarterback its Academy Award candidacy; she had earlier worked on Mephisto, Madame Rosa and Fanny and Alexander. "There's no mystery in what I do," Furst said in an interview. "Exposure is the key. I'll work around the clock to make sure every critic in New York and every member of the academy's nomination committee sees my film." Many Hollywood insiders thought Le Déclin's most serious rival for the Academy Award was the Czech film, My Sweet Little Village. They were wrong. The Oscar winner was The Assault, a Dutch film about the Second World War. Says Frappier: "We should have won the Oscar . . . . We don't even remember the film that won that year."

Attending one pre-Oscar breakfast, Arcand was approached by several producers, offering congratulations and insisting that Le Déclin was a film that never could have been made in their countries. That it was made in Quebec says something about the climate of confidence that developed there during the 1980s. In many fields, Quebeckers were proving that they could play the game on the international stage; cinema was no different. But that the film spoke so universally, Arcand believes, was largely a matter of timing. "There was a point in life, where people wanted to hear those conversations and to face that reality," he says. "Sometimes an artist has that insight. He has that inside of him and he must follow his inspiration to make the movie he really want to make . . . . [*Le Déclin*]," he once said, "is better than my other films because I'm older. I'm technically better. But my aim is the same. This is an extremely personal film. No one told me to do this, do that. I made it myself, in a spirit of absolute liberty. If that results in something more, commercially, so much the better."

Popular though the film was in North America, *Le Déclin* scored its greatest success in France. It opened in Paris on February 3, 1987, following openings in London, Germany, Belgium and Switzerland. The staggered premieres were part of Malo's release strategy—to build word-of-mouth, important for all films, but critical for a film like *Le Déclin*. As Malo put it at the time: "We're doing it in waves." The wave hit Paris like a tsunami, drawing more than 1.5 million patrons and grossing more than $10 million. Here, too, the advertising campaign was aggressive. A new poster was created. It showed a couple on beach chairs, reading books. On the cover of the woman's book was a penis; on the cover of the man's, a pair of breasts. The film was the fourth highest grossing film in Paris in 1987. Before the film was made, Malo had sent the script to Christian Fechner. According to Pierre Latour, Fechner liked it, and offered either to invest as a co-producer or act as a sub-distributor for France—or both. But at Cannes, Malo chose to give the film to another distributor, Yves Gisais, That ended Malo's relationship with Fechner for some years. Strangely, *Le Déclin* was unable to repeat its success in England. There, says Latour, it was "a total disaster," although Arcand's subsequent film, *Jésus de Montréal*, was a much bigger hit in the U.K. than it was in France.

DECLINE — THE SEQUEL Inevitably, perhaps, the film's success prompted Hollywood to think about producing an English-language version. Paramount Studios optioned the script, and Malo and Arcand flew to Los Angeles for contract discussions. A script doctor, David Geiler, was hired to retool the screenplay for the American context; Arcand, retained for about six months as a script consultant, was also given first right of refusal to direct it. Already a well-known and trusted name in Hollywood, Geiler had written *The Parallax View*, *Alien*, *Fun with Dick and Jane*; he was probably selected for *Le Déclin* because of his unproduced screenplay for Erica Jong's novel, *Fear of Flying*, which also dealt frankly with the subject of sex. "Eight academics talking about sex for an hour and half is is not anyone's idea of what makes a hit in Hollywood," Geiler said at the time. "Paramount is taking a real gamble."

Geiler wrote two drafts, polarizing the script and its characters, and making it, he said, "less poignant, but also funnier." To create dramatic tension, he added conflict, having some characters compete for the same jobs. And everyone in Geiler's version became "more outrageous and flamboyant" than in the original. At the time, Arcand said that if he could live with the new script, he would probably direct it, but added: "[Le Déclin] has been seen by more people than I ever thought would see it. Whatever happens with the remake, my film is already made." But he was never really convinced of the logic of "redoing your own film," and in the end he had problems with the script. The life of an academician in the United States, he points out, is far different than it is in Canada. The university is a more competitive environment, with no unions and no guarantee of tenure. "To have four or five teachers from the same department spending a long weekend together is unheard of," says Arcand. Moreover, in the years after Le Déclin's initial release, AIDS had appeared, "and people were not sleeping together as readily." The remake's coup de grâce was the departure from Paramount of its key sponsor, Ned Hannon, and the arrival of a new vice president, from Disney, who hated the original film and had no enthusiasm for its remake. After Jésus de Montréal, Arcand had other offers to direct in Hollywood, several of which are still pending. And given the right offer and the right script, he says, he would go. But in Montreal, "I can do what I want—make interesting films. I'm not as well paid as I might be in Hollywood, but as long as I'm comfortable, I don't need that much money."

FINAL TAKES Roger Frappier: "Everybody, when they see an unfinished film, wants to change it, make it their own, add things. So this film taught me a lot. It taught me a way of looking at things. To feel confident about what I was doing. To listen to other people, yes, but at the same time, to say, 'No, this is the film we made. This is how it will be. The producer's final, most important responsibility is to the film itself. You have to ask, 'what is best for the film? How can we do it? Do we have time to do it?' And you have to be there from the beginning to the end. I've seen Le Déclin 50, 60 times. But every time I see it, I always discover something else."

Denys Arcand: "Le Déclin was the first time I was making a film where I felt it was I who was in control, and not the film controlling me. Before, I'd arrive on location and say, 'shit what do we do now?' Here, I knew exactly the look I wanted to have. I made the actors run through their text while they were cooking and following a recipe, and it forced them to be absolutely natural, because you have to lift the crêpe, turn it over, pour the batter, the burner's on and the sauce will burn if they're not attentive. That's the kind of ability of directing you get after 20 years."

Where To
Find The Films

DESPITE THE PROBLEMS most Canadian feature films have in finding theatrical distribution and exhibition (problems shared by just about every other filmmaking cultures in the world), many Canadian movies are now available on video. If you can't find any of these titles in your local video store, try a specialty store, and if you can't find a "Canadian" or "Quebec" shelf look in the section that is most often set aside for Canadian cinema: "Foreign Films."

If the videotape you are looking for is unavailable locally, try contacting the following distributors:

For video distribution only

I've Heard the Mermaids Singing
Canada: Some Films Inc.
60 Millbrook Crescent
Toronto, Ontario
M4K 1H5
Phone: (416) 469–8063
U.S.A.: via Miramax
375 Greenwich Street

New York, New York 10013
Phone: (212) 941-3800

The Outside Chance of Maximilian Glick
Canada: Alliance Releasing/Home Video
355 Place Royale
Montreal, Que
H2Y 2V3
Phone: (514) 844-3132
FAX: (514) 284-2340
U.S.A.: Movie Group
1900 Avenue of the Stars, Suite 1425
Los Angeles, California 90067
Phone: (213) 556-2830
  or
South Gate International
7080 Hollywood Blvd., Suite 307
Hollywood, California 90028
Phone: (213) 962-8530

A Rustling of Leaves
Canada: Canadian Filmmakers Distribution West
100 - 1131 Howe Street
Vancouver, B.C.
V6Z 2L7
Phone: (604) 684-3014
FAX: (604) 684-7165
International: Kalasikas Productions
16 - 2137 West First Avenue
Vancouver, B.C.
V6K 1E7
Phone: (604) 737-2522

Les Noces de Papier / Paper Wedding
Canada: Office National du Film/National Film Board of Canada
P.O. Box 6100
Montreal, Quebec
H3C 3H5
Phone: In Atlantic Canada 1-800-561-7104
In Quebec 1-800-363-0328
In Ontario 1-800-267-7710
In Western and Northern Canada 1-800-661-9867
U.S.A.: Capital Home Video
4818 Yuma Street N.W.

Washington, D.C. 20016
Phone: (202) 363-8800
FAX: (202) 363-4680

Diplomatic Immunity
Canada: Astral Home Entertainment
7215 Route Trans-Canadienne
Montreal, Quebec
H4T 1A3
Phone: (514) 333-7555
FAX: (514-333-7309
U.S.A.: Alliance Releasing/Home Video
355 Place Royale
Montreal, Que
H2Y 2V3
Phone: (514) 844-3132
FAX: (514(284-2340

Comic Book Confidential
Canada: Sphinx Productions
24 Mercer Street
Toronto, Ontario
M5V 1H3
Phone: (416) 971-9131
FAX: (416) 971-6014
U.S.A.: The Voyager Company
1351 Pacific Coast Highway
Santa Monica, CA 90401
Phone: 1-800-446-2001 or (310) 451-1383
FAX: (310) 394-2156

Perfectly Normal
Canada: Alliance Releasing/Home Video
U.S.A.: Four Seasons Entertainment
Contact: Bialystock and Bloom Ltd.
18 Gloucester Street, 4th Floor
Toronto, Ontario, Canada
M4Y 1L5

Tales From the Gimli Hospital
Canada: Not in distribution at time of publication.
Contact: Norstar Home Video
5th Floor
86 Bloor Street West

Toronto, Ontario
M5S 1M5
Phone: (416) 961-6278
FAX: (416) 961-5608
U.S.A.: Zeitgeist Home Video
2nd Floor
247 Centre Street
New York City, NY 10013
Phone: (212) 274-1987
FAX: (212) 274-1644

Deadly Currents
Canada: MCA Home Video Canada
2450 Victoria Park Avenue
Willowdale, Ontario
M2J 4A2
Phone: (416) 491-3000
FAX: (416) 491-2857
U.S.A.: Alliance Releasing/Home Video

**Le Déclin de l'Empire Américain /
The Decline of the American Empire**
Canada: Malofilm Distribution
Suite 650
3575, boul. Saint-Laurent
Montreal, Quebec
H2X 2T7
Phone: (514) 844-4555
FAX: (514) 844-1471
U.S.A.: MCA Home Video
Suite 435
70 Universal City Plaza
Universal City, CA 91608
Phone: (818) 777-5539
FAX: (818) 777-6419

Index